Pete Brown is a Barnsley-born author, journalist, blogger and broadcaster specialising in food and drink. His approach takes in social history, cultural commentary, travel writing, personal discovery and natural history, delivered with the warmth and wit you'd expect from a great night down the pub. He is a regular contributor to BBC Radio 4's Food Programme. He was named British Beer Writer of the Year in 2009, 2012, 2016, and 2021, has won three Fortnum & Mason Food and Drink Awards, and has been shortlisted twice for the André Simon Awards. He blogs at petebrown.net and can be found on Twitter as @PeteBrownBeer

★ CLUBLAND ★

HOW THE WORKING MEN'S CLUB SHAPED BRITAIN

PETE BROWN

Harper
North

HarperNorth
Windmill Green,
Mount Street,
Manchester, M2 3NX

A division of
HarperCollins*Publishers*
1 London Bridge Street
London SE1 9GF

www.harpercollins.co.uk

HarperCollins*Publishers*
Macken House, 39/40 Mayor Street Upper
Dublin 1, D01 C9W8, Ireland

First published by HarperNorth in 2022
This paperback edition published 2023

1 3 5 7 9 10 8 6 4 2

A catalogue record for this book
is available from the British Library

PB ISBN: 978-0-00-845757-0

Printed and bound in the UK using 100%
renewable electricity at CPI Group (UK) Ltd

For Liz,
and for her membership of my local working men's club,
which is equal to my own.

'There is no true civilization, no true and lasting prosperity, unless the condition of the mass of people steadily improves, not only in material comfort or in security from destitution, but in all that makes life valuable.'

The 20th Annual Report of the Club and Institute Union, 1883

'I toyed with the idea of playing Ravel's "Pavane pour une infante defunte" but I couldn't remember if it's a tune or a Latin prescription for piles.'

Les Dawson

CONTENTS

PART ONE

THE SOUTH

1

THE CLUB AND ME

Staincross Working Men's Club, Barnsley

One of my earliest memories is of being held in someone's arms, in a space that glowed.

I know the memory is authentic because it's disjointed and incoherent, a bunch of sensory hollers from before I was old enough to link them together into a sequence that made narrative sense. It was mostly just colours and lights.

That's why it stands out.

When I was little, an oil crisis and a miners' strike combined to create power shortages and a three-day working week across Britain. I can just about remember winter nights when the black-and-white telly would snap off and the candles were lit.

For much of my childhood, the landscape was shades of black and grey, even when the lights were on. When I was born, in Barnsley, South Yorkshire, the town and its scattered satellite villages still owed their existence and modest prosperity to coal mining. We were promised they always would. At the bottom of our street squatted the 'muckstack,' a charcoal mountain of slag clawed out of the ground on the way to the rich coal seams beneath. It greeted us when we opened the living room curtains each morning, like a negative of the photo of an alp. Above the muckstack, the Pennine sky was a grey shell that rarely cracked. Our houses were (it turned out later) built of beautiful golden sandstone, but the soot from our chimneys had long since blackened them, as black as the faces of the miners when they came to the surface at the end of each shift. I'm conscious of the danger of laying this on too thick, but the main road that ran parallel to our street, connected to it umbilically by soot-blacked terraces, was actually called Blacker Road. This, then, was the stereotypical North, where, as The KLF reminded us years later, it was always grim.

And that's why Christmas blazed so brightly.

In places like Barnsley, the contrast between normality and Christmas was tuned so high, the colours bled. My proto-memory is of a large room in which every flocked wall, every inch of Artexed ceiling, is exploding with hanging decorations industrially cut from metallic paper. Technicolor tinsel drips from every corner and ledge. Perhaps there are fairy lights. Possibly – suicidally – it might be candles. But everywhere there is light, and every surface catches this light, refracts and multiplies it, until the air itself shines.

As a toddler, I have no concept of alcohol, no understanding of its power to liberate, no idea why we are here in this place. But I see it as a magical grotto that I never want to leave. (I might be embellishing now, but I think I bawl my head off when we eventually do). For the rest of my life, I will always scorn minimalist, supposedly tasteful, colour-coordinated Christmases, and regard any naked branch, wall or mirror in late December as an aesthetic and moral failing.

This wonderland transforms the people within it. Throughout my childhood, adults were stony-faced. Cracking a grin seemed like surrender, as if someone had breached their defences. When they spoke to each other they diverted their eyes to the sideboard or the mantelpiece. So to my infant eyes, the true miracle of the shining room is that now they are in it, these same people laugh. Faces that are usually lined and grey are now shiny and red. They lock eyes as they laugh. They are ostentatious in their generosity. The women are gorgeous in their long frocks, dangly earrings and blue eye shadow, and the men are open and warm, thawed out in the midst of the winter chill.

My childhood was not a happy one, and Christmas memories like these stand out as brief moments when everything was OK and everyone was bright and sparkling.

For a long time, I used to associate this first memory of what turned out to be Christmas with the pub. But as I grew older and began visiting the local pubs myself, I could never figure out which one it could have been. Obviously, the décor would have changed over the decades, but even accounting for the difference in scale perceived by a tiny person in an adult's arms and a gawky teenager, my magical glowing place had been much bigger than any of the boozers in our village, or even in the town centre. My dad has been dead for a long time now, and there's no reason why he'd remember one random Christmas from the late sixties or early seventies even if he was still around to ask. But thinking back, my parents hardly ever went to the pub at all. My dad, on the rare occasions when he drank, was a clubman.

* * *

Words are powerful. When you look at who controls their meanings, you can see where the power in a society lies.

Take 'clubman,' for example. Ask someone in the North what a clubman is, and they'll tell you it's a bloke who tends to do their drinking in a club – working men's club, social club, ex-servicemen's club, Labour club, whatever – rather than a pub. Ask an affluent, well-connected person in the South, and a clubman is a member of a gentlemen's club.

Fine – some words have different associations for different groups of people: Mecca is either a chain of bingo halls or the most holy city in Islam, depending on your point of view. But the *Oxford English Dictionary* defines 'clubman' as 'a man who is a member of a gentlemen's club' – and that's it, no possibility of a double-meaning. This is revealing of, at best, a profound ignorance of the reach and impact of the working men's club movement, and at worst, a deep institutional bias against the history and interests of the working class.

Likewise, ask a grizzled, veteran stand-up comedian, or a singer and TV personality such as Tom Jones or Jane McDonald what 'clubland' is, and they'll tell you it's a circuit of working men's clubs, mainly in the north of England. Ask the internet, and it's 'St James's, an area of Westminster in London where many gentlemen's clubs were located,' with no mention of its working-class equivalent.

Members of gentlemen's clubs tend to be influential people – aristocrats, politicians, and men at the top of the business, professional, and military worlds. So, of course, they get written about – in history, academia, memoirs, even novels: Phileas Fogg famously circumnavigates the globe in eighty days using Pall Mall's Reform Club as his start and finish point. There are enough books about the upper-class version of clubland to fill a small library. While the term 'gentlemen's club' is now, hilariously, used more often as an attempt to paint a veneer of respectability onto strip clubs and lap-dancing bars, London's lofty version of clubland is familiar to millions who would never actually be allowed through its doors.

However, if you want to read something about working men's clubs, you're going to struggle. There's *Clubmen*, an official history of the Club and Institute Union (CIU) written by George Tremlett and published in 1988; a self-published book by academic and lifelong club-goer Ruth Cherrington from 2012; and a hard-to-find history workshop pamphlet from 1971. Throw in two or three academic papers, an unpublished PhD thesis and the odd chapter in a sociology textbook from the seventies, and that's pretty much it. Of this collection, only Ruth's book is commercially available at the time of writing.

Does this imbalance, this domination of the idea of 'clubland' and 'clubmen' by the upper-class versions of those words, reflect the relative social and cultural importance of working men's clubs versus gentlemen's clubs?

Hardly.

At their height, there were around 400 gentlemen's clubs in London. The total membership of these clubs is not known, but let's be generous and say that in total it ran to the tens of thousands. Hell, let's pretend it's Christmas and say, for the sake of argument, that the membership of gentlemen's clubs at its peak topped 100,000. Or even 200,000 – but that's probably getting a bit silly.

At the time I was being held in all that colour and light, working men's clubs and social clubs were at their peak. In 1974, there were 4,033 clubs affiliated to the CIU, and at least as many again that were not affiliated to the Union. Over 4 million people – 10 per cent of the UK's adult population at that time – were members of at least one CIU club, with thousands more on waiting lists. Each of these working men's clubs had an impact not just on its members, but also their families, their wider communities, even the social life and popular culture of the nation, that far outstripped that of the comfortable colonnades where men of influence relaxed with the *Daily Telegraph*.

Today, this clubland peak – the peak of the *real* clubland, the one that matters – is frozen in time. In the popular imagination, if the gentlemen's club belongs to the late Victorians, the working men's club remains stranded forever in the mid-1970s, the preserve of dinner-suited comedians doing dodgy gags about 'the wife's mother' to a smoke-filled room of flat-capped men swilling pints of bitter and munching chicken in a basket, their wives beside them growing impatient for the bingo.

This stereotype may be accurate, as most stereotypes are. But it's also hopelessly incomplete. Safely in the past, and resolutely working class, this one-dimensional cliché gives us permission to laugh at the working men's club, and to kick down at previous generations of members who didn't define themselves by the brands they wore, couldn't name a single Instagram influencer or had never eaten sushi.

It's a stereotype that seems to have prevented any serious mainstream consideration of a movement that's now 160 years old and has had a profound impact on millions of lives, quietly shaping the cultural fabric of Britain in ways that still resonate today. As soon as you start to dig, it's frankly weird how little clubs are mentioned in books on Victorian leisure habits, or books celebrating everything important about the north of England, or books on what it means to be working class. Clubs had a far bigger and broader impact in the UK than, for example, the Cooperative Movement, which deservedly has page after page of books devoted to it on a cursory Amazon search.

And it's not like we haven't tried.

Ruth Cherrington spent a decade trying to get her book on the history of working men's clubs published before deciding to do it herself. I failed to interest publishers in the idea for this book for fifteen years before finally being introduced to the only one that saw its value. The rejections, all from London-based publishers, were always based on the same assumption: only old people in the north of England would be interested in reading about working men's clubs. And the problem with that is, they continued, old people in the north of England don't read.

Beneath the surface of the obvious issues with this statement, there lurks a telling insight into how we perceive the difference between history and nostalgia.

History is important. It helps us understand who we are, where we came from and how we got here. Only by knowing the past can we make sense of the present and prepare for the future.

We care about history so much it has become the battleground for present-day culture wars: removing a statue is erasing our history. 'Rewriting history' is a sacrilegious act.

Nostalgia, meanwhile, is the junk food, empty-calorie version of history. We look back to find comfort in the warm glow of a past that probably never existed in the first place, at least not as the golden light of nostalgia illuminates it. Nostalgia tells us nothing useful about the past, seeks to escape the present, and to resist the future.

For years, when I mentioned to someone that I was interested in writing a history of the working men's club movement, what they heard is that I wanted to embark on an exercise in nostalgia. A history of working men's clubs is, by definition, not proper history – it has nothing to offer the reader beyond prompting fond reminiscences of scampi and chips, Federation Bitter and Marti Caine. Like, say, a history of pubs, or fish and chips, the subject is not important enough to count as 'proper' history. It's primarily northern and working class, and because of that, it can't tell us anything useful about who we are, where we're from, or how we got here.

It's not just working men's clubs that fall foul of this bias: Professor Stephen Earnshaw, author of *The Pub in Literature*, and Professor John K Walton, author of *Fish and Chips & the British Working Class, 1870–1940*, both describe in their respective books how they were ridiculed by their peers for choosing these as serious areas of study. The latter even ended up in *Private Eye's* 'Pseud's Corner,' for daring to suggest that the foodways of working-class people in the early twentieth century was a valid area for a social historian to study.

This intellectual bias against the culture of the working classes is itself an integral theme that runs through the entire story of the working men's club movement – in fact, the whole story starts there, with middle-class people looking down on the 'lower classes' and their leisure habits, and failing to see anything they could recognise as culture or worthwhile leisure pursuits. So it's not surprising that this bias still exists today. When right-wing tabloids create a moral panic over a new form of dance music or portray young working-class people as drunken louts terrifying town centres, they're doing the same thing they've been doing since the 1820s, sometimes – as we'll see – even using the same language.

Outside academia, it's not surprising that clubs are dismissed, given that the few references to them anyone might see invariably freeze them at their 1970s peak. The flat cap and slopping bitter image of clubs has been stamped onto the minds of every living generation – if they have any image of clubs at all – first by older relatives who were clubmen and women, then by distant memories of the *Wheeltappers and Shunters Social Club*, which both celebrated and pilloried club culture on prime time TV between 1974 and 1977, and finally by Peter Kay's *Phoenix Nights* – a portrayal of club life in decline that absolutely had fondness at its heart, but allowed its audience to laugh at the characters portrayed at least as much as with them.

The irony is, the story of the working men's club movement doesn't start in the North at all, and it takes quite a while to get there. Both for southerners who look down their noses at the real clubland, and northerners who regard clubland as part of their identity, it's going to be galling to learn that the foundation and early history of the working men's club movement was overwhelmingly centred not amid the mills of Lancashire or Yorkshire's pits, but in the salons and coffee houses of London.

This is not just another example of London grabbing everything that matters and keeping it for itself. While clubs would go on to thrive around the pitheads, factories and furnaces of the North, London was the hellish laboratory where clubs were first perceived as necessary – in full, close-up view of a ruling class that had conflicting emotions about the new, industrialised workforce they had created.

I first became fascinated by working men's clubs while researching my first book, *Man Walks into a Pub*. I was tracing the history of licensing regulations and how they affected the evolution of the pub. In 1872, Gladstone's Liberal government introduced a Licensing Act that forced pubs to close from midnight in London (and 11pm elsewhere) until 6am. These restrictions were applied to the pubs where the working classes drank, but not to gentlemen's clubs. This hypocrisy let to rioting and attacks on clubs, and the eventual fall of Gladstone's government.

The working men's club movement was a decade old at this time, still small and struggling, and not really on the nation's radar. If it had been, the 1872 Licensing Act might have been worded a little differently. It didn't specify between different kinds of clubs, just stating that private members' clubs, because they were private, were exempt from the rules that applied to public houses. Working men's clubs pointed out that they, too, were private members' clubs, and should therefore be subject to the same rules as the gentlemen's clubs of St James's. Licensing authorities and judges were faced with a simple legal choice: recognise the equivalence of working men's clubs or change the law so that their own clubs would be subject to the same rules as pubs. Working men's clubs were duly recognised as being subject to club rather than pub regulations. While this ruling would be challenged many times over the next century and a half – not least by the breweries that owned the pubs – clubs found self-sufficiency through the profits on beer sold when pubs had to close, and their numbers boomed.

I loved this victorious defiance, at a time when the working classes had to fight for every scrap from the table, when people were transported or even executed for campaigning for every single right and comfort we now take for granted. It gave me the first inkling that there was something more to working men's clubs, that this was a social and cultural movement through which the working classes defined themselves, protected themselves and improved themselves.

Clubs were run by committees elected by and for their members. Downtrodden working men gained roles and responsibilities that allowed them to prove they weren't thick or incompetent, that they could run organisations with turnovers to rival those of some of the companies they worked for. Clubs offered dignity and status, cohesion and vital support to communities decades before the welfare state arrived.

And yes, they also sold cheap beer, and blokes went to clubs and got pissed on it, but maybe not as much as the stereotypes suggest. There are apparent contradictions in the story of working men's clubs, because they were more than one thing. In fact, at their conception, the whole point of clubs was that they were intended as a sober alternative to the pub. The founder of the working men's club movement, Henry Solly, wrote at the time of the foundation of the Working Men's Club and Institute Union in 1862: 'The Club Rooms in every locality will form the strongest counter-action to the allurements of the Public House. The desire for social enjoyment and the love of excitement are the impulses that habitually drive the Working Classes to visit the Beer Shop ... Until there shall be established in every locality an institution that shall meet these instincts with superior attractions, but without temptations to evil, it is unreasonable to expect a great diminution in the drinking customs of the working population.'

Compare that to what Les Dawson wrote a century later in *A Card for the Clubs*, the semi-autobiographical story of the rise and fall of stand-up comedian Joe King (geddit?) Here's 'Joe,' peering through the curtains as he's about to go onstage in one of Solly's salubrious club rooms: 'Friday night at any club, as artists knew, was idiot night. Morons in expensive suits sat in male-dominated groups, bleary-eyed and drunk, heckling the "Turns" and lurching to the gents despite the fact of an artist performing on stage. Good manners and decorum are totally unknown to these ignoramuses, who, unfortunately, were necessary to a club's survival economically.'

Solly was keenly aware of the apparent contradiction. Reflecting on his achievements towards the end of his life, he complained that there were two popularly held views of the working men's club. One, as 'a severe institute, wherein are gathered aesthetic miners, weavers, boot-makers or others, in continuous discussion of the Higher Criticism of the Greek Plays,' and two, 'mere dens in which besotted workmen horde in order to drink to excess and to greater depths than would be tolerated in a public-house.'

Neither, he argued, was fair nor true. Maybe they're not true as absolutes, as static, binary opposites. But I'd say each represents some-thing true about the working-class condition. 'Making something of yourself' is far from being a universal characteristic of communities where Tall Poppy Syndrome is rife, but it's not unknown, and it doesn't just mean getting out and going to university, like I did. It could mean a route into local politics via the club committee, or becoming a famous singer, snooker player, magician or comedian. The story of clubland is the story of people making things better for them-selves on their own terms rather than terms dictated to them from above, in ways Henry Solly never quite understood.

But at the same time, the uncomplicated joy of blind escapism is a necessary antidote to monotonous drudgery. Working men's clubs rose at a time when workers were starting to gain some basic rights and a disposable income, but the jobs they did were often physically demanding and boring. So what if they'd rather see a comedian than a lecture on monopoly capitalism? That didn't mean they were thick: it just meant they wanted to relax in their precious leisure time.

I find myself pulled in both directions. As a teenager, I desperately wanted to escape the confines of Mapplewell and Staincross, the merged villages five miles north-west of Barnsley where I lived between the ages of six and eighteen. I wanted to 'better' myself, to learn about drama and literature and find out what 'aesthetics' meant. I was frequently teased – or worse – for it. And yet, now I'm a middle-class writer, I've ended up writing mainly about pubs and beer because I adore that escapism, that first crisp pint on a Friday night, the loosening of shackles, and the democratic freedom of a holiday spent on a lounger in the sun with no obligation to visit the local museums or galleries.

Clubs spanned the whole range between these two positions, from intellectual stimulation to a few pints with your mates. The problem for both them and me was that, like most people my age, I had no idea they did.

* * *

My dad and I had an awkward relationship. When I was growing up, neither of us really understood the other. The best thing he ever did for me was to take me to join the village library. He followed this up brilliantly when I was 10 years old, by persuading them to let me take books out from the adults' section because I'd read everything that interested in me in the kids' section. But he couldn't fathom why I always read 'them thick books' instead of sticking to the pulp cowboy novels and comics about the Second World War that he taught me to read with. At fourteen, when I started bringing broadsheet newspapers home after my paper round, they formed a barrier between us that was both physical and relational.

After I left for university – another decision that confounded him – we each independently started to look for ways to grow closer. I hadn't become the man he had wanted me to be on his watch, but I became a man anyway, and I returned home during university holidays and stood before him, a beer drinker and an adult male. So he asked me if I wanted to go with him to the club.

For most of the time when I was a kid, Dad worked overtime at weekends. But by the time I was a student, the overtime had dried up and he had free hours he was forced to spend outside work. He'd joined the Mapplewell Ex-Servicemen's Club – 'The Tin Hat' – mainly for their Saturday fishing trips. But he got on with the blokes on the boats and started going down to the club on a Sunday lunchtime while dinner was being prepared – a rite that was observed by a large percentage of the northern male population at that time.

Like most men, Dad wore his suit and tie to the club. But under his jacket he wore a jumper, *because if tha just went art in thi shirt sleeves tha'd catch thi dee-ath o' cold*. Mum knitted all Dad's jumpers and she was very fond of big chunky patterns, so Dad's thick Arran cardie made his jacket look a little bulky and odd. Standing next to him dressed head to toe in black, my bootlace tie beneath my RAF greatcoat, my hair in a rockabilly quiff dyed blond on top, I thought at the time that he was the one who looked ridiculous.

His mates acknowledged me without really engaging with me, and I wonder now if he'd cleared it with them in advance or sprung me on them unawares. 'What's tha do, then?' one finally asked, about the third time I was there.

'I'm at college,' I said proudly ('college' being the catch-all term for any education after the age of sixteen. You just didn't say the word 'university').

'What's tha study?'

This was brilliant. A follow-up question! A real conversation with the lads. 'Management Studies,' I replied proudly.

An embarrassed silence fell immediately around the table. After a while, one of the other blokes, without lifting his eyes from his pint of John Smith's, muttered, 'Tha can't *study* management.'

And that was the end of it. I was never invited to the Tin Hat again. Dad and I never mentioned it again. I see now that even if tha could study management, tha didn't if tha wanted to go to t'club. If my appearance hadn't been enough, my words had marked me out as an outsider. I'd embarrassed my dad. Even though I grew up three streets from here and was still living on a fraction of what these men earned, I was already a middle-class wanker.

But I still hadn't quite got the message.

The following year, I stayed away during the Easter holidays, but was back in Barnsley for the summer, looking for a job to tide me over the sixteen-week break. By now, I was working behind the bar in the Niblick during term time at St Andrews, so when the woman in the job centre in Barnsley actually laughed in my face when I asked if there were any summer jobs for students, I looked for bar work.

I found it in Staincross Working Men's Club. No one knows really where Staincross and Mapplewell bleed into each other, but they sit on the southern side of a steep hill. Staincross is definitely the top of the hill, and Mapplewell is definitely the bottom. The Tin Hat was right at the bottom, just off the busy junction of Four Lane Ends, where all the shops are. Staincross Club was close to the top of New Road, which ran to the peak of the hill, in an otherwise residential part of the village(s). The club had just been rebuilt, the building finished a few weeks ago, and they needed new bar staff for the opening night. I was the only applicant with any previous bar experience, and I was one of about six new staff who were taken on.

The beer pumps were metered, so that instead of opening a tap, pouring beer and closing the tap when the glass was full, you pressed a button once and exactly half a pint came out. You pressed it again, and another half-pint came out. The glasses were over-sized with a pint mark about an inch down from the rim, so that if the beer was a bit feisty, there was room for a good head of foam without you losing any beer and having to top it up.

I'd never seen this system before, and no one explained it to us before our first shift, so the first time I poured a pint I pressed the button and kept it held down, the glass slightly tilted, until the pint was almost full, when I straightened the glass, gave the beer a perfect head that sat exactly between the pint line and the rim of the glass, and smiled as I passed it over the bar. My smile froze as I noticed that beer was still flowing from the tap, and I was soon standing in a widening, deepening pool of Stones Bitter.

'What's tha done?'

The bar manager came over as the other staff got out of the way of the flood.

'Your beer pump's broken,' I replied.

They'd never had any other kind of dispense in New Road Club, so it didn't occur to anyone that the most experienced member of staff on shift might be so clueless as to not know how the beer tap worked. 'Be more careful next time' was the only advice I got. It took two or three more goes for me to figure out what had gone wrong, and the rest of the evening to mop up.

I recovered from this and went on to increasingly enjoy the job over the next few weeks. I was fascinated by the queuing system in front of the bar that was enforced by metal railings, a form of crowd control more recognisable from stadium concerts or demonstrations. The punters didn't seem to mind it: they queued quietly, stoically, minds elsewhere, until it was their turn to ask for 'Two pints o' Stones's, luv.' (I'm sure I must have served other drinks apart from Stones Bitter at some point, but I can't remember specifically doing so). I got on well with the customers and had a bit of the banter that marks out a successful bar person from someone just enduring their shift. But I did confuse people, until one man broached the subject many of them had been pondering.

'Whee't'frum?' asked the old bloke in his seventies from under his flat cap as I handed him his pint of Stones.

'I'm sorry?'

'Wheer. Ter. Frum?' he enunciated, a little more clearly and loudly, as if to a foreigner.

Oh, *where are you from*! 'Braithwaite Street,' I answered.

'No! Not like that. Wheer ter frum *original*, like?'

'Braithwaite Street. I grew up there. Since I was nine.'

'What tha' talkin' like that for then?'

'Oh! I've been away.'

To this day, when I meet people for the first time, they remark on how much of my accent I've retained. Many professional contacts hear me speak over the phone or Zoom and assume I still live in Barnsley because they find it so strong. Back then, when I'd just about started to lose the tiniest bit of glottal stop and inadvertently introduced one or two diphthongs, New Road Club found me an exotic creature.

It was clear that, however capable and friendly I was, I didn't quite fit. After about three weeks I walked a female member of bar staff home and we lingered for a while on the swings near her house. (Neither she nor anyone else told me about her boyfriend). I told her I was a student, home for four months, but heading back to Scotland in October. It was still only early July, so that was ages away.

The next day, when I turned up for my shift, the bar manager took me outside. 'I've had to let one go, so I've had to let thee go.'

'Oh. Right. You're firing the only member of your staff with any previous experience. Um … why me?'

He stared at me and said nothing. I thought of some possible reasons why and mumbled them on his behalf. He said nothing more, simply stood and looked me in the eye until I turned and walked away, and I never set foot in New Road Club again, not even to say goodbye to everyone, until a few months ago.

That was the moment when I realised I wouldn't be going back home to Barnsley after I graduated. I never even went back during the holidays again, staying in St Andrews and going full-time in the Niblick instead. The Tin Hat, and now New Road Club, had made it clear that I didn't belong in Mapplewell and/or Staincross anymore, if I ever had.

* * *

Ken Green's early association with Working Men's Clubs was very different from mine, mainly because he's twenty years older than me. He was born in Cudworth (*Cud'orth*) about five miles east of Staincross. By the time I was flooding the bar and confusing the locals, he was secretary of his local Working Men's Club. He's now the general secretary of the Club and Institute Union, as well as being secretary of the South Yorkshire branch.

'The first thing me dad gave me when I were eighteen is me Associate and Pass Card,' Ken tells me over the phone. 'And that were fifty years ago. I've been involved in the club movement ever since. That rarely happens these days. Kids around here'll go out on a Friday night and blow a couple of hundred quid in one go, and then they'll stop in for the rest of the week.'

The difference between the then newly legal Ken and the eighteen-year-old drinkers in Barnsley town centre today is stark. You'd expect it to be, with over half a century separating them. But talking to Ken makes me realise my generation was closer to today's than to his. Okay, so when we went out our idea of a big night was twenty quid rather than £200, but my dad never gave me membership to the Tin Hat when I turned eighteen, even though I hadn't yet made a fool of myself in front of his mates. I doubt it ever occurred to him, but if it had, he would probably have realised that I didn't want it. And it wasn't just me.

By that point, I was becoming increasingly distant from the lads I'd played with in the street when I was growing up and spending more time with other people who were staying on at school and hoping to go to university. The Talbot in Mapplewell had a pub quiz on Wednesdays so the clever kids made that our local. The last few times I hung out with the kids from the street, we'd swapped hide-and-seek for going into the leather and chrome-decked theme pubs in the centre of town. These two friendship groups were very different from each other, and me and Mark Bedford were the only overlap between them. But in 1986, not a single person in either group so much as raised the possibility that we might all become members of the Tin Hat, New Road Club, or either of the other two clubs that then existed in Staincross and Mapplewell. It's not that we disliked the clubs or what they stood for: for us, they didn't stand for anything. It simply never occurred to us that they were worth thinking about.

Why though? This was when clubs were at their very peak, just on the cusp of decline, and I was growing up in their heartland. A sociological study of clubs in Huddersfield, just 17 miles across the hills, was published in 1968, the year I was born. At that time the town boasted seventy clubs, but in the words of the author, 'there is nothing here on the scale that takes place in South Yorkshire.' One drinker describes to him the nature of clubs in the coalfields: 'Ah were at a club in Barnsley at ten to two one day, and Ah thought the barman had gone mad. He started drawing pints and he went on until he had over a hundred standing on the bar. Then the miners came in. Straight back it went – to wash the coal dust out of their throats. Only four of them stayed.'

The 1984–85 miners' strike ended just before I turned seventeen. The closure of the pits would eventually destroy Barnsley's club life just as it destroyed so many other aspects of the community, but in 1986, the effect hadn't yet kicked in. The clubs were still going strong. And yet my generation of 18-year-olds was the first in the heart of clubland to turn our backs. We were part of the clubs' demise, and looking back as this project took shape, I didn't understand why. Was it me? Or was it the clubs?

* * *

People like me are often described as 'professional northerners,' our crime being that we're always banging on about where we came from, never letting anyone forget for a second. It's a curiously specific insult – you never hear someone described as a 'professional Londoner' or 'professional Oxford graduate,' despite these people being at least as eager to share their backgrounds as northerners supposedly are. The only group it's OK to insult in this way are northerners, and the people who call us 'professional northerners' are those who would consider themselves our 'betters.' Northerners who stay in the North and keep their heads down are fine. The Professional Northerner is someone who got out of the North and attempted to mix it with the Oxbridge graduates and Londoners. Those of us who dare to keep some of our accent and share our lived experience with others, just like people from any other background do, are somehow transgressing social norms.

It hits home for me, because coming from a northern working-class background, leaving that upbringing behind and then trying to write about it from an outside perspective, is a complex, guilt-ridden process. In *The Uses of Literacy*, Richard Hoggart – a working-class boy from Leeds who became a brilliant academic – argues that middle-class writers approach the working class either with too much of a romantic hue or too much caricaturing of what he describes as the 'salty' aspects of working-class life. (While most of what Hoggart has to say applies to working-class people anywhere in Britain, his focus remains largely on the North). Hoggart then goes on to say that being a writer of working-class origin, coming back to write about that origin from a current perspective, carries its own temptations to error. 'I am from the working classes and feel even now both close to them and apart from them,' he writes. While he has a deeper understanding of the subject than a total outsider, he feels a constant inner pressure to 'make the old much more admirable than the new, and the new more to be condemned, than my conscious understanding of the material gave me grounds for.'

The working men's club, for me, symbolises the break between me and my background. I rejected the clubs, and the clubs rejected me. Now, attempting to write about clubs, I must re-examine this break with my past and recognise that I'm not an impartial observer. The clubs helped make me what I am and my feelings towards them are complex. I resent them. I want to reconnect with them. I'm sad about their demise but did nothing to stop it. I think as institutions they can represent the very best of the working class but that's a class I chose to leave. I'm an unreliable narrator, with a conflict of interest, of a book I've spent fifteen years wanting to write.

* * *

I eventually joined a working men's club when I turned fifty, the same age as some of the younger men I briefly served at New Road. My club is the Mildmay on Newington Green, north-east London. It used to be known as the Mildmay Radical Club, famous in its day as part of the East End Radical Club movement that would eventually become a pillar of the fledgling Labour movement. Today, the Mildmay serves craft beer and holds jazz concerts, and has writers, teachers and people who work for the BBC on its committee. Some of the older members grumble about the 'yuppies' who have taken over. The area had gentrified over the last forty years, and if that's a problem, then I'm part of that, too.

A few years ago, a faction of the old guard of the Mildmay wanted to close it and sell it for redevelopment. This was quite a common trend at the time: a club's members are its owners, and if the membership has dwindled (and you don't allow anyone new to join) these valuable parcels of urban land could provide a nice boost to people's pensions.

Their argument was that no one wanted working men's clubs anymore. They were a relic of a previous age, when communities were different. The steady clamour from people wanting to join the club – partly just to save it – suggested otherwise. After years of trying, I finally succeeded in becoming a member, as those who got in before me widened the breach.

Were we joining ironically? There's a lot of that around in East London today. The Hackney Colliery Band, who I once saw, are either a jazz collective who are 'reinventing' the concept of the brass band for the twenty-first century, or a bunch of privileged middle-class twats culturally appropriating the musical heritage of the North for their own amusement, depending on your point of view.* Are we approaching working men's clubs with the same lack of respect as this lot were showing traditional brass band music? Am I still part of the group from the ad agency I used to work for twenty years ago, going to a bingo hall to see how our target consumers lived, smirking behind our dabbers?

As a relatively new member of the Mildmay, pulling more of my friends in behind me each time there's a new member's night, I don't think so. Stoke Newington has been gentrifying for decades, and we're all part of that process, but we all have our own point where we think 'Right, that's enough now, that's just right.' And yet it carries on, the original gentrifiers going native and joining the outcry against yet

---

* There has never been a colliery in Hackney, and if there ever had been, this lot would never have worked in it, so they're not allowed to call themselves a colliery band, OK?

more gentrification. The Mildmay is a bulwark against that (even if older generations see us as part of the gentrification that's ruining even that). It's a much more pleasant space to have a beer on a Friday night than any of the loud, tinny, over-expensive pubs in Stoke Newington. You're always bound to see someone you know. And you're very unlikely to have your evening ruined by someone who can't hold their drink.

The problem the Mildmay has is that many of its new members join, and then head straight back to one of those noisy pubs instead. They like the *idea* of being a member of a working men's club, even if they'd rather drink somewhere else. In the last few years, something has changed. Now, when I tell people I'm writing a history of the working men's club movement, their eyes light up and they are genuinely interested. Every single person I discuss it with in the brewing industry is eager to tell me their stories of the characters they met when they were just starting out and they went out on the drays doing deliveries to the clubs. Anyone with any connections to the music industry wants to tell me the same apocryphal story about what happened when Shirley Bassey played Batley Variety Club. Few, if any, of these people are members of a working men's club today. But many share similar backgrounds to me. The club is part of a life we left behind but are curious to reconnect with.

Like the new, absentee members of the Mildmay, I suspect most of us like the idea of the working men's club, in the same way that, according to a recent poll, a quarter of people earning over £100,000 a year describe themselves as working class. We have, until recently, enjoyed a period of unprecedented class mobility that has allowed elements from across Britain's class system to mix and merge. Perhaps, from a safe distance, we are finally romanticising the idea of the working men's club.

But the reality for clubs is that they have not survived this process: there are just over 1,000 clubs left in the CIU today, and most of those are struggling. At the time of writing, just before the CIU marks its 160th anniversary, it's hard to imagine it still being around for its 170th.

This book, then, is an attempt to give clubs their fair due, to tell the full story of their remarkable achievements, acknowledge their flaws, and argue for their continued relevance. Founded by what George Tremlett calls 'A group of young aristocrats and middle-class liberals,' challenged and fought against by almost everybody, the working men's club movement became the biggest ever working-class social movement, the largest ever British provider of live entertainment, the single biggest ever organiser of sports and games competitions, a body unlike any other in the world. For 160 years, it has given men – and, eventually, women – help and support, a voice, a place go and a place to be, and for those who wanted it, a dream, a chance to escape, to become a politician, an activist, an organiser, a writer, an entrepreneur, a champion angler, darts player or snooker player instead of – or as well as – being a miner, a steelworker, a housewife, or a hairdresser. It enabled Lynne Shepherd to become Marti Caine, Vera Welch to change into Vera Lynn, and Tommy Woodward to transform into Tom Jones.

The story of the working men's club movement is the story of ordinary people achieving extraordinary things. There are at least four people in this book who I had never heard of before I started researching it whose stories would make amazing movies or plays, and that's not even counting any of the singers, comedians or sportspeople who rose to fame and stardom from their clubland roots, shaping popular entertainment as we know it today. It really is bizarre that the clubs' role in shaping modern popular culture – not to mention society – hasn't been told in full, that even those with a nostalgic or ironic affection for clubs are unaware of their massive importance in shaping modern Britain. As someone with one foot inside the club and one foot outside, I'm going to try to change that.

2

THE CLUB AND THE INSTITUTE

Reddish Working Men's Club, Stockport, Lancashire

Reddish Club doesn't look like the oldest working men's club in Britain.

Claims like this are always hotly contested, but the consensus in clubland is that Reddish holds the title, even if its current appearance might make that seem implausible. The smart, modern, redbrick building stands on a leafy corner of two suburban streets, its ochre roof tiles giving a vaguely continental finish to resolutely English windowless brick walls. A row of slightly paler rectangles suggests there were once big windows looking out on the spacious car park, but that the club at some point had second thoughts about either the quality of the view outside, or the wisdom of letting passers-by peek within.

You can tell the club apart from the light industrial units flanking it along Greg Street only by the sign running just below the roof line:

WELCOME TO REDDISH WORKING MEN'S CLUB
Established 1857

And the faded Carling, Coors and Foster's logos beneath.

Next to it, a crumpled banner reads:

Greg Street Club
CABARET EVERY SATURDAY NIGHT
BINGO – OPEN THE BOX – ALL WELCOME
Live football. Function room for hire.

If it were not for these details, you might mistake the club for the flooring services company across the road.

The other units I passed walking here along Greg Street – the sawmill, the used car dealer, the car body repair shop and the self-storage complexes – stand in the dust of the soon-to-be-forgotten mills that long ago turned Reddish from farmland into industrial revolutionary hub. The writer Paul Morley grew up in Reddish just as its purpose was ebbing away.* To his eyes, it was 'too small to be called a town, and too big to be called a village … very neatly if haphazardly laid out, small streets nicely leading to other small streets without it getting too built up, the occasional giant dingy mill turning its back on the present.' Like the *Hitchhiker's Guide to the Galaxy's* review of Earth as 'mostly harmless,' during Morley's childhood, Reddish was 'largely unassuming,' but later acquired a 'tired, vaguely desolate atmosphere, where nothing was destined to happen now that Manchester, and Stockport, had spread this far, because they were full, and needed somewhere to deposit their leftovers.' It feels like it's on the edge of the action, but a more accurate description would be that Reddish is lost in the middle of things, as if it's slipped between the cushions in the middle of a northern sofa.

This loss of purpose doesn't yet seem to have spread as far as Reddish Working Men's Club (often referred to as Greg Street Club, to avoid confusion with North Reddish WMC up the road). Inside, the main bar, lounge bar and concert room are smartly decorated, the

---

* Despite growing up just a few hundred yards away from the oldest working men's club in Britain, Morley doesn't mention it once in the exhaustive, relentless descriptions of Reddish he provides in his 2013 book *The North (And Almost Everything In It)*. The working men's club movement itself is clearly victim to the 'almost' in the title: the book mentions working men's clubs, in passing only, five times over its 592 pages.

main bar quietly busy. The Farrow-and-Balled bar counters wouldn't look out of place in a gastropub. Chairs and banquettes are tastefully and recently upholstered: the whole place is spotless.

Ian, the club president, and Ged, the secretary, are waiting for me in the main bar. They're clearly proud of the place. 'We did a big refurbishment when we were shut with Covid,' says Ian, a fit-looking septuagenarian. 'A lot of the members are tradesmen. They got the materials at cost and came in and did it for nowt, basically.'

We sit down in the lounge bar with Ged, ten years Ian's junior. Ray, another sixty-something, and Jason, no older than his late twenties, sit on the fringes of the conversation, curious to see what this here visiting writer wants.

I explain that I'm here because this is the oldest club in the country. Everyone nods. 'We're not the oldest club in the CIU – Wandsworth club joined before we did,' says Ian. 'But we are the oldest overall. It's a close-run thing, there are a few others that are very close. But we were around even before the CIU set up in London. When the Manchester branch opened in 1865, we were the first to join.'

As a rule, working men's club records tend to be murky. In the early days, record-keeping and filing were non-existent, so any information that exists has been passed down orally through generations. The central office of the CIU kept better records, but many of these were destroyed by fire in 1978.

I suspect Ian is thinking of Walthamstow Workmen's Club rather than Wandsworth. Though both London clubs are mentioned in the very first CIU annual report, Wandsworth is listed as a club that has 'been established by the agency of the Union,' whereas Walthamstow is cited as a club that was 'already in operation' when the Union was founded. To make matters even more confusing, in 2012, on the 150th anniversary of the CIU, the president of Walthamstow Workmen's Club told local press that the club had in fact been formed personally by the founder of the CIU in 1862 (which it hadn't), making it the oldest working men's club in the country (which it wasn't). Even while claiming to be the oldest, it was selling itself short by two years, having actually been founded in 1860. The Holbeck Club in Leeds also claims to be the oldest, despite having been founded in 1877.

Meanwhile in 2014, the *Daily Mail* reported that 'Britain's oldest working men's club,' the Anstice Memorial Institute, was closing for good rather than complying with new equality legislation that required the club to admit women for the first time since it opened its doors in 1868. At no point have any of these clubs claimed to be older than Reddish; nor have they disputed Reddish's claim to have first opened in 1857. Given the scant internet presence of most working men's clubs, it seems likely none of them thought to check before making the claim.

'This is not the original site though, is it?' I ask.

'No, that was further up Greg Street, right among the mills,' says Ged.

No one is certain exactly when the club moved here, but it was 'after the Second World War.' That move may have been to this site, but it wasn't to this building. Ian shows me a picture of what seems to be a large white house at the end of a terrace. 'That's the car park now. When that terrace went, we built this place. Then knocked down the old one.'

If you were trying to take the title of 'Britain's Oldest Club' away from Reddish, you might try to argue that the change of location and subsequent change of building negates its claim of having been around since 1857. These are the kinds of tactics used in the parallel argument over which is Britain's oldest pub, with about five or six different pubs staking the claim according to competing angles such as 'There's been a pub on this site since …' or 'The cellar floor dates back to …' When I was writing *Shakespeare's Local*, a six-century history of the George Inn in Southwark, South London, I was confronted by the problem of whether a pub is still the same pub if, say, it burns down and is rebuilt, or if different parts of it are replaced more slowly over time, or if it changes its name. This took me, via Sugababes, *Only Fools and Horses* and John Locke's darned socks, all the way back to the philosophy of Ancient Greece, to Theseus's ship and Aristotle's thoughts on the four causes of being, and still some people weren't satisfied by my answer.*

With a club, the argument is more straightforward, because while we might refer to a physical building as a *club*, technically it's a *clubhouse*, the place where a club meets and carries out its business. Unless you're the New York Giants, Brooklyn Dodgers or MK Dons, no one argues that you're a different sports club if you move to a different ground. Arsenal were once The Woolwich Arsenal. When they moved to Highbury in 1913, changing their name in the process, no one argued that they now constituted a different football club. While some argue they lost something when they moved again to the Emirates Stadium in 2006, no one would claim that Arsenal FC dates back only to 2006. Yet we might argue that a pub can only be traced back to 1667 if that's when (some of) the current building was constructed.

A club is an organisational entity that can survive name changes, personnel changes, changes in ownership, purpose and location, whereas a pub is, strictly speaking, a building (though it can be argued that it is so much more). Reddish Working Men's Club was founded in 1857 and has continued to operate since then via a variety of different clubhouses. As we'll see, there were earlier clubs, but none of those survived.

If we go back to the time of Reddish Club's foundation, the story of its survival since then reveals itself to be remarkable.

* * *

The Industrial Revolution may have had its first stirrings in early eighteenth-century Britain, but it would take a hundred years for it to gather steam, to build its momentum until it truly was revolutionary, in the sense that it swept aside a way of life that had remained largely unchanged for centuries, fundamentally reshaping the nature of work and society within the space of a generation.

---

* While pedantic architectural historians disagree, by Aristotle's thinking, it's still the 'same' pub even if it's not entirely the same building.

After the Enclosure Movement destroyed the land rights of the rural population, farm labourers looked for better-paid, more reliable work in the booming factories and mills in towns and cities. Women and girls – who had previously worked alongside their fathers, husbands and brothers in the fields – saw opportunities in domestic service, in the houses of those who were growing rich off the labouring backs of their men.

In 1801, the first ever UK census showed that fewer than one in five people lived in towns and cities of more than 20,000. By 1891, that figure had risen to more than 50 per cent. London surged ahead, its population doubling between 1831 and 1861 to reach 2.8 million, 40 per cent of whom hadn't been born there. London had become the biggest city in the world.

What people found in the metropolis was not just a massive change in how and when they were expected to work, but a total eradication of the broader society and culture they had enjoyed in farms and villages. Their leisure habits simply disappeared and, eventually, were replaced by something quite different.

In the fields, work and social life blurred together. People thought nothing of a backbreaking ten- or twelve-hour working day during periods such as harvesttime (when the work was there and it needed to be done) but when there was less to do, they took it easy. Work itself was a social activity. Whole families would work the land, easing the physical labour with songs, storytelling, and the steady consumption of beer or cider. The calendar was generously studded with holidays that ignited a steep acceleration of the drinking, louder singing, and, especially around Whitsun, an enthusiasm for fighting and brawling, or watching others fight and brawl and placing bets on the outcome. As most of these festivals were derived from the observance of the Christian calendar, the clergy and other moral guardians regarded them with, if not approval, then paternalistic forbearance.

This began to change in the late eighteenth century, as Christianity entered a more fundamentalist phase and people began to notice that, if you looked a bit more closely, there was a fair amount of residual paganism hiding among all that feasting, drinking and fornicating. At the same time, the more formalised working patterns of industry allowed the ruling classes to micro-manage their workers rather than just leaving them to get on with the ploughing. The working classes needed to be controlled and regulated, and tolerance of their wild leisure habits turned into sour disapproval. What had once been harmless fun (give or take a few hangovers, cuts and bruises) was now regarded, in the words of historian Peter Bailey, as 'morally offensive, socially subversive, and a general impediment to progress.'

The best thing to do then, as far as the ruling classes were concerned, was simply to deny the working classes any leisure time at all. In the towns and cities, cyclical, seasonal labour patterns were replaced by long, regulated shifts. Production lines meant there was no longer a natural finishing point to the work – they could carry on being fed eternally. By the end of their shifts, men were too tired to do anything else. The only day off was Sunday, and that was theoretically spent catching up on domestic tasks, at church, or recovering from the working week. As is always the case with rapid societal change, regulation and infrastructure struggled to keep up with industry and culture, and it would take decades before industrial practices were regulated to make work safe and humane.

The social traditions of the countryside may not have survived the transition to urban sprawl intact, but they didn't go down without a fight. Early Victorian workers formed close-knit communities that often acted with one mind. The unofficial holiday of 'Saint Monday,' when workers who had laboured until late Saturday took off the first day of the week to continue Sunday's drinking, was tolerated by bosses who had no other choice if everyone did it. When an entire factory rushed out of the gates to go and see a celebrated prize fighter who had come to town, there was little the bosses could do: better to lose a day's productivity than fire the entire workforce and spend days or weeks trying to replace them. When regulation did finally catch up, limiting the length of shifts and instituting statutory time off, it was as much about trying to persuade the labour force to observe official working hours as it was about preserving their health and safety.

When free time finally re-emerged, it was strictly defined and compartmentalised: a five-and-a-half day working week, with timed breaks at work, a half-day off on Saturday, and the occasional bank holiday gradually replacing Saint Monday. All this was on the understanding that leisure time was separate from work: you didn't enjoy yourself at work, and you weren't meant to.

Having regulated the working week and clearly delineated leisure time, the ruling classes could now set about stamping out working-class leisure activities of which they disapproved – and they disapproved of all of them. In London, the famous Bartholomew Fair, which had run in Smithfield every August since 1133 and had enjoyed the patronage of leading civic figures such as the mayor, was now recast as an orgy of debauchery and disorder. The Common Council of the City of London slowly strangled it with the imposition of higher rents for stallholders, shorter permitted running times, and the enforced move to a less convenient site. It was abandoned altogether in 1855.

In industrial towns and cities across the country, newly incorporated municipal authorities clamped down wherever they could. In London, after 1829, the new Metropolitan Police descended on fairgrounds and racetracks, harassing the show people whom they suspected of criminal intent. Across the country, court records show police cracking down on dangerous criminal activities such as football, pitch-and-toss, street races and travelling street performers, on the grounds that these were nothing more than, respectively: obstruction, trespass, breaches of the peace, and vagrancy. Bolton banned pigeon-racing, stating that it was a public nuisance. In the streets of early Victorian Britain, play was effectively criminalised. The only exception was horse racing, which, by total coincidence, was also enjoyed by the upper classes.

How about a nice walk out to the country? While physically possible, the problem here was that with most poor people now safely confined in the cities, wealthy landowners took on a stricter interpretation of property rights. Access to footpaths, commons and public gardens was closed off, essentially stealing common land – because who was there to stop them?

The only leisure options left available to urban workers were the pub and the music hall. We'll look at each of these in some detail shortly, because each was a parent to the working men's club. All we need to note at this point is that the ruling classes, having driven working men to these places by robbing them of any alternative, strongly disapproved of both. They were dens of drunkenness, lewdness, and possibly even rebellion and anarchy.

As the nineteenth century entered its second half, an even more dangerous threat to society began to coalesce as an inevitable certainty, one that was capable of toppling the wealthy ruling classes from their lofty position. This gathering storm meant that working-class people – specifically men – simply couldn't be allowed to socialise freely on their own terms any longer. Something would have to be done – because the 'lower classes' were about to get the vote.

* * *

In 1832, at the third attempt, Earl Grey's Whig government succeeded in passing a Reform Act that made significant progress in modernising a deeply corrupt parliament. Up to this point, the right to vote had depended on where you lived, how much you earned, and who you knew. It extended to around half a million men in a total population of just over 20 million. In some scattered boroughs, all men and even a few women could vote. But in most, you only got the vote if you owned property or paid certain taxes. Some boroughs, such as those in the rapidly growing industrial towns of Birmingham and Manchester, had no MPs to represent them. Meanwhile infamous 'rotten boroughs,' such as Old Sarum in Salisbury, had two MPs representing just seven voters. There were also 'pocket boroughs,' in which rich landowners chose their own MP. On top of all that, if you were lucky enough to be able to vote, you had to do so publicly, leaving you open to harassment and intimidation if you didn't vote the right way.

As well as sorting out rotten boroughs, the 1832 Act extended the right to vote to any man who owned property or paid an annual rent of £10 or more, at the same time clearing up some ambiguity about the rights of female voters by defining 'voter' as 'male.'

Progressives had been campaigning for reform for decades, and for many, the Act didn't go nearly far enough. The vast majority of the population was still excluded from voting, thanks to the belief that only rich men were responsible enough to elect the right kind of people. In 1836, a London cabinet maker named William Lovett, inspired by utopian socialist Robert Owen, set up the London Working Men's Association with a group of fellow radicals. Two years later, the group drew up a 'people's charter' which demanded universal manhood suffrage (extending the vote to women was too extreme even for the radicals); equal electoral districts, vote by secret ballot, annually elected parliaments, paid salaries for Member's of Parliament, and the abolition of property qualifications for membership. This was the first political movement of working-class origin to spread nationally – it became known as Chartism.

In 1839, a petition with 1.25 million signatures was presented to parliament. Parliament promptly rejected it. In 1842, a second petition of 3 million signatures – the equivalent of one in every six people in Britain – was presented. This was also rejected. After each rejection, there was civil unrest, and at one point, every Chartist leader was jailed. After a third petition failed in 1848, the anticipated unrest didn't happen. A few years later, the Chartist movement faded away.

Often regarded as the first articulation of the voice of the working classes, history generally judges Chartism as a failure. But it had ignited something among the working classes: if they came together, they had a powerful political voice that maybe next time would be listened to seriously. Having found this voice, working-class people continued to use it. After speaking on protest platforms or articulating arguments in writing, former Chartists began to enter middle-class occupations such as journalism, the ministry or local councils, where they continued to press for the extension of the franchise. Some Radical MPs became convinced of the rightness of the Chartist cause, and started to advocate for it in parliament. Steadily, it became clear that extending the vote to the majority of men (but not women, don't be ridiculous) was a matter of not if, but when.

The 1867 Reform Act doubled the number of men eligible to vote from a million to 2 million, and the vast majority of the newly enfranchised were the working class. The third Reform Act of 1884 extended the vote to about 60 per cent of the UK's male population. Men who had simply been useful as soldiers or labourers now had a significant say in how the country should be run.

Well before the Acts were passed, the inevitability of widened voting rights created new headaches for the ruling classes. Both those who were sympathetic to the struggles of the working class and those who reviled them agreed that, if these people were going to be able to vote, they needed to be told who to vote for. They also agreed that the new voters mustn't get any silly ideas into their heads at a time when revolutionary fervour was sweeping across Europe. Working men now needed to be taught how to be good citizens and upstanding, moral members of society, whereas previously some had considered them little more than animals. If that sounds a little histrionic, an 1867 editorial for *The Times* comes close to suggesting sterilisation and concentration camps as the only viable alternative for changing the character of the slums: 'As long as these frightful dens exist in which a large part of our city population is now crowded we shall go on breeding a new criminal population every year. It is a mere physical necessity. As long as children are born and brought up in human rabbit-warrens, they will grow up into a kind of human vermin. We may catch a few of them and put them in cages, moral or legal; but the mass of them will remain in their savage condition.'

That such vermin might have a say, via the ballot box, about how to improve their situation was simply intolerable. If exterminating them might be seen as a tad extreme (who would we get to work in the factories?) they had to be trained and made obedient by their superiors.

The idea of 'good social citizenship,' in the words of social historian Brad Beaven, 'defined desirable patterns of behaviour in both public and private life which interlocked with the norms of a burgeoning liberal democracy.' The plan was that, in return for a stake in society, working-class people would commit to upholding and working as part of that society, rather than undermining it (via the new moral panic of 'hooliganism'), rebelling against it (from either the emerging far-left or far-right) or draining resources from it (as drunkards or feckless, undeserving poor).

Nineteenth-century social history has mainly focused on how this upheaval played out in the theatres of politics and work: the battle between Marxism and capitalism; the rise of the trades unions and the evolution of the Labour movement; and the gradual increase in living wages and workers' rights, partly because they were deserved, and partly to dissuade people from radical political action.

But leisure was also a key battleground for the hearts and minds of suddenly powerful working-class men. Free time was when working men gathered together and talked in pubs. From an upper-class perspective, this was the most dangerous thing of all, whatever your agenda. Capitalists worried that socialist agitators might be trying to indoctrinate working men down in the boozer – the Chartists had often held their meetings in pubs, because there was nowhere else to meet. To be fair, the capitalists were absolutely right – the socialists *were* propping up the bar, trying with increasing frustration to persuade working-class men that pub and music hall were no more than different brands of opium for the masses. Liberals, meanwhile, worried that the commercialisation of leisure pursuits – the pub and the music hall again, and, some time later, association football – could lead to a passive, apathetic audience of brain-dulled consumers who would prove a fertile recruiting ground for fascism.* Finally, evangelical Christians sent Salvation Army 'missions' into the pubs around the slums to save people from Satan, who seemingly not only had the best tunes, but also the best booze.

With all these people at the bar trying to save working men, it's a wonder any worker managed to squeeze their way through for a pint. Nevertheless, the one thing everyone agreed on was that they had to

---

* They'd have loved the impact of social media 150 years later.

be saved. At a time when the term 'pleasure-seekers' was coined as a derogatory phrase to describe the useless or even dangerous activities of the working class at play, the notion of 'rational recreation' became increasingly attractive as a solution. Leisure time should be enjoyable, useful and constructive. It was still to be enjoyed – as opposed to being a sticking plaster to help people blot out the depressing reality of the factory and the slum – but moral fibre could be built by exercise, sport, and culture, as long as it was the right kind.

Culture, of course, was what middle- and upper-class people liked. The poor wretches in the slums had never seen *King Lear*, never heard Beethoven, and that needed to change: as soon as working men were exposed to the good stuff, they would see the light and transform instantly into gentlemen. Whether or not working men actually wanted any of this was irrelevant – it was what they *should* want. Half a century before Eliza Doolittle became the first (fictional) woman to be made the subject of such a social experiment, the nation's working men were showered in paternalistic improvement schemes.

Such was the attention given to trying to civilise the working man that the already civilised men of *The Times* grew jealous of the inner-city slum-dwellers who were living it up and, seemingly, wanting for absolutely nothing: 'Who would not be the English working man? He is the spoilt child of the great British family. Though very well able to take care of himself, and with strong notions of independence, we are all striving to take him by the hand and do him some good or other. We build institutions for him, we present him with books, pictures and models, we read to him and preach to him, we teach him to make societies, we are bringing the franchise to his door and laying it on his table if he will but rise from his chair and take it.'

I mean, really. It's enough to make one dismiss one's servants, sell one's townhouse, and swap one's whole life for the dream of a one-room, rat-infested hovel and five-and-a-half days back-breaking toil in a factory, living a long, happy, malnourished life until one dies of cholera as an old, broken man in one's early forties.

The first of the major initiatives to improve the lives of the poor that so outraged *The Times* was the Mechanics' Institute, an outrageous and mollycoddling attempt to turn the poor into more educated, and therefore more effective, workers. Dr George Birkbeck began forming these institutes to teach working men the principles of their trades, and help them understand how their jobs fitted in to the broader economy. Reading rooms were opened across the country to give men access to books and newspapers. Politics and entertainment were banned, the emphasis being strictly on instruction.

Next came Mutual Improvement Societies, which met in school rooms for classes and discussions on interesting and improving topics. These organisations were initially aimed at 'the serious artisan' – the worker who was definitely not middle class, but was skilled or had a trade, and was therefore, to some extent and in some sense, already the recipient of education. Mindful that they weren't reaching the people who needed it most, some of these societies began taking their message to the workers more directly, organising events in factories.

Often, these schemes were instigated by well-meaning philanthropists who genuinely wanted to help the poor. But sometimes, employers who had a tight grip on working conditions saw institutes and societies as a way of extending their control over their workers – employers such as the Greg brothers of Reddish.

Reddish was a typical product of the nineteenth-century urban explosion. As a settlement it can be traced back to the early thirteenth century, but even in 1825, three decades after the Stockport Branch canal was driven through it, local historian John Corry wrote, 'The population of Reddish is but thin.' By the middle of the century it was still mainly agricultural, having 'neither post-office, schoolmaster, lawyer, doctor, nor pawnshop.'

This all changed with the arrival of Robert Hyde Greg. Robert's father, Samuel, was a pioneer of the factory system who liked to control people as well as capital. When he built the famous Quarry Bank Mill in Styal, Cheshire, he and his wife Hannah also built a model village for their employees. Conditions here were somewhat better than they were for the enslaved people on Greg's sugar plantations in the West Indies, and the couple were considered enlightened for their time. Sure, they forced young children to work seventy-two hours a week, but Hannah took a personal involvement in their education and well-being.

Robert Hyde Greg brought his parents' philosophy with him when he arrived in Reddish from Manchester and opened Albert Mills in 1845. Over the next thirty years, mill after mill opened up along the path of the canal. Between 1851 and 1911, the population of Reddish grew fourteen-fold.

Like his parents, Robert took a keen interest in the lives of his workers, acquiring land not just for more mills but also for rows of cottages. By 1857, the Gregs owned a third of all the land in Reddish. They generously threw in a park, but as liberal intellectuals and strict unitarians, they decided the population would not be allowed any pubs.

Robert Hyde Greg believed in the betterment of the working classes, just not on their own terms. He was a stout opponent of factory reform, trade unionism and health and safety legislation. In 1824 he helped found the Mechanics' Institute in Manchester, the original prospectus stating that it was: '... for the purpose of enabling Mechanics and Artisans, of whatever trade they may be, to become acquainted with such branches of science as are of practical application in the exercise of that trade; that they may possess a more thorough knowledge of their business, acquire a greater degree of skill in the practice of it, and be qualified to make improvements and even new inventions in the Arts which they respectively profess.'

When this tight brief was relaxed to include more general educational aspects such as a newspaper reading room, it succeeded in attracting working men to it, and Greg saw such establishments as the key to educating workers in the way he thought they should be educated. He saw pubs as the main threat to productivity, and having banned them from Reddish, in 1857 he founded, instead, a reading room offering newspapers, tea and coffee. Perhaps because there was no alternative, the millworkers flocked there and made it their club.

Today, no one knows when the club succeeded in reversing the alcohol ban imposed by the Gregs. 'The family is still around, but they don't own much any more,' says Ged. 'Back in the sixties we got our first pub round here, The Carousel, and they still had to get permission from the Gregs. These days there are two microbreweries on Greg Street. That's really rubbing their noses in it!'

With the mills long gone, Reddish is now a dormitory for people commuting into Manchester or Stockport. 'That's why we don't really open during the week,' says Ian. 'We used to open at twelve but there'd be about three pensioners in here, drinking halves. It's still a big housing area but everybody's at work somewhere else.'

Robert Hyde Greg's Institute survived by adapting, changing not just its location, but what it offered the workers of Reddish. Most other Mechanics' Institutes and Mutual Improvement Societies didn't fare so well. The talks and facilities were a great resource for people who were already interested in the subjects being discussed, but apart from places like Reddish, where there was nowhere else to go, working men – even serious artisans – remained in the pub. Some of the Mechanics' Institutes survived (Robert Hyde Greg must have been delighted to see a meeting at the Manchester Mechanics' Institute give birth to the Trades Union Congress in 1868) and evolved into educational centres that were patronised increasingly by the middle classes. Quite a few were acquired by universities, and survive today as departmental buildings. But as a means of bringing rational recreation to the broad mass of working men, the institutes had little discernible effect.

One man knew exactly why.

* * *

In the only photograph I've ever seen of him, the Reverend Henry Solly looks like Santa Claus – specifically, the *real* Santa, the one played by Richard Attenborough in *Miracle on 34th Street*. Twinkly eyes shine behind small glasses, framed by a bushy white beard and long, wispy white hair falling around a bald pate.

But like the real Santa, Henry Solly had a steely core beneath his cuddly exterior. He was a complicated and flawed figure – self-important and a relentless social climber, he brooked no argument with his ambition or his methods. The frustrating thing for his rivals was that, much of the time, he was right. He may have been insufferable at times, but his drive and energy were astonishing, and his motivation was sincere.

Solly was born in 1813 in London to a prominent Puritan family. He grew up in Walthamstow and went to the University of London in 1829, but his father wanted him to be a businessman, and he had to leave university to join, in his words, 'the counting house' of a ship-broker. Working in business, he became ever more 'conscious of intolerable disorder all around me, and an overpowering desire to right all wrongs in the universe.'

In 1840, Solly became a Unitarian pastor, with his first posting in Yeovil. The Christian Unitarians believe in one god rather than a Holy Trinity; that Jesus was a great prophet but not God, and that faith and belief can co-exist happily with science and reason. It's a more liberal, less dogmatic faith than Anglican Christianity, which was becoming more fundamentalist and evangelical as the nineteenth century went on, so it was a comfortable religion for those with more progressive views. In Yeovil, Solly became involved with the local Chartists and several other working-class groups. He was impressed by the moral force of their argument and the way they set about achieving their aims. Genuinely moved by the poverty of working people in Victorian England, he realised that this was the chief of all those wrongs he wished to right.

Despite Jesus having stated some pretty clear views on the poor, Solly's church didn't warm to his literal interpretation of Christ's teachings. The poor may have been due to inherit the Kingdom of Heaven, but as far as the local Unitarians were concerned, they were getting sod all out of Yeovil. Solly was forced out of his ministry for the crime of spending too much time with the poor and went to Tavistock. This was the start of a pattern. As Solly's commitment to his cause intensified, his popularity within the church fell correspond-ingly. He became interested in the Christian Socialist movement, which began in Britain in 1848 after the final defeat of Chartism. Rather than setting the classes against each other (the Chartists couldn't gain their demands without the rich losing something) the Christian Socialists believed all classes should work together to help elevate the poor, redefining capitalism with a moral duty at its heart. Their basic principle was that if everyone benefited from it, class harmony would surely replace conflict. This advocacy of peace, harmony and justice was simply too much for the church to bear, and when Solly was accused of heresy and forced to leave his latest posting in Lancaster in 1861, he was pointedly overlooked wherever a new vacancy arose. He realised he needed a new job and set about creating one for himself.

The Christian Socialist principle that the classes should work together to elevate the lowest remained with Henry Solly, and he decided to put it into direct action. He had been a big supporter of Working Men's Colleges and Mechanics' Institutes, but he could see where they had gone wrong. While they were mostly well-intentioned, they all missed the simple truth that what working men really wanted after a hard day's toil was 'unrestrained social intercourse, the means of chatting with one another, with or without refreshments.' This was why they resolutely preferred the pub over any institute or college offered to them. Solly, a devout teetotaller, felt that the pub was not the best place for working men to meet, chat and relax, but there was no alternative. What working-class men really needed was not an educational institute, but a club.

The *Oxford English Dictionary* defines a club as 'an association dedicated to a particular interest or activity.' While they may have been called different things over the centuries, this basic idea crops up in history wherever and whenever people start to come together in groups larger than a family or small tribe. Once humanity rose above basic subsistence and began to develop specialisms in trades, culture, politics, arts and leisure activities, there was a need for like-minded people who didn't share family ties to gather together. Clubs are primarily communities of interest, but humans are fundamentally social, so whatever the stated reason for their existence, relaxation, gossip, and the taking of food and drink together, usually define clubs to some degree.

The gentlemen's clubs of London rose out of the coffee houses of the eighteenth century. The discovery and sudden popularity of coffee and chocolate made them the most fashionable drinks in the capital. Taverns suddenly felt a bit dated. Coffee houses became centres of business, gossip and social advancement: there might be a famous artist holding court in this one, a wealthy merchant in the one across the road, each with their hangers-on.

The problem with coffee houses was they just let anyone in, which could harsh the buzz for those who needed to feel they were in the most fashionable spot in town. Politicians and courtiers encouraged their favourite places to evolve into private members' clubs – communities of interest that were not so much about who could join, but who could not. They centred around St James's Square, handy for the Royal Court. The newly wealthy industrialists and merchants who could not gain entry to these clubs by birth or placement formed clubs of their own. These were homes from home where they could eat, drink, even sleep, and socialise, read the papers, gamble (which was illegal in public) and – in a phrase that is applied far more often to the privileged than the poor – 'let off steam.'*

The ruling classes may have had the means to build elegant club buildings within staggering distance of Buckingham Palace, but the basic need to socialise around common interests is a universal human experience. In 1852, Viscount Ingestre opened the Colonnade Working Men's Club in Clare Market in the heart of London, which offered 'amusement and refreshment' as well as newspapers and books. It met with 'a tolerable amount of support.' Bastard's Club was

---

* Remembering that words have power, it's interesting to note that, even today, when climate change protestors block a road or Black Lives Matter advocates deface a statue, they are vicious thugs destroying property. But when Oxford's Bullingdon Club trash a restaurant, or supporters of foxhunting are arrested for violent behaviour, they are letting off steam because they are young and headstrong, and should, at most, be gently chided. In the eighteenth century, 'the Hellfire Club' was founded specifically on the premise of giving 'persons of quality' a safe space to indulge in what society perceived as immoral acts. These people of quality weren't perverts, demons, or hooligans – they were 'rakes.'

founded in Charlton Marshall near Blandford, Dorset in 1855 for farm labourers. It was named, as wags enjoyed explaining, not after its members, but after its founder, Mr Horlock Bastard, who 'made the means of conversation, combined with opportunity for obtaining refreshments, the primary object – newspapers, books, with chess and draughts, being at the same time offered,' according to Solly.

There was a smattering of other successful examples before 1860, so Solly can't be credited with inventing the idea of the working men's club, and he never attempted to – he offers a selective range of examples in his own writing. But he was the first to take an overarching look at the concept of the club as the ideal means of bringing rational recreation to the working classes, and to create something much bigger than one individual club.

Solly's version of a 'club' was, in reality, the fusing of two separate ideas. The gentlemen's clubs of St James's were all about relaxation, sociability and enjoyment – hell, how could the gentlemen who went there be 'improved' any more than they already were? If Solly's scheme was going to work, then these qualities also had to be at the heart of working men's clubs. Create a relaxed environment where men felt comfortable – but crucially, where alcohol wasn't present – and more serious, educational matters could gradually be introduced. Not so much an iron fist in a velvet glove, as a history lecture submerged in a nice cup of tea.

The second concept was the 'institute' – while it would always remain in the background, standing behind the club, the betterment of working men was Solly's ultimate goal. For him, recreation, temperance and education were like a three-legged stool – remove one and the whole thing would collapse. Healthy relaxation was necessary to social welfare, temperance was crucial to averting the worst excesses, and education was fundamental to development.

While continually stressing that working men should be free to organise and run their own clubs, Solly had some definite and detailed views on exactly what those men should be choosing to organise and run. 'Suitable premises,' he wrote, should contain: '... rooms to be used for conversation, refreshments, recreation etc., and others for classes, reading, lectures and music. A library of entertaining and instructive books, scientific apparatus, diagrams etc., a supply of newspapers, and some works of art should be aimed at. The services of efficient teachers, paid and unpaid, should be procured; Discussion Classes, to awaken thought and a desire for knowledge, should be established; readings from amusing and eloquent writers,* interspersed with music and recitations, should be given periodically.'

It's all he can do to stop short of specifying what colour the walls should be painted or specifying the biscuits that should be served with tea.†

Defining what the perfect club should look like down to the last detail was just one part of Solly's plan. Given some clubs already existed, more or less along the lines Solly was suggesting, the most important part of his vision was not the individual club itself, but the idea of a parent organisation that could help more of these clubs to get started, survive, and eventually prosper. In the summer of 1861, he met the Reverend David Thomas of Brixton, and 'found that gentleman as deeply interested as himself in the subject of suitable places of resort for working men.' Solly claims that Thomas suggested the foundation of a limited liability company with a working capital of £3 million (around £180 million today) which would build a chain of clubs for working men across the country. Solly, 'saw with great thankfulness that such an organization ... was the very thing required, but only if it were made a philanthropic society instead of a commercial company.' The two men set about writing a prospectus and raising support.

Their first coup was securing the agreement of Lord Brougham to be president of the new body. Elected as a Whig MP in 1810, Brougham campaigned against the slave trade and helped get the 1832 Reform Act passed, before being elevated to the peerage in

---

* Obviously, he's bang on regarding this point.

† Club biscuits, obviously. But only the orange ones and not the mint ones because if they'd existed in Solly's time, he would have considered them an offence to God. I imagine he would also have held a strong view that Jaffa Cakes were definitely cakes, not biscuits.

1834. In 1826, he founded the Society for the Diffusion of Useful Knowledge, which aimed to help improve the education of the working classes and self-educated, while providing an alternative to the dangers of radical pamphleteering, by publishing cheap, mass-produced versions of important scientific texts. These were snapped up by the middle classes, outraging the established publishing industry. But working-class people stayed away. The Coventry branch of the Society decided that if people wouldn't come to them, they would go to the people, and began visiting factory floors to spread the good news. The president of the branch conceded that this strategy 'did not succeed to any extent.' The Society was disbanded in 1846, another casualty of the urge to put improvement before relaxation.

But Brougham remained one of the most credible and celebrated names in progressive politics. With him on board as president, it was much easier for Solly – more of an outsider to begin with – to start recruiting further powerful, influential men to the cause by offering them the title of vice-president.

Next, Solly wrote a paper, *Working Men: A Glance at Some of their Wants with Reasons and Suggestions for Helping Them to Help Themselves.* Here, he publicly outlined his vision in full for the first time. The opening paragraph encapsulates the paternalistic attitude that dominated progressive thought at the time: above all else, the working classes had to recognise they needed help. While Solly firmly believed all classes should work together to benefit everyone: '... there can be no disguising the fact that, as a body, the working men of England are far too indifferent to their own mental and moral improvement, too little anxious to help others and themselves up the path which must be trodden by all who would rise above mere animal existence, and claim their spiritual privileges ... while my respect and regard for the working men of this country, as a class, has continually deepened, their own apathy with respect to efforts to promote their mental and moral elevation, appears to me to oppose the most formidable obstacle in the way of that elevation.'

The reason for this, of course, was drink. At the same time that Christian evangelicalism was dominant in society, middle-class people had a growing interest in scientific knowledge and the powers of sober reason. Drunkenness led people away from respectability into sensual, animalistic pleasure, which was a sin against both reason and religion. (Of course, whatever happened in the gentlemen's clubs of Mayfair and St James's stayed there). Because of this, a respectable Victorian would never set foot in a pub, so they didn't actually know what they were like – but they were obviously bad, and working men suffered terribly from being enslaved to them. Against this backdrop, Solly set out his vision, the contradictions within it just below the surface. Working men should absolutely better themselves, on their own terms. But they weren't capable of doing that, so the ruling classes had to do it for them, until they were able to do it for themselves at some unspecified future point.

Solly's speech was read out at a meeting of the Social Science Association in Dublin (also known as the National Association for the Promotion of Social Science, or NAPSS), another progressive group that had been created by Brougham, in 1857, 'to coordinate the efforts of the experts and the politicians on issues such as public health, industrial relations, penal reform, and female education.' Momentum began to build, and Solly created a prospectus for his new organisation, which begins: 'This union is formed for the purpose of helping Working Men to establish Clubs or Institutes where they can meet for conversation, business, and mental improvement, with the means of recreation and refreshment, free from intoxicating drinks; these Clubs, at the same time, constituting Societies for mutual helpfulness in various ways.'

He states that 'at least half' of the council should be working men. The objects of the Union included:

The dissemination of tracts, or special papers, on subjects lying within the sphere of the Society's operations.

Supplying instructions for the guidance of persons who may wish to establish Clubs or Institutes; together with rules to define their objects, and to regulate their proceedings.

Grants and loans of Books for Club Libraries, Apparatus, Diagrams etc., to Societies in membership with the Union.

This prospectus was distributed among all branches of the Social Science Association, and other potentially interested bodies such as Methodist and temperance groups, who were also desperate to save the working man from himself.

On 14 June 1862, the Association met again to discuss the formation of Solly's new enterprise. To prove his mission wasn't futile, Solly presented John Bainbridge, an upholsterer whom he had first met in his Yeovil days. Solly regarded Bainbridge as a case study in the improvement and emancipation of the working classes, if only they would embrace the principle of working with the middle classes rather than following the Chartists' course of agitating against them. Bainbridge followed Solly to London and became a kind of mascot in the early years of the club movement, paraded like Eliza Doolittle or Gerald the Gorilla as an example of what could be achieved through the teetotal magic of rational recreation. Bainbridge's speech was followed by another from Mr Bebbington, a costermonger and secretary to an existing working men's club in Duck Lane, Westminster.

With such proof that working men could be saved by rational recreation, the Working Men's Club and Institute Union was duly created, both 'Club' and 'Institute' enshrined in the name, which would go on to be referred to less cumbersomely as the Club and Institute Union, or CIU. Solly formally resigned from the ministry and took on the role of secretary on a salary of £200 a year, working from new offices acquired at 150, The Strand.

Whatever his faults – and he had many – no one can deny Henry Solly's absolute conviction to his cause and his astonishing work rate in making it happen. He often slept in his office, and in the CIU's first year he sent out 25,000 leaflets as well as a constant supply of long, wordy letters to every newspaper and magazine he could think of. He personally addressed over forty meetings, and three times that many in the following year. He was always asking people for donations and recruiting distinguished patrons for the Union. 'We printed [details of speeches] on "Occasional Papers," and sent them flying through the country,' he wrote in his memoirs, thirty years later, 'and into rich men's and titled men's homes, and money flowed in, and great men were added to our list of vice-presidents, and large numbers of working men and their wives blessed the day when they joined a club.'

After Lord Brougham, Solly managed to recruit thirty-three vice-presidents, including six peers, three MPs, and eight reverends. Of Britain's twenty-two dukes, Solly persuaded ten to contribute. By the end of its first year, the CIU had been instrumental in forming thirteen new clubs (including Wandsworth). Another thirteen pre-existing clubs had been persuaded to join the Union, ten more were forming under the Union's guidance, and another seventeen (including Walthamstow) had received guidance or assistance from the CIU's Council of peers, MPs and clergymen. In 1863, a further fifty-five clubs were established.

Solly's methodology stands in contrast to how trades unions were formed, and his early success seems to bear out his belief that more can be achieved if the classes work together for the betterment of all. Trades unions had to campaign and fight against the establishment, and early union leaders were threatened with prison, transportation, even death. The Combination Acts, which made it illegal for working men to organise and take industrial action, were repealed in 1824, but it was only the Trade Union Act of 1871 that gave unions legal status – and even then, activities such as picketing remained illegal. Solly worked with and from within the establishment. By doing so, his genius was that he made his cause fashionable in late Victorian society. He organised events full of 'elegantly attired ladies and faultlessly costumed gentlemen filing into the spacious hall in evening dress.' His incessant name-dropping about who attended, and who donated, and who told him he was doing a fantastic job, sometimes reads like Piers Morgan's 2012 diary, *Don't You Know Who I Am?*, in its needy validation via the famous and important people who are aware of his existence.

There were limits of course as to how far you could go with such a fashionable enterprise. Solly's rich patrons naturally wanted to see the fruits of their donations, so he would organise field trips to clubs in Westminster and Soho, to watch the enlightened working men at play. But because Solly's clubs had to be established in places where rich people were prepared to venture, the areas that needed them most were neglected. In hindsight, he admits: 'We ought to have worked the East End or South London more; but in those days the ladies and gentlemen who were anxious to promote the movement naturally wanted to see the progress of the work for which they subscribed their money, and the 'slums' were regarded somewhat with fear, as well as disgust, by even the most philanthropic of the upper classes …'

Like the man himself, Solly's work was brilliant, but flawed. As it gained more attention, people would soon begin to ask whether all this work really was being done primarily on behalf of the working man at all?

* * *

Among the institutes, reading rooms and fledgling clubs of the mid-nineteenth century, there were many that could have contested Reddish's title as the oldest club. There were certainly clubs and institutes before Greg founded his, but not one of those that predated Reddish Club has survived. Clubs are disappearing now, and even Reddish is not what it once was.

'Not long ago, you couldn't get a seat on a Saturday or Sunday,' says Ged. 'Christmas parties were booked up months in advance. I'm the concert secretary, and I used to have rock and roll bands, country and western, Irish. Acts from really good agents. It were a very full room in there,' he gestures to the concert room next door. 'Hundred and fifty people. Down to about thirty, now.'

The 2007 smoking ban comes up as a reason for the decline. It was a long time ago now, but its effect is still felt. In 2021, there's a worry that there will be a similar long-term impact from Covid-19.

'The older end don't want to come out, do they?' says Ian. 'Some of them haven't come back yet. These are all people double-jabbed. They've been isolated. But they've got out of the habit.'

'A lot of people are building their own bars in their own back yard,' says Ged. This prompts Ian to reach for his phone and show me his son's backyard pub, complete with working beer pumps. He's clearly very proud of it, but it's getting in the way of Ged's point. 'Some of them are lovely, I've seen them. Full size pool table. 60-inch telly. Proper bar. It's not the same though, is it? There's none of the social interactivity. People sitting in the background. You wouldn't get me in there. I like to come out and have a natter with the bar staff. I'm not sitting in my backyard, drinking. If you gave me free ale, I wouldn't do it.'

Crucially, while older people are staying away, their places are not being filled by younger generations. 'A lot of the young 'uns today, what they're doing is, let's have a few cans at home and then go into Manchester,' says Ged.

'Or they go to the pubs down the road,' says Ian. 'The pretentious lot. Only open late at night. Think they're something special.'

Writing about clubs in the 1950s, Richard Hoggart said even then that they weren't really relevant to people until after their 'courting days' were over. 'The majority of members seem to be family men; almost all on the far side of twenty-five,' he wrote. But this didn't necessarily mean clubs only appealed to an older generation. Rather, it was that clubs became more relevant when you settled down. The club was somewhere you could come as a couple, or even bring the kids if the club had a family room. This remains an unpopular idea at Reddish club.

'Another thing that's stopping younger generation coming in is you can't have children in after a certain time,' says young Jason. 'Older generation don't like kids.'

'We've had our kids,' grumbles Ian. 'We don't want to be crawling over every bugger else's to get a drink.'

Having said all that, there is a steady trickle of new members from the community. The main bar boasts three full-size snooker tables, and I'm obliged to go and look at one that sits apart from the rest. 'The last person to play on that before we got it was Joe Davis,' says Ian. Davis (no relation to Steve) is credited with pretty much inventing the modern snooker game. He persuaded the Billiards Association to recognise an official Professional Snooker Championship in 1927 and went on to win it every year until 1946, when he stepped back to allow someone else to have a turn. He remained a giant of the game until his death in 1978.

'We bought it from the King's Hall in Manchester. It's worth far more to the club than the price of a new table. Insurance value would be three grand, but at auction it would be a hundred.'

The King's Hall table is a totem to this club, a precious source of new members. 'People are interested in snooker and pool. They want to play the games,' says Ged.

They also want to watch them, and now Ray pipes up.

'I'm organising an exhibition match featuring Shaun "The Magician" Murphy,' he says. The posters for this are everywhere around the club. 'We had two already. They sold out.'

'We do a few things to get people in,' says Ged. 'Jason's trying this karaoke on a Friday.'

'Bank Holiday weekend it was packed,' says Jason. 'Then weekend after it was dead – absolutely no one in. So I suggested to Ged – why don't we try it on a Wednesday when there's nowt else happening?

Ged nods. 'Well, let's try it. If he wants to come across and have a go …'

'Yeah, I'm very happy to come across and have a go.'

These are not business people. They're members who do what they can for the club they love, just like the builders and decorators who refurbished it during lockdown. Most clubs I will go on to visit share a similar mournful loss of the good old days, and I suspect some of them won't be there by the time I finish this book. The smoking ban and Covid hit everywhere, but while the smoking ban is still blamed for the closure of many pubs and clubs, many more survived. The same will be true of Covid. So what's the difference between those that die and those that survive?

Clubs resemble the human body in some ways: I've always wondered how, if it's true that all our cells are replaced over a seven-year cycle, old scars don't disappear over this amount of time. The body knows the scar is there, so it replaces old cells of scar tissue with new ones, creating a continuity of identity. Over a longer period, every single member of a club is similarly replaced by someone new, but the club retains its character, its tradition and quirks. Reddish Club has, until now, survived longer than any other working men's club. Maybe survival is simply part of the genetic code that is passed on.

Or maybe I'm over-thinking it. As we all make ready to leave, Ray offers me a lift to the train station – he's heading that way anyway. 'I don't live in Reddish. Never have. But I've been coming to this club thirty-seven years,' he says.

'Wow. Why?' I ask.

He answers in the way northerners do, saying little on the surface, but everything in the subtle intonation he gives to the words.

'It's alright.'

3

THE CLUB AND THE PUB

Sheffield Lane Working Men's Club, Sheffield, South Yorkshire

The autumn months of 2020 were not the best time to start the research for a book on working men's clubs.

I knew the stereotype of chicken in a basket and dodgy comedians that remained in popular imagination was not totally inaccurate, but it was definitely incomplete, like a TV quiz show where you're shown one square portion of a bigger picture and you have to guess what the whole will turn out to be. To fill in the gaps, I wanted to visit a broad cross-section of clubs: clubs that were failing, clubs that were succeeding, clubs that were proud members of the CIU and clubs that had, for whatever reason, declined to join. Clubs that had great sports teams, clubs that still booked talented (or even not so talented) live acts.

Soon, I revised my hopes downwards: I would be happy speaking to any club that was still breathing.

Repeated enquiries to the CIU went unanswered. Google searches returned local newspaper articles that always seemed to be about the closure of a historic club I had been hoping to visit. On the few occasions national newspapers have mentioned clubs this century, they've effectively been obituaries for the entire movement – some of them mournful, others wishing good riddance to what they saw as an unwelcome reminder of an outmoded white, male, working-class bastion that had no place in a modern, multicultural, aspirational world.

The country drifted in and out of Covid-19 lockdowns, through tiers, alert levels and metaphorical traffic systems. The hospitality industry was punished far more than any other despite a complete absence of evidence that it was particularly responsible for the spread of Covid. Against this backdrop, most clubs remained closed, unable to operate under – or even keep up with – the constantly improvised restrictions that were imposed on them by a government that had no idea what it was doing.

About half the clubs on the first list I'd drawn up to visit would never reopen.

In the first months of 2021, as the third and most brutal lockdown fell on the country like a blanket of crap grey snow, I needed something positive, some good news about clubs. As that lockdown eased and pubs and clubs began a hesitant reopening, the CIU remained resolutely incommunicado. I scanned every page of their ancient-looking website to see if I could find contact details for current members of the national executive. I managed to find their names, but a day's searching suggested not a single one of them had any presence on Twitter, Facebook or LinkedIn. There didn't seem much point trying TikTok, YouTube or Snapchat.

Eventually 19 July 2021 rolled around – the date the British government insisted all lockdown and social distancing measures would be scrapped, no matter what the pandemic figures were, under their avowed strategy of following data, not dates. Everything opened back up. I wrote one last time to the CIU, pointing out that a history of their movement would look a bit weird without any contribution from them, and finally I received a response. Their head office put me onto Ken Green, fellow Barnsley lad, and current occupier of the post created by Henry Solly – General Secretary of the Working Men's Club and Institute Union.

A lot of what Ken had to say confirmed how bleak things were looking for clubs. So I said, 'There must be some clubs that are successful. Can you tell me of any that are still doing really well?'

'You could try Sheffield Lane,' said Ken. 'They take about 2 million quid a year over the bar. Which is not bad when you consider that they're still selling beer for not much more than two quid a pint.' I couldn't see how that was possible, so I decided to go and see them to find out.

First, I find their Facebook page, which was last updated in 2015. There's a link on it to a website, but it's dead. The emails I send to the address on the Facebook page go unanswered. Finally, with time running out before I'm due to catch a train to Sheffield, my wife Liz becomes exasperated with me and phones the number on the Facebook page.

'They said to pop in any time after twelve tomorrow,' she says ten minutes later. 'Ask for Tim, he'll be behind the bar. He sounds nice.'

Ah. So that's how you do it.

* * *

Of all Henry Solly's firm convictions about what was wrong with the working classes, the most fixed of all was that they needed to be rescued from pubs. A devout teetotaller himself, as he put it, 'the social and moral elevation of the hard-working industrial classes' could only be achieved by 'helping them to throw off the wretched and degrading bondage of the public house.'

He understood why men went to pubs, arguing that the 'wealthier classes have places to go, in their homes and outside, but the working classes don't.' The rapid growth of the cities was as unregulated as early industrial working practices had been, and most of the working poor lived in warren-like slums. Even as late as 1902, when the novelist Jack London visited his namesake city, Thomas Cook refused to provide him with a travel guide to the East End, suggesting he ask for a police escort instead. He eventually persuaded a cab driver to take him to Stepney, which he described as: 'One unending slum. The streets are filled with a new and different race of people, short of stature, and of wretched or beer-sodden appearance. We rolled along through miles of bricks and squalor, and from each cross street and alley flashed long vistas of bricks and misery. Here and there lurched a drunken man or woman, and the air was obscene with sounds of jangling and squabbling.'

Multiple families lived in one cold, damp room. If you were a young, single man you'd be lucky to have even that: many men were housed in temporary lodgings where they were only permitted to be in their rooms during sleeping hours. As Solly pointed out, many men had 'no place to go of an evening but the street corner or the public house.'

Solly believed most men were decent at heart, that 'by far the larger number of men who frequent the public house go there for the company rather than for the drink.' But once they got there, they were corrupted by cynical publicans, who would put salt in the beer to make them drink more, and encourage practices such as 'treating' (the buying of rounds). Everybody had a slightly unrulier comrade who would urge them to stay for just one more. And as cities grew, a new mutation of the traditional public house would turn disapproval of the pub into a full-blown moral panic.

Learning from bitter (sorry) experience, the one thing successive eighteenth- and nineteenth-century governments got right about booze was that it was better to have the masses drinking beer than gin. Beer wasn't just an intoxicant: it was a source of calories and B-vitamins, and even an essential source of hydration in urban areas where wells and water pumps could carry diseases such as cholera. Gin, meanwhile, had one function: to get people pissed as quickly and cheaply as possible. The gin epidemics of the eighteenth century prompted a fall in average life expectancy, and Britain struggled to recruit troops who could stand up, let alone fight.

So, in 1825, eyebrows were raised when duty on gin was slashed from 11s 8¼d to 7s per gallon. The idea was to harmonise duty rates across the UK and Ireland to reduce smuggling from Scotland and Ireland into England. The Treasury insisted gin consumption wouldn't increase, because it hadn't in other countries which had done the same thing. But this wasn't other countries: gin consumption soared.

At first, the gin shop was very different from the traditional alehouse. An alehouse was a place to linger, a relaxed environment with lots of seating, and potboys delivering your beer from the cellar. Gin shops were exactly that: a shop with a counter, harking back to when everyone pretended they were buying gin for medicinal purposes. You bought your prescription, downed it at the counter, and either bought another one straight away, or left.

Every hardcore drinker has a keen appreciation of the most efficient bang for their buck. From a drinker's point of view, a penny's worth of gin topped up with water was more potent than a penny's worth of beer. From a publican's perspective, you got people in, drunk and out with far less effort. Grotty old pubs were demolished, making way for glitzier establishments. Sir Richard Birnie, a magistrate, was a fierce critic of the gin shop. In 1829, *The Times* reported that Sir Richard was walking through Long Acre and noticed that 'a little common public-house had been taken down and a building erected in its stead which had more the appearance of a palace than a gin shop.' Thus, the moral panic of the 'gin palace' was born.

In an attempt to fix the problem caused by poorly thought-out legislation, Wellington's government passed some more poorly thought-out legislation. Rather than increase the price of gin, they reduced the price of beer, with the Beerhouse Act of 1830 slashing beer duty, and allowing any rate-payer to apply for a two-guinea brewing license and open their own beer house.

Now faced with competition not only from gin palaces but also a deluge of small beer shops, forward-looking publicans began adopting the look of gin palaces, while gin shops simultaneously began acquiring licences to sell beer. Eventually the two merged. Italian architects and craftsmen who specialised in churches would be commissioned: gin palaces soon boasted ornately engraved mirrors and windows, carved animals, tiles and mosaics. Outside, huge, bright gas lamps burned.

All this investment demanded higher returns to pay it back. The dram shop's counter became the gin palace's bar, introducing this physical division between servers and customers to pubs for the first time. Seats were removed so that more people could be squeezed in to stand and drink at the bar. Frederick Hackwood, in his 1912 book

Inns, Ales and Drinking Customs of Old England, says of the gin palaces: 'The repeated order is the condition of a continued welcome. This attitude of the management is betrayed by the inhospitable seatless bar, specially designed for "perpendicular drinking."'

Reformers and moralisers were aghast. The ever-reliable *Times* fretted that the magnificent decoration once reserved for gentlemen's clubs and hotels was now being used by publicans 'for the benefit (or rather corruption) of the lower classes.' The materials used and the style of decoration of the gin palaces were exactly the same as those found in 'respectable' West End shops, and this was the problem – the fact that mere public houses could afford them was an affront to middle-class sensibilities.

As historian Lee Jackson points out, the spread of gaslight in particular was a perfect example of Victorian hypocrisy. At this time common street lighting was rare, and gaslight was synonymous with progress – crime plummeted wherever it was introduced. But as soon as gas globes appeared outside gin palaces they were considered a bad thing, luring people into drunken misery.

The rational recreationists tied themselves in knots. They wanted working men to gain an appreciation of fine art and culture. But if working men embraced fine architecture and design on their own terms, rather than those dictated to them, they were defiling it.

Jackson points out that the only way some commentators could deal with gin palaces was simply to argue that their glamour wasn't real. Despite being built from the same material as middle-class haunts, sometimes even by the same architects and craftsmen, contemporary accounts such as that in John Hogg's *London As It Is* describes gin palaces' 'mock' finery and ornament: 'We've seen an arched light roof, supported on Corinthian columns; Classic displays thickly sculptured on the walls, chandeliers of crystal and lamps of bronze suspended by thickly gilt chains; and stately mirrors on all sides reflecting the mock grandeur of the scene.'

At the same time, critics of working-class habits couldn't quite work out what kind of bad things happened to people who drank in pubs and gin palaces. Drinking to excess apparently not only made men go home and beat their wives, but it also made them less productive at work, lazy and listless, not even bothering to turn up after a heavy weekend. At the same time, pubs were where men went to agitate and organise, to disseminate radical pamphlets and have meetings about how to overthrow the ruling classes.

Here then, was Schrödinger's Pub-Goer: a drunken deadbeat, little better than an animal drinking till he was sick, and then returning to his vomit (a metaphor used to the point of cliché in writing about pubs in the mid-nineteenth century). And somehow, at the same time, he was an organised, political actor, plotting revolution behind the closed doors of the public house. He was a brute, incapable of appreciating aesthetic beauty, while at the same time helplessly drawn to a 'mock' version of it. No one explained how he could be performing all these contradictions. But clearly, he had to be stopped.

It's easy to characterise pubs as sordid drinking dens and nothing more, especially when, like Henry Solly, you had no personal experience of them. To him, beer and gin were as bad as each other, wherever they might be found. Even as he documented the unscrupulous machinations that got people to drink more than they had intended, he simultaneously maintained that beer itself was the problem. In creating the CIU, it never occurred to him that you might be able to curb the excesses of the gin palace if you sold beer in a different environment. The working men's clubs had to be dry: 'The Club Rooms in every locality will form the strongest counter-action to the allurements of the Public House. The desire for social enjoyment and the love of excitement are the impulses that habitually drive the Working Classes to visit the Beer Shop … Until there shall be established in every locality an institution that shall meet these instincts with superior attractions, but without temptations to evil, it is unreasonable to expect a great diminution in the drinking customs of the working population.'

* * *

Sheffield Lane Club has no bright gas globes hanging outside – nor anything else. My maps app shows me that it stands on the top of a hill on what used to be the main road from Sheffield to Barnsley. It's a densely residential area, with some of the UK's first ever purpose-built housing estates sprawling away down the slopes. At Lane Top, there's a busy four-way junction surrounded by fast food shops, off-licenses and convenience stores. One corner is dominated by Sheffield's biggest KFC, which boasts a drive-through. A couple of small takeaways stand in its shadow at the start of Hatfield House Lane, which winds eastwards from the junction, heading deeper into the housing estates. After the takeaways there's a car fitting centre, and then a building twice its size, set back about ten feet from the road, about a hundred yards down from the junction. This, allegedly, is Sheffield Lane Club.

The thing is, walking down Hatfield House Lane, you would only guess that this was Sheffield Lane Club if you already knew it was. It's a blocky, municipal building of redbrick and uPVC windows. You could probably build an exact replica of it from old-school, basic Lego, without using any of the new fancy, customised bricks. Different shades of brick suggest various bits have been bolted on over the years. There are no lights, no signs, no gaudy decoration, nothing to suggest there's a club here at all. This is a club in urban camouflage, skilfully designed to look like – well, nothing, really.

Then, I spot four empty beer kegs hanging around outside a fire exit, trying not to draw attention to themselves. Aha, so someone is serving beer here somewhere.

Encouraged, I edge closer, and spot a door hiding behind a pile of steps, railings and ramps. As I get closer, I can see a tiny Carling logo next to it, no bigger than the Chubb burglar alarm box fixed to the wall a few feet away.

I enter, expecting to be stopped and challenged. There's a reception area, but it's deserted. Through a wide pair of double doors I'm in a big, spacious, mostly empty bar. Tables and chairs line the walls. There's a dance floor at one end. TVs tuned to NOW 80s provide the atmosphere.

The bar itself is about 25 yards long, lined with fonts for Foster's, Carling and a wide array of other lagers, all sitting behind Perspex shields. Every five feet, there's a hole through which drinks can be passed, framed by black-and-yellow hazard tape. The only bit of this long bar that isn't fenced in by screens is the hatch where the barman gets in and out. Naturally, this is where everyone queues to get served.

I decide not to assume the familiarity of a regular, or just to follow the rules, and go to one of the serving hatches in the Perspex wall. I don't really know. I'm acutely self-conscious, clearly an interloper in a close-knit members club. It's worse here than Reddish, because this is where I'm supposedly relatively local, but I haven't lived anywhere near here for most of my adult life. The memories and the anxiety of being a teenage barman in New Road flood back. *Wheet'frum*?

I order a pint of Stones bitter, cementing the link with the past. It costs £2.20. It's the smoothflow version rather than 'proper' real ale, served filtered, pasteurised and very cold from a pressurised keg, with a mix of carbon dioxide and nitrogen to give it the half-hearted illusion of being fresh cask ale with a smooth body and creamy head. I haven't drunk a smoothflow beer for twenty years, because as well as being cold and tasteless, they're usually also old and stale, the wet cardboard tang of oxidation being the only detectable character. So I'm surprised when my Stones tastes cool, fresh and mellow. It can only taste like this because the pipes are clean and the beer is flowing quickly through them.

The barman who serves me is in his sixties, sporting close-cropped hair and a darts shirt. 'I'm looking for Tim?'

His mouth moves and I hear noises. I shake my head, try to lean in with my good ear, and eventually move round to the Perspex-free hatch where everyone queues to get served.

'Are you Tim? I'm Pete. My wife phoned yesterday.'

I feel like Withnail talking to the farmer, biting my lip to prevent myself yelping, 'I'm not from London!'

'We were expectin' thee at twelve,' Tim replies. 'All t'old uns were in then. Tha could have talked to 'em.'

'Oh, sorry, Liz said any time *after* twelve.' Tim nods. 'I thought that meant … never mind. I only just got into town and I came straight up here as quick as I could.'

I explain what I'm up to with the book. 'Well there's nowt much I can tell thee,' says Tim, 'I only joined in 1982.'

I try a different tack. I explain that I'm here because this is one of the most successful clubs in the country and ask Tim why that is.

'Cheap beer,' he replies simply.

My pint of Stones seems to have disappeared. I pull out my wallet to pay for another, and sense something slip through my fumbling fingers. Sure enough, a voice from the banquette across the room calls, 'Tim, he's dropped summat.'

This takes me back, a northern tic: this helpful man doesn't know me, but he knows Tim, who is talking to me. He knows I can hear him, but custom dictates that, for whatever reason, he has to speak to me indirectly.

'Yer need to speak to Glyn,' says Tim. 'He's secretary. 'E'll be in abaht one tomorrer.'

That kind of finishes our conversation, so I take my pint and sit at one of the tables opposite the bar. The carpets are 1970s paisley. The walls are grey. The banquettes have a kind of *fleur-de-lys* pattern that fights the carpets for supremacy. The lighting is fluorescent and halogen, a pasty replica of natural daylight. Apart from the multiple TVs playing Kylie and Jason videos, there's no attempt to create atmosphere. Like the outside, it all feels municipal, utilitarian. This place wasn't built for aspiration or escape. There's no attempt to lure you in or deceive you. There's no need. It's the anti-gin palace.

* * *

Three years after the formation of the Working Men's Club and Institute Union, its future was looking as shaky as it would in the winter of 2020. Henry Solly was still working tirelessly, roaming the country, giving lectures, hitting up queens, bishops and earls for donations, and opening club after club. The problem was, as he hurried to open the next one, the ones in his wake shrivelled and died. After the initial fanfare, working men simply didn't turn up, and the rich patrons got bored and moved on. Of the fifty-five clubs that had been established in 1863, few survived two years later. Solly had his face set firmly forward, evangelising his cause, forever taking it into new territories. He was oblivious to what was happening behind him.

When the CIU's council finally brought the issue to his attention, he answered that the clubs were failing because of 'the absence of resident gentry,' which was precisely why he needed to keep hobnobbing with them. Had he stopped to reflect, he might have asked himself if what he was doing were any different from what had happened with the Mechanics' Institutes and Knowledge Societies. He fully understood that they had failed because middle-class patrons weren't giving working men what they wanted. Was it possible that his clubs were falling into the same trap? No – simply because Solly seems to have been immune to self-doubt.

A modern market researcher would immediately suggest interviewing those who had given clubs a try and then lapsed, and finding out why, but this never occurred to anyone. Ten years later, one artisan who had stuck with clubs for as long as he could told *The Times* that they merely offered a secular version of the Church's 'cup of tea and tract formula.' He meant that the CIU dictated what kind of recreation was and wasn't allowed in its clubs, banned political discussion, and – most egregious of all – banned alcohol. Sure, fledgling clubs were getting support that was otherwise unavailable to them – premises, loans, legal help – but the price of this was being told what to do by their social superiors – the very thing they wanted to get away from after they had finished work.

Solly had been shrewd enough to recognise that men wouldn't bother with an institute that didn't offer informal recreation and relaxation, but he simply couldn't see that for working men, beer was part of that relaxation, that it was so much more than just a means of blotting out reality. In many workplaces, the moderate consumption of beer was allowed throughout the working day: even those who had taken the temperance pledge argued that this was an inalienable right for their colleagues.

Of course, beer can lead to drunkenness, alcoholism and anti-social behaviour, but for the vast majority of people who drink it, for most of the time, it's a source of quiet solace, a small treat, a toast with friends, that doesn't often lead to drunken excess. There were few such pleasures available to the working classes. Beer, however, was cheap, readily available, and for most of the time at least, a pleasure to drink. And as historian Peter Bailey pointed out, not every pub in the new industrial slums was a gin palace: '... in an age of social dislocation the pub remained a centre of warmth, light and sociability for the urban poor, a haven from the filth and meanness of inadequate and congested housing, a magnet for the disoriented newcomer and the disgruntled regular alike. "There is plenty of gas and company to keep us alive," explained the customers ... "there is always society in the pubs, and the men there are so very agreeable."'

If you wanted to prise working men out of these hostelries, you had to offer something at least as attractive. Lord Brougham, the president of the Union, and his friend, Lord Lyttelton, were enthusiastic supporters of Solly's cause. But to them, the cleverness of the plan was in basing the model for the working men's club on the gentlemen's clubs, where alcohol flowed freely. They believed that drink, consumed in moderation, had a natural part in any kind of social life.

'The beer question' was later described by Solly as 'the greatest controversy in the club world.' He insisted that the main reason clubs could not survive was that there were not enough rich patrons pumping money in. But he never asked himself why clubs couldn't survive without financial patronage. Why could they not be self-sufficient? The answer became increasingly obvious to everyone apart from Henry Solly.

In 1865, Lord Brougham convened a special meeting of the CIU Council to discuss the beer question. Finally, and 'with the greatest reluctance,' Solly gave way. The meeting concluded that if clubs were to survive and spread nationwide, they must have the freedom to decide for themselves where they stood on the drink issue.

This was Henry Solly's first great defeat, the first time he had been challenged and overruled. His iron grip on the CIU had been weakened.

Solly the great political operator sensed this and wasted no time in spinning the decision as a great victory not just for the club movement, but for his personal vision. It was a *brilliant* idea for clubs to serve beer, because drinking beer in clubs was a completely different experience from drinking beer in pubs. Why, he should have thought of this years ago! In fact, he probably did – hadn't it been his idea all along?

He certainly did a good job of trying to imply this, without ever quite overtly claiming it. Speaking to working men, he found many who were keen to swap the pub for somewhere calmer, where commercial imperatives didn't pressure them into drinking more than they intended. Later, Solly remembered one meeting in Leicester where:

> One man after another got up and stated simply and straightforwardly his conviction that the cause of Temperance as distinguished from Total Abstinence had been greatly promoted by members being able to get their pint or their glass at the club instead of having to get it at their old haunts. One man in particular I remember – a thoughtful man, with a will of his own – telling us that before he joined a club, he regularly got fuddled every Saturday night, but that since he became a member he had never once been intoxicated the whole year through – adding, however, that if he couldn't have got a glass of ale there he should never have become a member.

Henry Solly's complete and almost instant failure to create a network of clubs that would reduce drunkenness among working men by getting them to spend their leisure time in a place that didn't sell alcohol was in fact a triumph – a network of clubs that would reduce drunkenness among working men by getting them to spend their leisure time in a place that sold alcohol.

Possibly the greatest obstacle to the survival of clubs had been removed. Clubs needed enough money to cover their running costs, but as they were owned by their members, and run on a voluntary basis, there was no need for them to make a substantial profit, so no need for dirty tricks and peer pressure to drink more. Clubs could buy beer for the same cost as pubs and sell it cheaper. Cheap beer meant more people came more often. Finally, the clubs had the means to be self-sufficient.

If things were looking up for individual clubs, the finances of the CIU itself were increasingly shaky. In 1874, Queen Victoria donated £50 to the movement, and the Duke of Bedford £100. It was great (in the eyes of some) that the Queen was so supportive, but together those two donations constituted a third of the Union's entire income for the year, and between them didn't even cover Solly's salary. The Council started trying to get increased subscription fees from its member clubs, and then one new Council member – E. Eisenhardt of the Bedford Club – suggested that an associate and pass card could be introduced. For the payment of a small fee, this card could grant access for all members to any other club in the Union. A competition to design the card was won by Henry Hill of Ashton-under-Lyne, who received a prize of two guineas. His design is still in use today.

Initially, the pass card got you into other clubs, but didn't legally allow you to buy drinks there. Then, the Union's lofty patrons came in handier than they ever had. Sir Harcourt Johnstone MP was one of the Union's innumerable vice-presidents, and a close friend of Stafford Northcote MP, the chancellor of the exchequer, who would also become a CIU vice-president in time. Together, they smoothed through parliamentary approval that the pass card should legally confer the right to buy drink and cigarettes at any member club.

This was fundamental for the Union. If a member paid for the pass card, they could now drink cheap beer freely not just in their own club, but in hundreds of clubs across the country. Sales of the pass card soared, and each time a club sold one, it paid a one-shilling levy to the CIU. The income from pass cards almost instantly outstripped subscriptions and donations, and by 1905, the CIU was making over £3,000 a year from the cards, compared to just £20–£40 a year from subscriptions and donations. Suddenly, the organisation and its clubs were independently financially viable.

But the beer question hadn't quite finished with the club movement just yet.

* * *

While beer may not have been the curse people like Solly thought it was, even the brewers had to admit there was a drink problem in Victorian Britain. It may have been exaggerated, spun and distorted to promote political or religious agendas, much like it still is today, but only a fool would claim it didn't exist at all. The poor lived in dire conditions with little hope of betterment: of course some of them drank harmfully.

The Gladstone government's 1872 Licensing Act contained a wide range of measures to curb public drunkenness, the chief of which was to declare it illegal. Since 1872, it has been a criminal act to be drunk in a pub or anywhere else in public, and an even more serious offence to be drunk in public while in possession of a loaded firearm or in charge of a horse, a carriage, a cow (or other cattle) or, God forbid, a steam engine.

The Act also forced pubs to close from midnight in London and 11pm elsewhere, until no earlier than 6am. Pubs had never been subject to such stringent controls before, and they were outraged. It's interesting to note that London – not big cities, just London – got an hour longer than everywhere else, and difficult to understand that logic as anything other than favouritism. Angry mobs took to the streets of cities like Liverpool, Coventry and Wolverhampton, chanting, 'Britons never shall be slaves,' seeking out teetotallers on whom to vent their spleen, until troops were called in to disperse them.

But the greater example of hypocrisy was that this new legislation applied to pubs but not to private members' clubs, which because they were private, were stipulated to be exempt from licensing law governing public houses. These clubs just happened to be where MPs, ministers, clergymen and the judiciary did their drinking. In a scene that's impossible to imagine in the twenty-first century, government ministers were free to party when the general public could be fined or even arrested for doing the same thing at the same time. Pub-goers spotted this straight away. In cities across the country, clubs were singled out and attacked by protestors and forced to close.

The CIU was only 10 years old at this point, and not really on the radar of legislators or the general public. It didn't take long for clever working-class people to work out that the new law made a distinction between private members' clubs and public houses, without making any kind of distinction between different types of private members' clubs.

In his history of the CIU, George Tremlett credits the massive spike in club membership in the closing decades of the nineteenth century to the spread of democracy in the club movement, with members eventually gaining a say in how their clubs were run. We'll discuss this soon, and it undoubtedly had a powerful effect. But Tremlett doesn't mention the separation between clubs and pubs under licensing law as a factor in their phenomenal growth. How do we know it was a factor, and not just coincidence? Simple. Because when the establishment caught up with working men and realised that their clubs could operate on the same terms as gentlemen's clubs, they were fucking livid.

Gentlemen's clubs were respectable places where respectable people gambled freely and drank copiously until the small hours. The 1872 Licensing Act specifically preserved their right to do this. But when working men's clubs did exactly the same thing, some thought they were cynically exploiting a loophole and had to be prevented from doing so.

The 1872 Act had also placed licensing powers with local authorities, with their decisions to be enforced by the local police. The police had the power to enter pubs and close them down if necessary, but no jurisdiction over private members' clubs, and this infuriated them.

Their argument was that if someone wanting to open a pub was refused a license – say, on the grounds that they didn't seem a suitable person to hold one – that person could simply open their premises as a club instead, and the police couldn't touch them. These working-class drinking clubs could charge a negligible joining fee and exist solely for the purpose of getting drunk.

Of course, some people did exactly that, and unlicensed drinking clubs sprang up across the country. But they were few in number compared to bona fide working men's clubs where, as Henry Solly was slowly realising, people really did go to wind down and play a game of dominoes over a pint or two without getting drunk, now that the option was available to them. Nevertheless, the authorities persisted in painting every single working men's club as no more than a private drinking den.

They moved quickly to try to establish a legal precedent that would stop working men's clubs from supplying drink. In 1882, the Grosvenor Club in London – which sounds like a gentlemen's club but was actually a working men's club – was sued for supplying drinks to its members. The case was successful but the club appealed, and the appeal judges ruled that the club had not broken the law because the transaction did not constitute a 'sale,' given that the members owned both the club and its assets. This established one of the basic principles of club law and succeeded in strengthening the rights of all private members' clubs. It's worth noting that if anyone had ever brought a similar action against a gentlemen's club on exactly the same grounds, for doing exactly the same thing, then of course this legal precedent would already have been established. But for some reason, no one had.

The vendetta from the police continued – and indeed would continue for over a century. The history of the CIU beats to a regular drum of attempts by licensing authorities and police to gain more control over clubs and, for the most part, being rebuffed.

My favourite example is the Royal Commission on Licensing Laws that was convened in 1896 – yes, I know how that sounds, but stay with me on this, it's worth it, I promise.

The commission comprised one-third of representatives from the licensed trade, including brewers, distillers and publicans, one-third temperance bodies, from moderate temperance supporters to hardline prohibitionists, and a third of 'non-interested' parties for balance. One of the first decisions the Commission made was that clubs – all clubs – should be included within the remit of the investigation.

The make-up of the commission demonstrates how, for pretty much everything it was discussing, it was anticipated to be a bunfight between the licensed trade and the teetotallers, with the neutrals in the middle trying to calm everything down. But when it came to discussions about working men's clubs, an extraordinary alliance was formed. The case against the clubs was led by the teetotallers and the police superintendents, but the publicans chipped in, helping them to collect evidence of the clubs' shortcomings and crimes. These shortcomings and crimes were so extreme, so widespread, so blatantly obvious, that the coalition had to advertise in the press to ask people to come forward with examples of them, because the 'secretive nature' of clubs meant they couldn't find any. These drinking dens were so dastardly, the police didn't even know the names and addresses of the clubs that were supposedly doing so much harm. B. T. Hall, who was at this point the secretary of the CIU, was happy to help. He wrote to the commission enclosing 'a list of names and addresses of over 500 clubs, into whose conduct you may enquire, and I will be glad to assist your inquiry in any way.'

When the evidence came before the committee, the Chief Constables of Manchester and Leeds led the charge. The former argued that every single example of late-night drunkenness in his city was the fault of the clubs he could neither find nor document. It had to be, didn't it? They were allowed to stay open later, and obviously all the pub-goers went straight home with their cows, horses, carriages and steam engines rather than risk being found drunk on the street with them. It was definitely only the club-goers who were still out drinking.

One of the commissioners asked if some of the drunken behaviour might not be due to brothels and other 'night houses' in the city. Huh, as if! The Chief Constable replied that there were no such things as brothels or night houses in the whole of Manchester, seemingly – and you have to hand this to him – with a straight face. When it was subsequently discovered that not only did brothels exist in Manchester, but the main ones were owned and run by senior members of the city's detective service, and furthermore that all the pub-owning breweries were paying bribes – sorry, 'subsidies' – to all members of the police force on a sliding scale from constable to detective, the case for trying to demonise working men's clubs as the source of all the alcohol-related ills in British towns and cities fell apart.

The commission reported its findings in 1899 and formed the basis of a yet another new Licensing Act, which became law in 1902. The only bit of it that really concerned working men's clubs was that if they were selling alcohol, they simply had to register with their local licensing authority, which they didn't mind, as this was a way of distinguishing between a respectable working men's club and an unlicensed drinking den. Both the temperance movement and the licensed trade were a lot less happy with the Act than the clubmen were and continued desperately to try to squeeze something into it that would hurt clubs. But when the Bill reached its third reading in the House of Commons, its author, Home Secretary C. T. Ritchie, put them in their place, saying: 'I am sure that the House will agree with me that we must enlist on our side in this matter the best opinion of the best clubs, including working men's clubs. I know that that great organisation – the Club and Institute Union … is as anxious as the House can possibly be that the evils we complain of should be suppressed. If we do not carry the favourable opinion of these clubs with us, harm will result …'

The clubs were being taken seriously. They were respected, part of the solution, not the problem. This was deserved, because it turned out that most men really did drink more moderately in clubs. But it also must be acknowledged that Reverend Solly's social climbing had ultimately paid off. Potentially, clubs could have been screwed by any government: the Liberals were closely aligned with the temperance movement, while the Tory party contained so many peers and MPs who had made their fortunes from brewing that it was often jokingly

referred to as 'the beerage.' The unholy alliance between these opposing forces had just spent six years trying to stitch up clubs using every
means possible. If they had been able to lobby their respective political parties successfully, working men on their own would have been
powerless to resist. But the CIU had spent its entire forty-year history
making friends in high places. Even after Solly's departure, this opened
doors. Lord Rosebery, the CIU's first president, even served as prime
minister from March 1894 to June 1895. When working men were
still being demonised and their leisure pursuits vilified, Solly's principle of working from inside the system and getting powerful men
onside had helped win a crucial victory.

* * *

The licensed victuallers who campaigned so hard against working
men's clubs did so because they were a threat to their business. For
most of the twentieth century, Britain's brewers either owned the pubs
that sold their beer, or 'tied' them with loans the publicans used to
finance the extensions and adornments that turned them into gin
palaces. The clubs, operating outside this system, were draining profit
from it.

Today, there's much less difference between pubs and clubs. The
majority of Britain's pubs are no longer owned by the breweries, but
by private pub companies with whom the brewers must negotiate
bulk deals and discounts. The CIU could, if it wanted, behave in the
same way, negotiating the supply of beer to 1500 clubs. But it chooses
to let each club negotiate its own deals.

When clubs begin to struggle financially, the brewers do what they
did with pubs in the age of the gin palace and offer loans in return for
exclusive deals. From the club's perspective, what seems like a short-
term fix creates two longer-term problems. One, clubs often take
these loans to consolidate existing debt, rather than fixing the problems underlying their decline. Two, as a condition of the loan, brewers
tie the clubs to paying fixed prices for their beer that become increasingly uncompetitive over time, because there's no scope for

renegotiation or playing one brewer off against another. This means the cheapest prices are no longer guaranteed. Put these together, and a loan can often accelerate the decline it was supposed to fix.

Glyn Bradshaw has been a member of Sheffield Lane Club since the mid-nineties. As soon as he arrived, he could see the problem: 'When I got here we were giving money away. It was a shambles. A cattle shed. The place was filthy and we were £9k in the red. In 1989 we had to borrow £200,000 off Bass and we'd been paying it off since. By 1997 all the money from the loan was all gone, frittered away. So I became treasurer that year, and secretary in 2000. We weren't getting any discount on the beer because of what we still owed on the loan. And I saw that if we didn't get that discount, we were done.'

Under the terms of the loan, Bass (now Molson Coors) held the deeds to the club. Glyn took out a loan from the Co-op bank, paid the brewery loan back, regained the deeds, and freed the club to negotiate better deals on its beer supply by talking to other brewers. Molson Coors still supplies Sheffield Lane with their lead brand Carling, and it's still the biggest seller. But Heineken-owned John Smith's is on its tail.

'But it was still a cattle shed,' continues Glyn. He gestures to the main bar from his cluttered office, the desk covered in paperwork. 'That was a plain room, with oil cloth on the floor instead of carpets. We put carpets in, did the whole room – it cost £80,000, and this time we paid it all up front. Then we spent another £90,000 doing the concert room.'

This time, the investment paid off. The bars take between £19,000 and £20,000 a week, most of it in Carling and John Smith's, which sell in volumes that far outstrip most pubs. 'And we didn't put the price of beer up for ten years, between 2009 and 2020,' says Glyn. 'It was £2 for a pint of Carling, £1.80 for Marston's Smooth. Cheapest pint in Sheffield.'

There are three officials of the club: Glyn, the president, and a treasurer – plus four other committee members. The committee meets every Sunday morning, 'without fail,' and keeps a close eye on what's happening, ensuring the club never starts creeping back to its previous shabby state. 'If anything gets grubby, we redo it.'

We leave Glyn's office so he can show me the concert room. It's twice the size of the huge main bar. A wide stage runs down the long wall opposite the bar, an old keyboard sitting in one corner. A sort of church pulpit next to the bar has a state-of-the-art mixing desk where the lectern should be.

'We used to have a house drummer and organist. Organist's been here since 1978. Drummer died. We didn't replace him.'

'Well, the organist can do all that now, can't he?'

'Aye. We also still have top-class acts,' says Glyn. 'The Fortunes, Amen Corner, Union Gap. We always have rock bands on a Friday. We don't charge admission, but the bar take will go up from £15k to £19 or 20k.'

I express astonishment that some of these bands are still going. It turns out that, like Sugababes, there are few, if any, of their original members left, but they still belt out the hits the ageing club audience remember from their youth.

'We were full on Saturday night. Union Gap – well, they're called From the Gap – 450 people in, we did £3,500 on the bar; 150 for a Sunday act and we took £4,000. Amen Corner cost us £1,500 but it was absolutely packed.'

Every time Glyn opens his mouth, numbers spill out. It becomes a little dizzying, but it's this attention to numbers, to detail, that means Sheffield Lane Club is still here. It makes me wonder how many clubs disappeared because they didn't have someone like Glyn turn up to be on their committee.

'Bingo, acts, and beer, that's why people come.' he says 'We have karaoke on a Tuesday, that brings in £2k on the night.' He pauses and reflects for a second. 'Well, it's got to the stage now where it's not really karaoke. They're too good.'

I wonder if there are other factors at work. When I left here last night after talking to Tim, I did what I do whenever I'm somewhere new and asked Google Maps to show 'pubs near me.' And there were none. The nearest pubs are about a mile in any direction. There are two big off-licences around the corner, offering treats such as two bottles of Black Tower for £11 or three litres of Lambrini for £5.99. But apart from that, it's as if the local area were built by temperance campaigners like Reddish's Greg family. Is that part of the club's success? They simply don't have much competition?

'Oh, there used to be plenty,' says Glyn. 'That big KFC on the corner – that were a pub till not long back. There were other clubs as well. You know the Shire Green Club? Where they filmed *The Full Monty*? That were just down t'road. Do you know what they got from *Full Monty*? 150 quid and they lerr'em keep curtains. But it's all drugs round here now. They get into the pubs – or clubs – and when they start dealing in there that's it, you end up closing down. Happened everywhere except here.'

Suddenly, the strange anonymity of the building outside makes sense. 'How did you survive, then?' I ask.

Glyn thinks, answers slowly and quietly, choosing his words carefully. 'We have some very good security on the doors.'

I wish I could stay here till tomorrow, when a live band is on. I've timed my visit badly. But I don't want to leave yet. After Glyn completes the tour by showing me the new snooker room upstairs, I head back into the bar and buy another pint. The place is filling up a little, and I realise I need to be careful.

Once – a long time ago – I went to my local Wetherspoons at lunchtime. To paraphrase the legendary comedian Bill Hicks, I wasn't proud of it but I was thirsty. The vast drinking hall had about seven people scattered among its two-hundred-or-so seats, and I was the youngest by about thirty years. I chose a small table, well away from anyone else, and got out my book. When I was about halfway down my pint, a woman in her seventies came in, bought herself a gin-and-something, walked over and sat down so closely to me, our thighs were touching.

I could no longer concentrate on my book. I pretended to keep reading it anyway. There were acres of empty seats around us, no one else within about ten yards. Over the next ten minutes or so, she greeted other men who came in, bought pints, and sat alone at tables well apart from each other. But she said nothing to me, didn't look at me. The other men she greeted were the early day regulars. They all knew each other. But they didn't sit together when they found each other here. They had their daily ritual, not just the greeting, but the pattern of owning the space.

I was sitting in this woman's seat.

Slowly, without making any sudden movements, I finished my drink as naturally as I could, made sure I had everything, and stood up. As soon as I did so, the woman slid across six inches into the space where I'd been sitting. From the corner of my eye, I could see her body relax. I almost ran when I got to the street.

I'm conscious of the lesson I learned that day as Glyn heads back to his mountain of paperwork and I head to the serving hatch at the end of the Perspex-covered bar. Tim isn't on the bar this time, and none of the people from last night are here now, so I'm anonymous once again. I quickly betray my status as an outsider by asking for a pint of 'Stones' instead of 'Stones's.' The seating arrangements, though sparser than the Wetherspoons, are being used in exactly the same way, each person occupying their own space. I sit on a newly reupholstered banquette in the most anonymous-looking spot I can see, an outlier in a scattered constellation of day drinkers.

'There's only one person I know and that's Mark wi' a van,' says a man sitting alone at a table near the bar, talking into his phone. It takes me a second, and then I adjust: he's not saying the only person he knows is this guy Mark, who happens to have a van. He's saying the only person he knows with a van is this guy Mark.

I pretend to mind my own business. It takes a few seconds to tune in to the chatter that takes place between the tables. It's guarded, modest, shy, and, perhaps, considerate. You sit on your own, not bothering anyone else. If there's someone you know sitting at another table – and if you're a regular here, there always is – you might say something to them. But you don't get up and walk over uninvited, and you don't invite them to your table. Either move might look a bit too forward. So you chat across the room, because you can, because the music's not too loud, and because there's no reason to keep anything you're saying private from everyone else. This way, the conversation can stop and start at any time. There's no need to try to continue it if there's a lull. Once you've both say what you had to say, you can switch off, go back to your pint, or gaze at the screen, which today has gone forward a decade to NOW 90s, until someone has something else to say.

They talk about football, neighbours, relationships, and the past. The hospital and the buses. They people they love. The people they've left. Hedge trimmers. Ailments and illnesses. The traffic. Vans. They talk about Rambo, who was meant to be coming in.

'Rambo was meant to be coming in.'

'Was he?'

'Said he'd be here by two.'

'He's not normally late, is he?'

'Wheer's he got to?'

'Said he'd be here by two.'

At 2.17, Rambo arrives, grizzled, head shaved, in haste, to growls of 'First blood!' from around the room. He drops into a seat opposite the man who was wondering where he'd got to, and chats away for ten minutes before remembering to go to the bar for a pint. Relieved, the room falls back into its fragmented conversations.

They tell longer stories, of people they know who have made fortunes, lost everything, had accidents, had builders in, had Covid, had the vaccine, got married, got pregnant, got divorced, got a new phone.

Sure, Tim, the booze is cheap here. But it's even cheaper at the off-licences around the corner at Lane Top. People don't come here for cheap booze. They come to be out of the house. They come to be close to others, if not quite with them. They come not just for the Carling or the John Smith's, and they certainly don't come here to get drunk. They come to talk, to share, to relax, to live with the beer and over the beer. But not because of it.

4

THE CLUB AND
THE MUSIC HALL

Newcastle Labour Club, Newcastle upon Tyne

I briefly wonder what to wear for a whistle-stop tour of clubs around Newcastle and Gateshead. I want to blend in if I can, a northern middle-aged bloke in a northern middle-aged bloke's world. With a shapeless fleece covering a T-shirt and V-necked jumper, I feel classless, placeless, faceless.

It totally doesn't work.

We arrive at Newcastle Labour Club at 6.30 on a Friday evening, pay a quid each to sign in, handing the money to a tall, elderly man who has a little trestle table by the door, and head for the main bar. As we walk through the doors, the entire room turns to watch us make our way to the bar at the far end. It's a long walk, and every one of the hundred or so people in the bar gets a good look at us as we thread our way between their low, round tables.

As I dare to lift my head from the carpet to return their gaze, several things immediately become obvious. One: Ben, Dave and I are the only people in this packed room with beards, and Dave's in particular is full and lush, Edwardian in its ebullience. Two, we're the only people whose hair is not full-on silvery white. (Ben and Dave's heads are also covered by a baseball cap and a flat cap respectively – the only head-gear in the room). Three, our casual dress choices are way off the mark. Women outnumber men in here two to one, and each of them looks their very best, all made up and sporting jewellery, some in dresses, others in smart tops. The men are mostly in suits or blazers, all of them at least wearing shirt collars, many with ties. And finally, we're strangers. Everyone here knows each other. Apart from us.

While it pains me to say this as a Yorkshireman, the north east of England is the undisputed heart of clubland. The Northumberland Branch of the CIU boasts 92 clubs, most of which are in and around Newcastle, while the neighbouring Durham branch has 142 – the highest of any branch. By comparison, at the time of writing South Yorkshire still scores a respectable 79, but West Yorkshire – another bastion of clubland – can only manage 37 these days. As branches are closed and merged in other parts of the country, the north east surges on.

Dave Stone owns Wylam, Newcastle's finest craft brewery, and Ben is his head brewer. Dave is a scouser who turned up in Newcastle with a van load of PA equipment and has never left. Ben grew up here, in the clubs. When I announced I was writing this book on social media, Dave insisted on organising a driver to take the three of us around the clubs that mean the most to him and Ben.

The Labour Club is our first stop. If it were not for the big sign outside sporting the famous Newcastle blue star, and the letters 'C-I-U' picked out in the brickwork, you might mistake it for a public library built in the 1980s. The building is certainly big enough to be the main library for a city like Newcastle. It takes up half of one side of a street in the city centre, a hundred yards away from St James's Park, home ground of the beloved Toon.

In the main bar, a karaoke machine is set up down one side of the room. As these things go, it's quite elaborate: the speakers would be sufficient for a full band in a venue this size. Extra screens are rigged up so that everyone in the room can see the words to the songs and sing along if they wish. An elderly woman is gamely wrestling with Patsy Cline's 'Crazy,' the whole room behind her as she fights to hit each high note. There's something of David Lynch in the way she stands close to the screen, her posture like a hunter about to strike, leaning forward to read the lyrics and singing in a fragile but intact voice. A huge round of applause greets her final 'crazy for loving you,' and the DJ-cum-Karaoke MC says, 'How about that! 81 years old and still belting them out!'

A bloke in his sixties is obviously next in line. He stands too close to the 81-year-old woman, intruding on her spotlight, eager for his go. Between songs, the screens showing song lyrics flip to a slideshow of photos of the people sitting in the room now sitting in the room some other time, in the same seats they're sitting in now, wearing the same clothes. I feel momentarily trapped in a shadow world created by two mirrors facing each other.

Dave, Ben and I are eyed suspiciously as we order our three pints of McEwan's Scotch Ale – another beer I thought had ceased to exist a long time ago. We get stiffed, only receiving £2 change from a tenner, victims of a Stranger Tax that tops up the guest admission we paid at the door. The beer tastes surprisingly decent – fresh, malty and treacly, but quite light. Perfect for an October night, and only slightly spoiled by being served in branded Woodpecker Cider pint glasses.

So as not to try to compete with the karaoke – which would not go well – we head into the smaller bar, which is still massive, and has been designed like the departures lounge of a provincial airport, decorated as a shrine to Newcastle United, and lit like the Sahara at high noon. I mention the lighting – which has been the most consistent aspect of all the clubs I've visited. 'You can't look your best unless you're under the fluorescents!' says Dave. 'It's Friday. That's when you were given your packet and you took it home. Pay your keep. Get washed and changed and go out with the rest.'

Dave and I know each other only through the medium of the craft beer revolution that has swept through the UK over the last decade. In here, we feel a very long way from that world.* Clubs feature in

---

* Later, I tweet that, to my surprise, I'm actually enjoying the taste of the beer in the clubs. Some of my craft beer followers tell me that I am mistaken: I couldn't possibly have enjoyed them, because they were smoothflow beers brewed by macro brewers.

the deep pasts of all three of us, and there's a sense of relief in acknowledging and re-engaging with this shared history. We quickly get the obligatory craft beer gossip out of the way.

I've visited quite a few clubs by now, and am starting to get over my imposter syndrome (tonight's wardrobe disaster notwithstanding). I am a bit nervous about being here with other outsiders, because there's always the risk that you'll 'enjoy' situations like this in an ironic fashion, smirking behind your pint. So I'm glad when I see the other two start to thaw with the surprise that this is an enjoyable experience on its own terms. Clubland and craft beer don't mix well because craft beer takes the beer too seriously, whereas in most social situations the beer plays a supporting role, acting as a facilitator, a catalyst, to something bigger, something more important.

Something like singing your heart out.

* * *

The term 'moral panic' first came into modern, mainstream use around 1972. But it was describing a societal phenomenon that had been familiar for at least 140 years by that point.

Inspired by the seaside clashes between mods and rockers, Stanley Cohen analysed a series of outbreaks in his book *Folk Devils and Moral Panics*, and looked at where they come from and how they behave: 'A condition, episode, person or group of persons emerges to become defined as a threat to societal values and interests; its nature is presented in a stylized and stereotypical fashion by the mass media; the moral barricades are manned by editors, bishops, politicians and other right-thinking people; socially accredited experts pronounce their diagnoses and solutions; ways of coping are evolved or (more often) resorted to; the condition then disappears, submerges or deteriorates and becomes more visible.'

Examples from recent decades include Satanic messages hidden in heavy metal music, Dungeons & Dragons warping players' minds, binge drinking turning town centres into no-go zones for decent people, video games turning children into mass murderers, and rave music and ecstasy culture rotting people's brains, killing them, compelling them to tear the heads off pigeons, and all manner of outlandish behaviour, much of which never happened.

These all arose as threats from outside what is considered to be the mainstream, and were defined as threats by the self-appointed moral arbiters of the mainstream. Even as the nature of the threat changes, it's usually the same people and the same newspapers provoking a response among their readers of 'It's disgusting and it should be banned. Now, what is it, exactly?'

Moral panics need mass media to breathe and grow, so we think of them as a late twentieth century phenomenon. But newspapers and magazines were flourishing throughout the nineteenth century, and they have left plenty of evidence to show that moral panics were alive and well in the rapidly growing towns and cities of the late Industrial Revolution. As we've seen, in a climate that we'd view today as religious fundamentalism, with constant tensions between the classes, pretty much everything the working classes did in their leisure time created a moral panic. The gin palace was a big one. Association football would become another. But the biggest of them all, the gravest threat to Victorian society, was the music hall.

Today, if we have any opinion on music hall at all, we see it as a quaint old tradition, the good old days of wholesome entertainment, sanitised by time and familiarity. It's difficult to imagine what could have been so threatening about it. If a well-dressed lady standing on a small stage singing 'Any Old Iron' or 'Down at the Old Bull and Bush' seems like an improbable threat to civilisation, that's because music hall eventually won the argument. But it didn't do so on its own terms. After it had scandalised Victorian Britain for decades, the Edwardian establishment tamed it, neutralised the threat and turned it into respectable entertainment. Music hall had its roots in the fields where the pre-industrial working class toiled, and flourished for a while in towns and cities on their terms, in the shape they determined. This was unacceptable. But when this independent, subversive model of entertainment was finally gentrified, its spirit went underground, into the places no one was writing about, and there it continued, shaping modern popular culture in a way no one really noticed.

* * *

Before they moved to the cities, working-class people pretty much entertained themselves. Singing communally was just something you did, and there'd always be someone who had a particular talent who could be called upon to do a solo number such as 'Greensleeves' or 'Early One Morning,' with everyone joining in on the chorus. They sang about their shared experience, tales of love and loss, work and sex, drinking and celebrating, and songs were passed orally from one generation to the next.

This form of self-entertainment translated pretty easily into the urban pub. People would take it in turns to stand at the piano to sing, on evenings that became known as 'Free and Easies.' These were usually male-only events, free of charge, but often with exhortations to drink more quickly. Proceedings were overseen by a chairman, who introduced the rotating acts, or 'turns,' ensured there were plenty of breaks for drinks to be topped up, and set a personal example by always being ready to accept a pint from the audience. According to one Lancashire magistrate, such chairmen were: '… diverting pleasant fellows who had what is called "the run of their teeth;" that is, they were allowed to eat and drink, and they were employed by the publicans to sing songs and tell stories, and badger any country fellow who came till they made him drink.'

Now, you might think there's nothing wrong with a sing-song around the old Joanna, but these were Victorian working-class men, remember, so anything they did was, by definition, bad. *The Town* reported in 1837: 'The epidemic of vocal music has more particularly spread its contagious and devastating influence amongst the youth of the Metropolis, the London apprentice boys. These young gentlemen generally give vent to their passion and display their vocal abilities in the spacious room appropriated to that purpose of some tavern or public house and these meetings are most aptly denominated Free and

Easies: free as air they are for the advancement of drunkenness and profligacy and easy enough of access to all classes of society with little regard to appearances or character.'

This despicable practice of people singing to each other in a space that welcomed anyone and had no dress code has reappeared numerous times in history. *The Sun* used very similar language to *The Town* when it sent its intrepid reporters to a rave in 1989, and brought back tales of 'spaced-out young girls, some as young as twelve, rubbing shoulders with sinister drug dealers while drug-crazed youths writhed to alien rhythms.'

That word 'alien' comes up again when J. Ewing Ritchie, who took a very close interest in everything filthy and obscene he could find in London, describes the denizens of a Free and Easy in 1858's *The Night Side of London*. But he doesn't lay all the blame for their wretched condition at their own feet: 'The reader will see from these specimens how alien the costermonger race is in sympathy and life from the respectable and the well-to-do. Their songs are not ours, nor their aims nor conventional observances … Society will not educate its poor; wonder not then that they educate themselves, and that after a fashion not very desirable in the eyes of the friends of morality, of order, and of law.'

Each writer is describing music, and people enjoying it as a shared, communal experience. None of them seems to witness anything worse than that happening, so sensationalist language is employed to do some really heavy lifting to help make singing and dancing feel like a sinister threat from outside our safe cultural space. Whether it's happening behind the closed doors of a pub you'd never dream of visiting or a disused airfield in Berkshire you'll never find, the publication brings these revellers into your home, stoking the fear that contagious, alien beings are coming for you and your children.

Even worse than the Free and Easy was the Judge and Jury, a kind of mock trial where – if you're of a sensitive disposition, you may want to skip this bit – men would dress in costume and make rude jokes about each other. I know, right? J. Ewing Ritchie was even more disturbed by these than he was by the costermongers singing, but you can't help suspecting there's some knowing titillation of the delicate reader going on here: 'I dare not even attempt to give a faint outline of the proceedings ... the Judge and Jury Clubs make you familiar with the manners of the stews [brothels]; and I solemnly believe that in Sodom and Gomorrah nothing more filthy could have been talked about, and that this side of Pandemonium there is nothing more debasing or debased.'

The proprietors of the most popular Free and Easies soon began to find their premises too small. The Eagle in Shepherdess Walk, East London, erected a pavilion in its gardens that became known as the Grecian Saloon. John Hollingshead, proprietor of the Gaiety Theatre, later dubbed the Grecian 'the father and mother, the dry and wet nurse of the Music Hall,' but the Canterbury in Waterloo is generally considered to be the first proper, purpose-built music hall. In 1852, publican Charles Morton knocked down four skittle alleys at the back of his pub and built a music hall that seated 700 people. The Canterbury Music Hall proved so popular that four years later, Morton demolished the whole thing and built a new hall that replaced the pub altogether. It was so grand that even J. Ewing Richie felt it had an air of respectability: 'A well-lighted entrance attached to a public-house indicates that we have reached our destination. We proceed up a few stairs, along a passage lined with handsome engravings, to a bar, where we pay sixpence if we take a seat in the body of the hall, and nine-pence if we do the nobby and ascend into the balcony. We make our way leisurely along the floor of the building, which is really a very handsome hall, well lighted, and capable of holding fifteen hundred persons ...'

Aside from the stage and the balcony, music halls continued to echo the pubs they had evolved from: instead of theatre-style rows of seating, the main floor was still filled with chairs and tables, eating and drinking still being very much part of the deal. Servers wandered among the tables, and the acts had to compete with general chatter and people milling around.

The acts were a mix of amateurs from the Free and Easies and, increasingly, professional entertainers, all still overseen by the chairman. The singers began with the songs people knew – the folk tunes they had been singing in the fields for centuries, taking the audience back to an earlier, simpler life, delighting them with sentiment. Lyrically, the most popular songs commented on the ups and downs of working-class life. New songs such as 'Glorious Beer' and 'Champagne Charlie' were commissioned specifically to keep the bars busy. From America came songs from a different tradition, spirituals sung by enslaved people in the cotton fields that were popularised by wandering minstrel shows. These blended with different styles such as the Eastern European polka and waltz, and the Irish jig, giving birth to a sort of proto-world music.

The best performers soon made names for themselves, and some would start doing patter between the songs. With no microphones, a solo performer had to be gifted to be heard above the noise of people eating, drinking and carousing, and a form of raw humour developed that was able to cut through. In a tradition that continued with comedians such as Billy Connolly, for some, the patter eventually pushed out the songs altogether. The most successful performers learned how to work with the crowd rather than compete against them, encouraging the audience to sing along with the choruses. The lyrics to songs like 'Champagne Charlie' or 'Come Along My Boys Let's Make Some Noise' acknowledged and celebrated the desire to drink away the workday grind. Comedians developed catchphrases the audience could wait for and then call out.

Music hall became the highlight of the working man's week, and the halls spread rapidly around the country, particularly in large industrial cities. While halls such as the Canterbury sought and won some respectability – Morton actively encouraged women to attend in the belief they helped create a more genteel atmosphere than the male-only Free and Easy – it didn't take long for them to generate middle-class opposition.

The managers of West End theatres worried that some of their respectable middle-class patrons were being lured away by the baser delights of music hall – even the future Edward VII was a fan. The most common accusation was that the open, mingling layout of the halls was a fertile ground for prostitution. To some extent this was true, but magistrates turned a blind eye – it was going to happen somewhere, and better here than in the dark alleys of the slums. Next came accusations of lyrical inanity and obscenity, the idea that the very nature of the entertainment was immoral and corrupting of any who witnessed it. Music hall also popularised what were known as 'sensation acts.' These were entertainments that appealed to base emotions rather than the intellect. Acts such as trapeze artists and tightrope walkers were immoral because they apparently indulged the more animalistic, less rational side of our natures, getting the heart racing. At a time when women in particular were regarded as nervous creatures prone to fainting, even Charles Dickens worried about society reverting to these 'barbaric excitements.'

The audience wanted more, and each new twist to keep them satisfied was duly condemned for its degeneracy. 'Black-face' minstrels were shocking not for their racism, but because their comedy was slapstick and their words crude. Contortionists, clowns and clog dancers were all slammed for their lack of intellectual worth. The singers were the worst of all, especially the women. Marie Lloyd was famous for using innuendo and double-entendres in her songs. 'Don't Dilly Dally on the Way' – the story of a midnight flit to avoid paying the rent – was written for her and would have been identifiable for every man in the audience. When she sang about being a naïve young woman on a train who had 'never had her ticket punched before,' she used what Monty Python would later codify as 'nudge-nudge, wink-wink' to suggest to the audience what she was really talking about. When a Licensing Committee tried to use her lyrics as evidence of lewdness and justification for refusing to renew a music hall licence, she demonstrated how her act relied on these cheeky gestures and the building of a conspiratorial relationship with the audience rather than the content itself. She sang a few of her more notorious numbers without any of this, and the committee had to accept there was nothing they could find a problem with. So then she sang a very respectable standard of the time, Alfred Lord Tennyson's drawing room ballad 'Come into the Garden, Maud,' with leers, nudges and winks, and made lines such as:

And long by the garden lake I stood,
For I heard your rivulet fall
From the lake to the meadow and on to the wood,
Our wood, that is dearer than all

sound absolutely filthy, before telling the committee that any obscenity was all in their dirty minds.

Music hall entertainment was coarse because it reflected working-class life and was a product of it. It never occurred to moralisers, philanthropists and reformers that it was speaking truth about the lives of the audience. What the critics saw as a complete absence of worthwhile culture was in fact the culture of working-class life being honestly represented, but it was a culture that was very different from the one the middle classes wanted the working classes to aspire to. Even worse, it was so popular that it would go on to create the first ever entertainment 'celebrities' or 'stars,' terms which first came into service to describe the biggest music hall acts. Dan Leno created a cast of comic characters the audience would have found familiar from their everyday lives: the henpecked husband, the railway guard, the policeman and the gossip, Mrs Kelly. His patter was often surreal: 'Then comes the egg. That is the egg I am talking about. That is the egg that causes all the trouble. It's only a little round white thing, but you can't tell what it's thinking about. You daren't kick it and you daren't drop it. It has got no face. You can't get it to laugh. You simply look at it and say, "Egg!"'

Today, comedian Stewart Lee describes music hall as a 'a kind of working-class surrealism.' Even now, when such comedy is celebrated, he tells me that historians of comedy talk about it as 'happy accidents created by gin-sozzled proles who don't understand their own gifts until the middle classes start doing them and writing about them.'

Eventually, this kind of working-class entertainment would go mainstream. Comedians from the Goons and Tommy Cooper, through Monty Python, to the surrealism of Noel Fielding, Ross Noble and Reeves and Mortimer, the observational humour of

Michael McIntyre and Peter Kay, and the characters created by Catherine Tate or *The Fast Show*, can all trace a lineage back to Dan Leno. Meanwhile in pop and rock music, the rhythms and arrangements of music hall can be heard on classic albums by everyone from the Beatles and the Kinks, to Queen and Blur. It's hard to imagine just how alien and dangerous it was to the Victorians, and staggering to consider just how much this degenerate moral panic underpins modern mainstream entertainment.

*   *   *

For reformers, the problem with music hall was that it was the entertainment equivalent of empty calories, commercialised leisure that offered no rational self-improvement. Leisure time had to be useful and constructive. Why? Because otherwise we'd be back to Schrödinger's workers again, a population simultaneously lured into bored apathy and incited into violent rebellion by the sinful sensationalism they were all gorging on.

The kinds of people who agreed with the sentiments regularly expressed in *The Times* did their best to ban music hall. Failing that they attempted to at least regulate it and control it. The more well-meaning rational recreationist reformers reasoned that, as with pubs and gin palaces, if they wanted working men to forsake them, they had to offer a more attractive alternative.

Some believed this would be easy – after all, there was 'proper' culture everywhere! Listening to a song about a poor East End lad pretending to be a fashionable dandy may have corrupted the soul but watching a play about a grief-stricken prince pretending to be mad would make you a better person. People just needed to be exposed to the right stuff, and they would be instantly enlightened. As one organiser of a Midlands Penny Entertainment tellingly put it, 'the very beasts of the forest would sit entranced when [proper] music's gentle strains were heard.'

After the failure of Mechanics' Institutes and Knowledge Societies, rational recreationists realised they needed to add something a bit more entertaining if they wanted working people to sit and be lectured at. Across the country, various philanthropists founded clubs and societies – including some working men's clubs – that explored 'lighter' forms of recreation, with music and singing acting as bait to get people into lectures.

In 1854, Samuel Taylor, secretary of the Mechanics' Institution in Hanley, Staffordshire, hit upon the idea of reading out extracts from *The Times* in the market square (presumably choosing his passages very carefully so as not to let his audience know what the newspaper thought of them). There was some interest in this, as many working men could neither read nor afford to buy a daily newspaper. By adding literary and musical entertainment to the news, his events became so popular he could charge a penny admission. These 'Penny Readings' spread across the Midlands, attracting crowds in their thousands and eventually moving indoors.

One reason Penny Readings worked initially is that they conformed to some of the traditions of working-class entertainment. Like the singing saloons, they were held on a Saturday or Monday evening, and unlike theatre or opera, the organisers were careful to inform the audience that there were no reserved seats. Those working men's clubs that still had a thing for improving the working man cautiously adopted them.

Two areas of conflict swiftly emerged. The first was over the kind of entertainments that were suitable to show. The clubs quickly adopted the idea, asking for material to be submitted in advance for approval. Hodgson Pratt, the CIU secretary, advised readers to 'try to keep up a high standard in the selection of pieces, and do not, for the sake of popularity, imitate the vile taste of the London music halls.' In 1862, the Coventry Working Men's Club initially attempted to stick with recitations of 'higher literary works,' but as soon as they added musical entertainment – a move that divided the club's committee – they had to move their events to the local corn exchange to accommodate crowds of two thousand.

But a bigger problem was that people weren't just enjoying the wrong entertainment: they were enjoying it in the wrong way.

Comfortable in an environment that felt familiar, the audience brought their traditions with them, shouting for encores for acts they liked, and coughing and stamping through an act they didn't. Critics of the Readings noted that the crowd resorted to 'disgraceful' behaviour such as 'ironical clapping,' and that by doing so, they dragged 'all down to their ignorant level,' 'inflicting their vulgar tastes' on any middle-class people who had ventured into an event that was aimed squarely at the working classes. One former club committee member complained that after three series of readings, the organisers were now: '… the servants of the mob. The chairman at present is a mere sign post – an illumination for the programme instead of being there to direct the meeting and to keep order … If he finds it impossible to keep order, let him at once dissolve the meeting and leave the chair, and let the Police clear the room.'

That a working men's club committee member felt that the police should be called to break up a mob of people clapping ironically at someone reading something shows just how paternalistic the early clubs were. If the bit about the beasts in the field were true, and instead of being entranced, the mob reacted with shuffling, coughing, wisecracks and ironical clapping, it followed that the working class were less cultured than animals.

These accounts resonated with my own working-class experience of having someone else's culture forced on me by people who still thought they knew what was best for me and my peers.

My school was designed to equip working-class kids with the skills they would need to be good, hard-working citizens when they left at sixteen to work in a mine or factory. 'English' meant learning grammar and composition rather than an appreciation of literature, and music was something they never quite figured out how to teach, and pretty much gave up on by the time you were closing in on your exams. One or two of the younger, hipper teachers who had gone to redbrick universities in the mid-1970s were starting to whisper the heresy that maybe the Beatles were actually talented musicians rather than just long-haired hooligans, but Joby was not of their number.

Joby wasn't our music teacher's real name, but in the parlance of form 2D, 'he looked like one.' Grey and stern from the tips of his wiry hair to the heels of his polished brogues, he was a cross between Jack Nance's character in *Eraserhead* and the 1990s *Spitting Image* puppet of John Major. Attitudinally, he came across as a Victorian Baptist preacher who had been sent to save the poor as a young man and had over the years slowly come to fear and despise them for their abject resistance to redemption.

In his music lessons, Joby alternated between making us sing folk songs that we hated because they had nothing to do with our local traditions or lives and making us sit through his record collection. In each case, he would tell us nothing about why the music was important, or where it came from, or how it fitted into the broader canon. He might go so far as to tell us who the composer was and what the piece was called, but that would be it. He wouldn't even answer direct questions from the two or three people interested enough to ask them. Queries such as 'How did Beethoven write music when he was deaf, Sir?' were merely proof of our ignorance, and not worthy of engagement.

Perhaps Joby was hoping that he didn't need to bother to actually teach us anything about music because all we needed was to hear it, to listen to it, and we would somehow be entranced by it, and then develop an innate understanding of it. Instead, he managed to create a hearty antipathy towards classical music among every single person in our class.

How does an audience react when 'culture' is used as a form of assault upon it? By clapping ironically. By coughing, by hiding jokes and insults under that cough, by trying to explode the suppressed laughter in those sitting near you with a perfectly-timed gag or observation. And when asked to sing along to someone else's folk music, by taking the piss, by twisting the words wherever you can, seeing how far you can push it before eliciting a spittle-flecked diatribe: 'I heard you! I can hear you! And don't think I daren't say it! I dare! I can hear you singing '*In Dublin's fair city, where girls are so SHITTY!*'

The inhabitants of inner-city slums rejected each and every attempt from outside to 'improve' them. Eventually even the socialists, who arrived in the slums with the aim of defending those being exploited by an unjust economic system, ended up condemning the poor for their lax morals and their determination to kick back and enjoy themselves whenever they could. Whatever was thrown at them, the working classes showed what Brad Beaven calls 'a remarkable propensity to manipulate the entertainment offered to coincide with their own cultural preferences.'

Having said that, just as some clubs were boozier than others once they were able to serve beer, the range of entertainments was not uniformly lowbrow. Left to their own devices, men didn't inevitably drift towards the drunken, the lewd or the profane. For some, higher culture was fine – so long as they were choosing it for themselves, on their own terms.

John Taylor, a lifelong clubman who in 1972 wrote the pamphlet *From Self-Help to Glamour: The Working Man's Club 1860–1972*, observed that while the Penny Reading was imposed from above, the Free and Easy was an example of entertainment that 'forced its way up from below' into clubs. While the old singing saloons had become glitzy music halls with professional artistes, the simple Free and Easy was still fondly remembered. If it lost one home it would simply find another, and so it became a mainstay of club entertainment. Taylor himself remembers the Free and Easy still going strong in the club he first attended with his dad in the 1930s and 1940s:

Adopting very much the same approach as that in the Music Halls, the chairman for the night would take a seat on the stage with his beer and a small brass bell on a table before, him, cast his eyes around the hall, and write in his notebook the names of probable performers: there were always plenty ... an appeal for 'the best of order' was as much a part of the evening's entertainment as the songs themselves ... 'For our first turn tonight, I would like to call on our old friend ...': the summoned singer would take the last swig of his beer and amble towards the stage for a whispered discussion with the pianist. This was an often unnecessary ritual as most of the singers had their well-known favourites which were trotted out week after week. This in no way detracted from the enjoyment given: there was a kind of reassurance in this repetition.

The songs club members chose to sing were a mix of music hall standards, with titles like 'The Flea that Bit Poor Nora' and 'Knocked 'em in the Old Kent Road' folded in with political anthems like 'We've Worked Eight Hours This Day' and 'Strike Boys Strike.' What the political songs and the lighter entertainments had in common was that they were rooted in lived experience, culturally specific, and in that sense, no different from anything else that we consider folk music today.

From here, self-generated clubland entertainment soon spread to include more 'sensational entertainments,' which prompted that terrible and dangerous thing, a state of excitement. Hodgson Pratt didn't like these either, warning that 'steady and reliable members are kept away rather than attracted by Negro melodies and mesmeric seances, while the unwholesome passion for excitement destroys a taste for recreation of a quieter and more refined kind.'

Judge and Juries were also revived in clubs in the 1880s and 1890s and seemed to be less lewd than those held in pubs fifty years before. The 'Judges,' 'Learned Counsels' and other officials were selected from club members, who tried their peers for crimes such as 'not uncovering their heads in court.' Local politics might creep in with issues such as 'Billiard Players v. The Rest of the Club.' These evenings were often reported in the *Club and Institute Journal*, and the accounts make them sound like jolly affairs. One of the researchers employed by Charles Booth for his epic nine-volume study of *Life and Labour of the People in London*, published between 1892 and 1897, disagreed, describing them simply as 'filth.'

At what many would see as the other end of the spectrum, more serious dramatic performances also became prominent in some clubs. These began with 'Elocution Classes.' Richard Gaston, a 'serious artisan' who would go on to become editor of the *Club and Institute Journal*, lamented the fact that there were 'very little pains taken to amuse the working class,' and in the 1860s, he and some friends began forming amateur dramatic societies. When clubs became more established, they became the main venue where these groups performed scenes from Shakespeare plays. Again, 'higher culture' worked, when the club chose it rather than having it imposed.

Entertainment was starting to prove a big draw for some clubs. But to realise its full potential, better facilities were needed. By this stage the early patrons of the club movement weren't interested in putting any more money in unless they could take control of what it was being spent on, and they were never going to approve of lewd and corrupting entertainments. Ambitious clubs followed the path of the gin palaces, taking loans from breweries to improve their premises, in return for being 'tied' to that brewery and only being able to sell their beers.

The newer clubs of the late 1880s sported halls that could seat two or three hundred, with a proper stage as opposed to a platform. Clubmen – many of them tradesmen – would build and paint the scenery, with the establishment of each new scene drawing gasps and applause. The *CIJ* reported in 1886 that at the Borough of Hackney Club, 'Critics who predicted that it was presumptuous and absurd for an amateur company to play "Hamlet" were loud in their praises.' Whether it was building the scenery, designing costumes or learning lines, club members were acquiring new skills and getting to show them off to everyone else. The new emphasis on entertainment was promoted by some as more than just mere pleasure seeking. One club told the *CIJ* in 1885 that: 'Saturday evening concerts have become quite a feature of recent months, and they not only provide an agreeable and refreshing change after the dull monotony of our work-a-day lives, but they tend to promote brotherly feeling and mutual regard.'

By 1888, the *CIJ* claimed, 'there is hardly one club, however small, but boasts a stage and scenery, and a band of amateurs, giving periodical performances to their fellow members.'

But success created its own problems. Back with a simple Free and Easy, repetition of a single song was comforting. But when you were putting on more fully fleshed-out and ambitious entertainments, clubmen only wanted to see their mates reciting a play a certain number of times. The better performers formed companies and would tour other clubs, or members with their pass cards would go and check out the turns in another club down the road. By the late 1870s, amateur thespians and singers were sharing the spotlight with a smattering of professional acts borrowed from the music halls, often under the pretext of a fundraising benefit – Marie Lloyd herself appeared in 1891 at the Netherlands Club in aid of their children's party.

According to Richard Gaston, by 1894, potential new members want to know 'not what sort of members belong to [a club], but what kind of entertainment it puts on.' Charles Booth gave this description of East London clubs in 1887: 'The entertainments are sometimes dramatic, but more generally consist of a succession of songs, comical or sentimental, the comic songs often being sung in character with a change of dress. A Music-Hall entertainment is the ideal aimed at. A chairman presides and keeps order, as at the free-and-easy or benefit performances held at public houses, and as till recently was invariably the practice at the public music halls.'

The home-made nature of entertainment had pretty much vanished by the turn of the century, replaced by concert parties, comedians playing characters, female impersonators, ventriloquists, and at the Borough of Hackney Club, a boxing kangaroo. According to Gaston: 'The entertainment manager becomes the most important official of the club, for he knows the power he has of attracting hundreds of members belonging to the club and affiliated to it. The political secretary and the manager of the evening classes are looked upon as superfluous, and rather as encumbrances than any assistance.'

Here then was a huge step away from the original self-improving nature of the working men's club movement. While that idea of betterment could be argued for in the self-generated entertainment, others argued that the club was becoming just another aspect of the consumer capitalism and mass entertainment industry invented by the Victorians. The *CIJ* lamented in 1891: 'There seems to be an unsatiable [*sic*] thirst for amusements, and those of the lightest kind, so that the educational side of club life is quite forgotten. As is well known, lecturers have a poor chance of getting an audience, no matter how clever or gifted they may be, while the comic singer and the sketch artiste, however lacking in real ability, can always draw a hall full.'

These clubs were looking for audiences rather than members, people who parted with money to be entertained rather than people looking to join in with a programme of mutual aid and improvement.

But is this criticism entirely fair? The few historians who have covered this aspect of working men's clubs tend to be left-leaning sociologists, and they portray the evolution of entertainment in clubs as a lost opportunity, just another example of the masses turning into consumers of capitalist product. I don't think it's as simple as that. Clubs were competing with pubs and music hall for the attention of their members. Between 1850 and 1900, wages rose in real terms by 80 per cent, but work for many was still low-skilled, strenuous, repetitive, and lacking any job satisfaction. Working men began to see commercial entertainment as a right rather than a luxury. If they wanted to watch a comedian rather than debate politics, who could blame them?

As for the clubs, the counter-argument was that clubs as communities of interest had to reach out beyond their core membership and be relevant to a broader audience in order to be able to afford to provide services to that core. It's also worth noting that in these notoriously male-only establishments, it quickly became customary for men to bring their wives and families with them to big concerts. For a young woman in particular, it was far more respectable to be seen at a club than a music hall or gin palace.

Finally, it's a mistake to see this kind of entertainment as passive and apathetic. The big concerts didn't entirely replace the Free and Easy – they happened on different nights. And even when working men and women were mere audience members, they made their presence known. They were sitting in their own clubs – if they wanted to shout for an encore, or clap ironically, or even talk through the performance, it was their choice.

Back in the music halls that the clubs were now competing with, the story was taking a different turn.

* * *

Just as the gin palaces could only offer 'mock' glamour in the eyes of their critics, so the music hall, with its bar, long trestle tables, waiters serving beer, and its atmosphere of conviviality and informality rather than reverent silence, was a grotesque parody of 'proper' theatre. The irony of the situation was that this all made music hall far closer to what theatres such as the Globe in Southwark had been like in the Elizabethan era, when plays like *Hamlet* premiered to a room full of chatting, eating, brawling Londoners who would be back the following day to watch a bear being poked with a stick, or a pack of dogs chase a monkey tied to a horse's back. But cultured Victorians weren't big on irony: such entertainments led straight to hell.

The casual atmosphere of music halls had encouraged working-class audiences to play their own roles as chorus, critic or controller of what went on next. And this seems to have been the part that reformers and campaigners really couldn't bear. The censors of the Penny Readings in working men's clubs may not have approved of disruption from the audience, but in the music halls, active audience participation was dreadful behaviour even when it was clearly called for by the act on stage. One reporter at an East End show in the 1870s gave a scathing review of a comedian called Fred Molloy – or rather, of the audience watching him. When Molloy reaches the chorus of a song: 'The audience are invited to join, Freddy giving them encouragement by a 'Now then – all together' and a stamp of his foot. And they do, the imbeciles ... Encore! Encore! Encore! Here he is again!'

The idea that you would have to be mentally challenged, or morally degenerate, to want to sing along to a well-known tune, or shout for more when it had finished, seems bizarre in an age when this is common behaviour everywhere from pantomime to the proms. But the interaction between audience and performer was simply too much, and if it couldn't be changed by asking people to sit and listen properly and proprietors couldn't call the police every time someone clapped ironically or asked for an encore, then the physical space of the music hall itself would have to be changed. Under the pretext of improving safety, the bar was removed to the foyer. The long, communal tables were replaced by rows of theatre-style seating. Different classes of seats were created, priced according to how comfortable they were and what kind of view they had, so audiences could be separated and regimented.

There's no evidence that a greater focus on safety was needed, or that the behaviour of the crowd was becoming more unruly. The efforts of moralising reformers to have music halls closed down were mostly ineffective. Rather, it's a case of music hall managers becoming more ambitious and wanting to be taken more seriously (an ambition shared by big stars such as Marie Loyd, and Dan Leno, the latter eventually suffering a breakdown over his failure to be regarded as a serious actor). Behaviour that might have been considered robust larks in the 1850s was dangerous delinquency by the 1880s, when evangelism was at its peak and everything respectable people disapproved of was, by definition, the work of Satan.

By 1889, J. L. Graydon, secretary of the Proprietors of Entertainment Association, was reassuring our old friends at *The Times* that: 'It is not the desire of the proprietors and managers of the music halls to attract a minority of dissipated or half-tipsy youths. The patronage we seek is that of the immense majority of respectable artisans, assistants and small tradesfolk with their wives and families who, after all, are the pillars of a music-hall's propriety. The more respectably a music-hall is conducted, the greater is the profit.'

Era, an influential weekly magazine for the theatrical profession, suggested notices in artistes' dressing rooms reading 'no language in song or speech is permitted on the stage which the most refined ear may not listen to.' Local councils pressured music hall proprietors to ban certain songs or comic skits – the incident where Marie Lloyd was called upon to defend the supposed lewdness in her lyrics was just one example of a nationwide crackdown.

The chairman, reminding the audience to drink, was replaced by the slick celebrity compere. A wider range of acts was added, including jugglers, magicians and hypnotists – but none of them too sensational – and music hall gradually morphed into what was loosely termed 'variety.' This less gaudy, more respectable form received establishment approval in the form of Royal Command Variety Performances. George V attended the first one in 1912, by which time alcohol had been banned from the auditorium and relegated to the foyer bars. Pointedly, Marie Lloyd was not invited to perform.

This sanitised version of music hall succeeded in attracting a more genteel audience, with more money to spend. New theatres such as His Majesty's and the Palladium closed the deal on variety's respectability and sophistication. The standard variety theatre compere's greeting – 'My lords, ladies and gentlemen' – could not be further away from the earthy spirit of old-style music hall.

When radio came along, the stars of variety would go on to form the basis of 'The Light Programme,' further sanitised by Reithian values not too dissimilar to those of Henry Solly and his rational recreationists. In turn, TV would take the best from radio and variety theatre, eventually killing off the theatres in the process.

In pursuit of money and respectability, music hall cut itself adrift from its roots and, arguably, abandoned its audience. In his book *Palaces of Pleasure: How the Victorians Invented Mass Entertainment*, Lee Jackson argues that the audience was changing too. He quotes music hall impresario William Holland who calls the 1890s an 'age of luxury' thanks to rising incomes. We should consider the possibility, Jackson continues, that 'customers from all social classes were perfectly happy to trade the more rowdy, boozy, 'traditional' music-hall experience for the luxury of the palace of varieties.'

No doubt some were. But a self-identified 'common man,' writing in the *Daily Mail* in 1913, complained: 'In the name either of art or public morality they have improved the style of entertainment to a point at which we cannot understand it and cannot afford to pay the price of admission … the improvement of the entertainment amounts to no more than the exclusion from the auditorium of the vulgar working class population.'

Like most students of music hall, Lee Jackson follows its path to variety theatre, then on to radio and TV light entertainment as a logical progression. But if he had taken even a cursory glance at working men's clubs as part of his otherwise brilliantly researched examination of gin palaces, music halls, Free and Easies, association football, seaside holidays and every other conceivable aspect of Victorian leisure except working men's clubs, he may have reached a different conclusion.

Variety theatre was not a continuation of music hall; it was an abandonment of everything that made music hall what it was. The participative, sometimes anarchic nature of the proceedings, the Free and Easy, the surrealist streak, the bawdiness of songs and jokes, the chairman on stage introducing 'turns,' the waiters coming around tables serving beer, the closeness to the stage thanks to the absence of an orchestra pit, the booziness, the banter and joining in with a good performer, the voluble displeasure of the audience with a bad performer, were the hallmarks of original music hall entertainment because they all grew from the idea of the participative, informal culture that had been brought by working-class people from the fields and into the pubs where music hall was born. Every single bit of this was excised from variety theatre – and every single bit of it became a defining feature of working men's club entertainment for the entire twentieth century.

The BBC TV programme *The Good Old Days* ran for thirty years and was billed as an authentic recreation of the Victorian music hall. To borrow from the sentiment, if not the exact language of music hall: was it bollocks. With its neat rows of seating, theatre boxes, audience in fancy dress as well-to-do Edwardians, orchestra pit and pre-watershed-friendly acts, *The Good Old Days* was a wonderful recreation of the gentrified variety theatre that bore no resemblance to mid-Victorian music hall. If any 1970s TV viewer wanted to see an accurate evocation of music hall as it really was, they would have needed to turn over to Granada TV, and joined the much earthier *Wheeltappers and Shunters Social Club*.

* * *

After a couple of pints, walking back from the lounge into the main bar at Newcastle Labour Club feels like wading into a warm bath.

'It's a living room,' says Ben.

'It's therapy!' replies Dave.

By now the boys are euphoric. 'I'm going to do this again,' says Dave.

'When?' says Ben.

'Next week. Every week! It's so life-affirming. So welcoming. This is the best night out I've had in years!'

The karaoke has grown and mutated into a new stage – thanks to elderly karaoke's unlikely gods.

The scene is weirdly reminiscent of a time when Liz and I once stayed on a caravan park in West Wales. The clubhouses on caravan parks follow the working men's club modus operandi very closely, with bingo and live entertainment most nights during peak season. The night we dropped in, there was a duo belting out popular hits to an audience that seemed to consist of grandparents without enough kids to go around between them. One young lad of about six had the dance floor to himself, staring at the band through jam-jar bottom specs, doing the same moves to every song they played, and clearly freaking out the female singer. Then, the band launched into 'Human' by The Killers, and the tiny dancer was almost crushed by the stampede to the dancefloor. Whole tables of people in their seventies and eighties were up, bending their knees, waving their arms in the air like they really didn't care, and mouthing along to every single word of the song. When it finished, they all sat down again and didn't move for the rest of the set.

Polls of 'best karaoke songs ever' often have The Killers' other biggest hit somewhere near the top, and it probably is with a younger demographic, as immortalised by the headline on spoof news website *The Daily Mash* announcing 'Twelve dead after hen party hears first notes of Mr Brightside.' But clearly there's just something about 'Human' that sends older people barmy. This is almost certainly not the same bunch of people Liz and I saw at the holiday camp clubhouse ten years ago, but they look the same, and they're doing exactly the same thing to the same song. This time, instead of what clubland invariably refers to as 'a talented musical duo,' the song is being sung by another octogenarian woman, or maybe even the same one as earlier. It's hard to tell, because her voice is drowned out by the crowd, and it's difficult to see her through the geriatric moshpit. People are dancing in the aisles and at the bar. Three or four grumpy blokes sit staring at their feet, scowling each time a swinging hip or elbow jostles them. Everybody else is up, most doing a kind of gentle swing dance that's completely out of time with the beat, everyone singing or shouting every word of the song.

Karaoke is, obviously, not exclusive to clubs. It's rivalled only by the pub quiz as the most popular form of participative entertainment in the UK, with about one in five adults saying they enjoy a regular session. It cuts across both age and class – I've witnessed karaoke in dockside pubs in Leith being belted out by young single mums, and in smart, private booths in Islington full of advertising executives. But it's an absolute constant in working men's clubs across the country, one of the biggest draws they have. It is, quite simply, the modern continuation of the Free and Easy – a ritual that has never gone away. The idea of being called upon by our friends to sing them a song is a form of entertainment that stretches back as far as we can fathom. It came in from the fields to the pubs of the city, spent a while in music hall, and then made a switch to working men's clubs once music hall abandoned its roots. It remains alive and well, a draw to clubs matched, perhaps, only by bingo. If Friday night in Newcastle Labour Club is anything to go by, the answer to the eternal question is, emphatically, 'dancer.'

5

THE CLUB AND
THE RADICALS

The Mildmay Club, Newington Green, North London

When you compare old photographs of the Mildmay Club on Newington Green to how it looks today, it's as if the entire building has taken a step back from the road. When it was built in 1901, the current club dominated the north side of Newington Green, its three storeys capped by a gabled roof with an octagonal tower perched on top. Its elegant Queen Anne-style, eight-bay frontage is discreetly set back a few feet from a boundary wall topped with railings, but the main entrance bay juts forward, framed by elegant white columns, announcing the club to the world. Today, newer buildings neighbour it to the west, built right to the street boundary. A few years ago, the shop fronts here were disused, but in this rapidly gentrifying area, they're now all tasteful flower shops, bakeries, patisseries and bike shops. The Mildmay's dirty red brickwork is dowdy by comparison. If you weren't looking for it, you might not notice it if you walked past. It's not trying to hide, like Sheffield Lane seemed to be. It just looks faded and forgotten, its windows shrouded, the paintwork peeling around the door. Even though – when you actually stop and look at it – the club looks large and architecturally impressive (it's Grade II-listed) its anonymous exterior, in common with many clubs, gives no clue of the delights inside.

The first time I visited the Mildmay Club was to organise my wife's fiftieth birthday party. We knew the space from TV. The comedian Stewart Lee lives in Stoke Newington, and he had chosen the Mildmay as the location for his BBC TV show, *Stewart Lee's Comedy Vehicle*, which ran for four series between 2009 and 2016. The series had been filmed in the main function room (there are two) and this is where we had Liz's party.

You climb a wide staircase towards the main hall, and when you enter, you step back in time. This is why Stewart Lee wanted to film here. 'There's a '70s ITV variety show, called *The Wheeltappers' and Shunters' Social Club*, set in a terrifyingly accurate studio-replica of an old-school Working Men's Club,' he wrote for *Chortle* magazine in 2013. 'I loved it as a child, when I was too young to baulk at Bernard Manning, and think I have spent my whole adult life trying to recreate it. It's probably not a coincidence that Comedy Vehicle came to be filmed at The Mildmay Club, one of the last unspoiled Working Men's Clubs left in London.'

There's a big sprung dance floor in the middle of the room, with small round tables lining the wood-panelled and flock-wallpapered walls. The stage at the front is five feet high, backed with a curtain of shiny multi-coloured strips that immediately takes me back to that first memory of the club at Christmas. There's a small bar at the back, stocked with some surprisingly great beers.

Loads of our guests at the party asked me how to book the place for their own events, or even join the club. Towards the end of the evening, I started chatting to our bartender.

'How do we go about joining?'

'Oh, it's not like this all the time you know.'

'Yes, I know. I organised this, so I get that. But I'd still be interested in joining.'

'Well, we only have new membership nights once or twice a year. You have to come in then.'

'When's the next one?'

'They put a poster up downstairs in the main bar.'

'But I can only go in the main bar if I'm already a member.'

'Yes, that's right.'

'So there's no way of me joining unless I already know someone who is a member who's prepared to let me know.'

'They need to nominate you as well.'

'Right.'

With no website to check, and no email address to write to, it would take me another four years to finally join the Mildmay. There was a changing of the guard on the committee. Some new people set up a website and even a Twitter account and started announcing when the new members evenings were. Eventually someone knew someone who knew someone who knew a member, and the chain finally reached me.

I had no idea then just how important, how significant, my new club was, and the role that it had played in the last great struggle over the control and direction of the working men's club movement.

* * *

The great Beer Question had handed Henry Solly his first major defeat. At first he simply took it in his stride and carried on evangelising, keeping to his relentless schedule of touring, lecturing and letter writing. But his position had been weakened, and on top of that, his newly opened clubs were still closing. The next great argument – the one about who should actually be running the clubs – was on its way.

Before the introduction of associate and pass cards, the CIU had two sources of income: the donations from the rich and powerful, and the annual subscriptions from member clubs. The idea was always that the subscriptions would eventually make the donations unnecessary, but in the early years, this wasn't happening. In 1863, the Union had received £14 6s in subscriptions, against an estimated budget of £500 a year. The following year that sum halved. In 1866 it fell to £4 15s. Solly, meanwhile, continued to insist that he needed a substantial pay rise to continue his great work.

Solly still maintained that the problem was 'the absence of resident gentry,' but there was growing dissent against this view. At the 1866

Annual General Meeting, George Howell, a bricklayer, was minuted grumbling about 'the patronizing spirit which was too much shown to the working class.'

Solly simply couldn't make up his mind about working men. In writing, he insisted that the aim of the Union was 'in all cases … to help Working Men to help themselves,' but in practice, he showed no sign of doing anything to make this happen. Instead he regaled the Union Council with the news that he'd managed to raise £300 from a dinner presided over by the Duke of Argyll, that the Prince of Wales had given a personal donation of £21, that the Earl of Shaftesbury had agreed to join the long list of vice-presidents, and that Henry Solly was friendly with lots of very important people.

In 1867, subscriptions fell to just £1 17s 6d. The problem for Solly was that, despite his efforts, donations from the wealthy were falling too. They weren't seeing good enough results in return for their largesse. Of the 280 working men's clubs involved in the Union in 1867, only five would survive the next few years.

Not only was the amount of money coming in falling, the cash in the organisation wasn't being managed properly – it seemed to just melt away. Solly's skills as an orator and a campaigner had been essential in establishing the vision for clubs and then getting people on board with that vision. But now the Union existed, it needed a different set of skills to bring stability and order – and Solly was no administrator.

Hodgson Pratt had been a civil servant in India, a job that set people up for life. After fourteen years in Calcutta, Pratt didn't need to work again, and retired at 38 years old. He kept himself busy with the Cooperative Movement and various other initiatives to educate and empower working-class people. Pratt met Solly in 1864 and joined the Union Council soon after, where in many ways, he was Solly's opposite – a great organiser rather than a proselytiser. Along with Thomas Paterson, a furniture maker initially recruited by Solly, he persuaded the rest of the Council that the future lay not in founding more clubs, but in nurturing the ones that already existed, and getting the Union's house in order. Pratt was inspired by the

Cooperative Movement, which had begun in the late nineteenth century as a way for poor people to club together and buy things in bulk and gone on to provide a number of schemes where working-class people pooled their money and energy for mutual benefit. Cooperatives were independent and non-hierarchical, and Pratt believed that member clubs of the CIU should have a much greater say in how things were run.

The only surviving account of Solly's departure from the Council is his own, from his memoir *These Eighty Years*. Written twenty-five years later, it's clear to see how much pain the schism caused him, and it sees him at his rhetorical best in painting his ejection from the body he founded as a victory for both the Union and himself.

According to Solly, through no fault of his own, some Council members simply wanted to save the expense of a salaried secretary. Yes, there were some, he admitted, who 'thought, quite honestly, that the Society could be better managed under their own immediate direction than under mine,' but only a few. Others were concerned about poor old Solly himself, worrying that if he gave up his 'travelling propagandist work' to become a mere administrator, his immense talents would be wasted. 'Thus there came to be on the Council a relatively strong party that desired to see my services dispensed with.'

Once again, this was not failure, but a perfect example of just how successful Solly's scheme had been. His 'first thought' on realising people wanted him out was 'one of genuine satisfaction that the Society had grown strong enough to be able to dispense with my services.' Of course, he could possibly have stayed on in a voluntary capacity, but unlike some people he could mention (*cough* Hodgson Pratt) he didn't have 'a private fortune,' and was therefore 'obliged to earn my own living and contribute to that of my family, and was unable to serve the Society without taking pecuniary compensation.'

And so Henry Solly tendered his resignation from the organisation he had founded. It was accepted by the Council, but only 'by a narrow majority,' and only because 'many of the most influential members, and many who deeply regretted my action, were absent.'

So in fact, it was Solly's own decision to leave his post, and the only reason he did so was that he was too damned good at it to carry on.

Hodgson Pratt succeeded Solly as honorary secretary, working for free, and paying his own expenses as he travelled the country giving lectures at clubs. Solly, clearly desperately hurt despite his bravado, accused others of having frittered away the funds he had so carefully saved, and stormed off to form a rival organisation, the Social Working Men's Club Association. Several key people and many members went with him. But when no one really seemed to mind, he brought them all back to the CIU, and continued to quietly raise funds for the Union until his style of fundraising was no longer necessary.

With Solly's grip broken, the working men's club movement could move into the next phase of its existence. But the big battles weren't over yet: as the growing pains continued, the Union would come close to tearing itself apart.

* * *

By the early 1870s, a widespread 'revolt against patronage' was sweeping through the club world. Hodgson Pratt and his Council were committed to accelerating the evolution of the CIU to a point where it could run on democratic lines, with the member clubs calling the shots. But Pratt believed that he could only nudge the Union in that direction if there remained a broad coalition of interest behind it, a view illustrated brilliantly by his welcoming of the support of the Archbishop of Canterbury at the same time as accepting a donation from Charles Darwin. He was personally committed to change, but that change had to be gradual to keep such breadth of support on board. For some, it wasn't quick enough.

Control of the CIU via direct representation on its Council may still have been some way off, but the revenue from the bar meant that, at an individual club level, there was the possibility of financial independence. The working men's clubs of Maidstone told the CIU's *Workman's Magazine* in 1873 that, 'The members have made the discovery that the profit in beer is about 30%, and brings them double what they have to pay for rent,' adding quickly, to reassure any reformers who might still be reading, 'though the quantity sold does not average two pints per person per week.'

Some clubs started to vote out their 'sluggish gentlemen patrons' and take on the committee roles themselves. Solly writes in his memoirs of a club in Scarborough where revolution gave way to compromise, and two separate committees were formed: one of wealthy patrons and one of working men. You can imagine how well that worked.

Other clubs were now founded by groups of working men with no outside help from the start. John Taylor gives a touching account of the formation of the Great Wigstone Working Men's Club in Leicester in 1875, by 'a few youths of the village tired of being chased around by the village constable.' They borrowed four shillings and sixpence to pay the fee of a bellman to walk around town, ringing his bell and announcing their first meeting. This paid off, and a group of men duly convened in a draughty old room. The first member to arrive lit the fire and put the kettle on, and became the steward for the night. When they decided to try a small barrel of beer instead of tea, success came instantly.

Established clubs, having learned lessons the hard way, gave new start-ups any help they could. Members, many of them being tradesmen, improved or even built the rooms in which they met. The working classes were proving that they did have the skills to run individual clubs after all. With beer at their heart, the case for patronage from above was starting to look shaky.

In 1875 – the same year Gladstone reflected that his government had been swept away on a tide of gin and beer – Hodgson Pratt finally signalled a new direction for the CIU. At that year's AGM, the CIU as Solly had built it was still reflected in the Annual Report, which showed that the Union, still under the presidency of Lord Rosebery, counted among its vice-presidents four dukes, a marquis, and nine earls. The Union Council consisted of three bishops, nine lords, various assorted reverends, clergymen and judges, thirty MPs, eight knights, and among its seventy-five members, just twelve men (and one woman) without some kind of title or honorific.

The keynote speech given by Lord Rosebery, however, which was almost certainly written by Hodgson Pratt, rang the changes: 'The principle upon which the Working Men's Club and Institute Union is based is that working men are to be raised by their own endeavours, and are not to be patronised, and fostered, and dandled. All that is to be done for the working men is to be done by themselves. What a man does for himself is worth ten times as much as what can be done for him by anyone else ...'

After this opening salvo, he outlined three qualities that he believed were essential for a successful club:

The first is that each club should be altogether free from all vexatious infantile restrictions on the consumption of intoxicating drinks and all similar matters – restrictions which tend to make these institutions moral nurseries rather than clubs intended for the use of citizens of a great empire.

Secondly, if they are to be a great success they should be self-supporting.

Thirdly, they ought to set before their members some object higher than the mere social object of getting a comfortable place in which to meet. At the same time it will be very easy to aim at too much. From time to time one reads in the papers of persons discoursing to the members of these clubs, and drawing pictures of enlightened miners returning from their underground toil to the consumption of the aesthetic tea or the discussion of the subtleties of Hamlet or the mysticism of Greek literature.

Pratt couldn't have been any clearer in his intentions. Ten years after removing Solly's ban on beer, any such restrictions were now regarded as 'vexatious and infantile.' The second point was telling the wealthy they would soon no longer be needed, and the third was a swift cut to the rope tethering the club movement to the Victorian rational recreationists, even mocking them slightly. The future of the movement would be written by the working man, as well as for him. This was enshrined in the Union's first constitution, written that year, which laid out a path for representatives from member clubs being included on the Union Council for the first time. If any of the dukes, earls and reverends supporting the movement with their money or time were unhappy with this, they knew where the door was.

By 1878, around 52 per cent of all clubs were self-supporting. Five years later, Hodgson Pratt reckoned it was closer to 75 per cent. Finally proving that the sticking point had been the presence of resident gentry rather than any absence of them, the numbers started heading up: the total membership of working men's clubs grew from 90,000 in 1874, to half a million by 1883.

But for many of the men in those clubs, things were still moving too slowly. By the early 1880s, these new clubs only had minority representation on the Union's Council, which still read mainly like the lyrics from a really posh version of 'The Twelve Days of Christmas.' Many of the new clubs, particularly those that were springing up in London, were political in nature and deeply pissed off about the middle- and upper-class monopoly on the Council that supposedly represented them.

The 1870s had been a turbulent decade, with Britain and other world powers going into overdrive invading and then sending 'civilising missions' across Africa and Asia. Britain was the greatest empire the world had ever seen, but little of its amassed wealth seemed to be making it back to the working classes. Working people were broadly supportive of the Empire, and felt personally invested in it: the soldiers who upheld Britain's authority, the shipbuilders of Tyneside who built the ships that made up the world's most powerful navy, the steelworkers of Sheffield who created the materials for those ships, the miners in Yorkshire and Nottinghamshire who dug the coal to power them, the bicycle-makers of Coventry who got those workers to the factory, and the millworkers of Lancashire who clothed them all, felt entitled to share in the rewards of what they'd helped create. What these millions of workers got instead was a financial crisis in 1873, followed by a long period of recession which, of course, hit them harder than anyone else. It had always been thus. But this time, with trades unions having been given legal recognition in 1871, even unskilled workers were getting organised, and strikes and protests were spreading. Karl Marx was living in exile in London and had just published the first volume of *Das Kapital*, which sold out its print run quickly.

Many of the new clubs that were being formed around this time were, unsurprisingly, political in nature. As John Taylor explained: 'There is no doubt that the new-found independence of the clubs, when working men began to run them, was itself a stimulus to political activity. These were truly worker's clubs – self-governing, self-expressing, and increasingly class-conscious.'

By 1883, the CIU realised that if it was going to keep these clubs on board it had to pick up the pace of change. The Third Reform Act was well on its way to being passed the following year: with millions of men about to get the vote for the first time, the Union could not afford to be seen as being even slower than parliament. A special meeting with the members was convened to explore the issue.

The meeting was preceded by a survey of all clubs, but only 106 clubs – about a third of the total – bothered to fill it in. Mainly these were the clubs that thought of themselves more as Institutes, still hoping to 'improve' the working man. The self-sufficient clubs let their silence speak for them.

When the conference was convened, members' grievances were given full vent. One working-class delegate took to the floor and put the issue in simple terms: 'The Union has reached a crisis in its history. It must either be patronising or self-supporting. It cannot be the former and must either become the latter or cease to exist … A great deal has been said about abolishing class distinctions but under the present system these exist in the constitution of the Union itself.'

Another delegate, Mr Fletcher Pape from the Commonwealth Club, got up and suggested the principle of 'federalization,' in which 'the Clubs of each district should group themselves together and elect delegates to a district delegate meeting, and from these district meetings the central body should be formed.'

This was considered to be such a good idea that it was immediately formalised into a resolution stating that it was time to make the Union 'what it has hitherto been only in name, i.e. a Union of Clubs and Institutes,' that should 'not be exclusive on social, political or religious grounds.' This resolution was passed, kickstarting reform that went much further than the conference had originally intended. Putting the resolution into effect would still take time, and a lot of work. Following its passing, a barrister, William Minet, introduced an efficient bookkeeping system for the first time, then created model rules for clubs to show them how to keep accounts. Hodgson Pratt resigned as secretary (though he would return as president two years later) to be succeeded by J. J. Dent – the Union's first working-class secretary. Over the next ten years, Pratt and Dent oversaw steady change: the model rules helped clubs run themselves in a democratic fashion, and by the mid-1890s, those clubs would be running the Union that represented them, taking it in a very different direction from the one originally envisioned by Henry Solly.

* * *

If there was one thing that Solly, Dent and Pratt all agreed on, it was that the Club and Institute Union should be apolitical. If working men wanted to found clubs that were political, they had the freedom to do so, and those clubs were welcome in the CIU. But the Union was there to help any and all working men's clubs. Whatever aims a club had, the CIU existed to help working men run that club – and that was all.

The East End of London in particular saw an explosion of radical clubs. Well to the left of the Liberal Party, but sometimes also opposed to socialism, these clubs marched through the street carrying banners, agitating for change. The Borough of Hackney Club, founded in 1873, was regarded as the 'Mother' of other clubs that sprang up in Bethnal Green, Islington and Walthamstow, exploring political education for the working man by getting radical thinkers to come and speak to them. It turned out working men were interested in having lectures at their clubs after all – they just had to be the right kind of lectures. For a while, as Taylor puts it, 'Shakespeare rubbed shoulders with socialism.' The Borough of Hackney Club merged the politics and entertainment with the formation of a band that became notorious around the neighbourhood for its enthusiastic renditions of the 'Marsellaise.'

Some eminent speakers got more – or less – than they bargained for when they visited these clubs. In his diary of 1887, William Morris describes an experience that will sound painfully familiar to any entertainer who played clubland at its 1970s peak: 'I gave my "Monopoly" at the Borough of Hackney Club, which was one of the first workmen's clubs founded, if not the first; it is a big Club, numbering 1,600 members: a dirty wretched place enough, giving a sad idea of the artizan's standard of comfort: the meeting was a full one, and I suppose I must say attentive, but the coming and going all the time, the pie-boy and the pot-boy was rather trying to my nerves: the audience was civil and enclined [*sic*] to agree, but I couldn't flatter myself that they mostly understood me, simple as the lecture was.'

While not all clubs held the same beliefs, the rising voice of secularism was common to many. The late nineteenth century saw the peak of evangelical activity in Britain, with churches deciding that it wasn't enough to open the doors and welcome anyone who wanted to come and worship – they had to go out into the community and harangue people into realising that they could only be saved through almighty God. If labelling this as religious fundamentalism sounds a bit much when applied to Christians, it's worth noting that some Christian groups commonly referred to clubmen and other secularists as 'infidels.' The London City Mission – a Christian evangelical group that today still targets the poor for salvation, wrote in their report for 1885–86:

Infidelity is still actively propagated in some quarters, especially in connexion with the Working Men's Clubs, which are a fruitful source of evil in many neighbourhoods. Private in character, these clubs are … under no magisterial authority or police control, and only those who are privately admitted by members can fully estimate their injurious influence among the morals of the people. The German element* in the clubs gives, as a rule, an impetus to their sceptical and infidel tendency, and unless some corrective to their baneful influence is speedily applied, it is impossible to exaggerate the evil that may result.

This literal demonisation of clubmen beautifully disproves its own final sentence. It employs the same rhetoric the anti-club police commissioners on the Alcohol Commission would use a decade later, but in a more deranged fashion: we can't get into the clubs, so we have no idea what they're up to in there. But whatever it is, it's definitely evil – there can be absolutely no doubt about that.

The following year the Mission doubled down, calling clubs 'modern hells,' and lamenting that 'the labouring classes have their rights as well as the rich, and there seems, therefore, no remedy for this terrible evil, except the more persistent and earnest preaching of the Gospel wherever opportunity offers.' Just as when Solly upset his Unitarians, here's a group that seems to believe it follows the teaching of Christ, lamenting the fact that the poor have basic human rights.

In early 1887, the Hackney clubs, convinced that the CIU 'knew nothing at all about the wants of the East-End clubs,' organised a Social and Political Federation of East-End Clubs within the CIU to handle their own affairs, and withheld their subscriptions, demanding representation. Hodgson Pratt's new direction just about managed to keep them from breaking away altogether – instead, the radical clubs were given representation on the Union Council.

Most of these clubs had republican sympathies as well as being secularist, and their presence on the Council made the remaining establishment patrons increasingly uncomfortable. This came to a head with what club historians George Tremlett and John Taylor refer

---

* There was a radical school of Unitarian religious thought in Germany at the time which had a significant influence in the UK. For example, it was German philologists who demonstrated that the Bible, the unique source of authority to Unitarians, was in fact the product of numerous authors at different times.

to in passing as 'The Bradlaugh incident,' an ideological clash that briefly tore the Union apart, and threatened to end the movement permanently.

Charles Bradlaugh was an atheist, secularist republican, who founded the National Secular Society in 1866 and, a decade later, scandalised decent society by publishing an American book called the *The Fruits of Philosophy, or the Private Companion of Young Married People*. This was a summary of what was known about conception, included advice on infertility and impotence, and explained a method of birth control. Widely considered to be blasphemous, it saw Bradlaugh and his colleague Annie Besant unsuccessfully prosecuted for obscenity.

After defeats in 1868 and 1874, this obscene blasphemer, republican, trade unionist, supporter of Irish home rule and universal suffrage, was elected as the Liberal Member of Parliament for Northampton in 1880. To take his seat, like all MPs, he had to swear a religious Oath of Allegiance to the Queen. Bradlaugh believed this would be hypocritical for him to do. Having worked as a legal clerk (he had a brilliant legal brain, but was too poor to train as a lawyer) Bradlaugh pointed out that the courts offered an option of a secular affirmation of loyalty, which carried the same legal weight, but didn't involve swearing by a god he didn't believe in. Why couldn't he do the same in parliament?

That this may seem perfectly reasonable now is testament to how hard Bradlaugh fought. The Tories despised him, scented blood, and resisted every attempt at compromise or reform by Bradlaugh and his supporters, leaving him with the choice of betraying his principles, attempting to take his seat illegally, or standing down. Bradlaugh did attempt to take his seat and was arrested and briefly imprisoned for doing so. The issue would take eight years to resolve, during which time Charles Bradlaugh was repeatedly arrested, fined, prosecuted and beaten up. As a result, he had to forfeit his seat repeatedely, and was re-elected by the people of Northampton four times over. When he relented and said okay, fine, I'll take the Oath, parliament decided that he was no longer allowed to. He became a hero of the working classes, and there was fury on the streets each time he was refused his seat in parliament.

In 1885, the East End clubs successfully campaigned to add Bradlaugh to the list of vice-presidents of the CIU. By this time the clubs of the Union were electing their own Council, but the rest of the vice-presidents were still the great Lords, earls and bishops. The resolution was carried by one vote, after which many of the nobles, including Solly's main ally Lord Lyttelton, the honorary secretary, the Duke of Westminster and various other vice-presidents resigned their positions. This was swiftly followed by the wholesale secession of branches of the Union such as Worcester, Hampshire and Kent. The CIU, at 23 years old, was on the verge of collapse. Bradlaugh had been a long-time supporter of the club movement, and was dismayed that it was tearing itself apart in his name. He withdrew his name from the list of vice-presidents, stating, 'My only desire is, and has been, to befriend the clubs. I shall be as ready to help in my poor way without holding office.' And help he did – not just by stepping down to save the uneasy truce within the Union, but by using his fame to hold lectures, for which he charged admission, and donated all proceeds to the CIU.

Bradlaugh was finally allowed to take his seat in parliament in 1886, and in 1888 succeeded in passing a new Oaths Act that made it legal to affirm loyalty rather than swear to God. He died, three years later at the age of fifty-seven, physically and mentally shattered by his ordeal. His funeral was attended by 3,000 mourners, including a 21-year-old Mohandas Gandhi.

J. J. Dent, the general secretary of the CIU at that time, came from a working-class background, having trained as a bricklayer before moving to London to become involved in radical politics. Sympathetic to the aims of the radical clubs, he realised the Union needed them, but also persuaded them to work with the rest of the CIU, changing it from within. After the Bradlaugh incident, he persuaded most of the clubs that had seceded to rejoin, along with the radical clubs of the East End, who had also briefly left. The uneasy alliance held, but the radical clubs were increasingly shaping the focus of the club movement.

As Dent was still trying to build bridges, 1887 saw Queen Victoria's Golden Jubilee. Celebrations were, obviously, planned across Britain, and some clubs immediately protested the Union having any part in this or spending any of their members' funds on it. On 13 November, the London radical clubs held a major rally, converging on Trafalgar Square.

It is entirely plausible – even probable – that the clubs intended this rally to be peaceful. However, there had been mass rioting in the centre of London the year before. Apart from the recession and the glaring lack of any evidence of the British Empire's immense wealth, immigration into the East End and emerging rivals to Britain's trade dominance raised the spectre of mass unemployment, and in February 1886, a meeting was held in Trafalgar Square where socialist and radical speakers gave 'exciting and provocatory speeches' urging the working classes to make their voices heard. Angry rioters, soon characterised by the press, without foundation, as 'the East End mob,' roamed the streets smashing windows and damaging buildings. They specifically targeted the gentlemen's clubs of St James's and Pall Mall, and according to the *Illustrated London News*, 'at the Carlton Club the vast crowd, which had now increased to several thousands, stopped, and several of the Socialist leaders climbed on to the railings, and one of them waved the small red flag.' The police seemed unprepared, and the riots led to the resignation of the commissioner, Sir Edmund Yeamans Walcott Henderson. His replacement, Charles Warren, made a point of stamping on anything that had the potential to turn into a civil disturbance.

Almost two years later, the West Marylebone Liberal and Radical Club assembled on Paddington Green and set off marching along 'as orderly and as comfortably as possible' until they reached the Guards Crimean War Memorial in Pall Mall, where they were baton-charged by the police, who then also began beating up bystanders on the pavement. The West Southwark Liberal and Radical Club reached London Bridge before they were 'charged by the police, brutally maltreated and scattered in all directions, maimed and wounded.' The East Finsbury Club and the John Bright Club gave similar accounts to the

CIJ. Often, it seemed that the police were specifically targeting the banners each club carried, brightly embroidered with scenes such as Liberty triumphing over Despotism. Members 'stuck to the banners as long as they could,' despite the bearers being 'truncheoned in a most merciless manner' until 'our banner was torn from us.' The clubs therefore had no doubt that the violent assault by the police on what they came to call 'Bloody Sunday' was politically motivated, rather than simply being a botched attempt to 'keep the peace.' The North Camberwell Radical Club subsequently passed a resolution denouncing: '… the infamous tyranny of the Tory Government, and the cowardly attacks made today by the police and military, acting under orders, on crowds of unarmed Englishmen, peacefully exercising their legal rights of procession, and endeavouring to hold an orderly meeting …'

The following year, the Star Radical Club in Herne Hill, south London, created a list of demands which they published in the *CIJ* that included home rule for Ireland, votes for all men and women, abolition of the House of Lords, free higher education for all, the nationalisation of the railways, and 'legislation for the masses and not the classes.'

All of this was faithfully reported in the *CIJ*. Its editor, Richard Gaston – who we last met when he was setting up drama troupes in the clubs – remains a vital source on the machinations of club life towards the turn of the last century, and told us a great deal about early club entertainment in the last chapter. As well as being an 'actor and reciter,' he was an effective writer too. A poem of his, first read at the United Radical Club in 1885, shows that the clubmen were not oblivious of how they were seen by polite society:

We working men are often called hard names by jealous scribes,
And made the butt of many jokes, and sneers and cruel jibes;
We are 'the mob,' the 'great unwashed,' sometimes the 'dregs'
    and 'scum';
As if they thought from working men no good could ever
    come.

But if we drink we also think; we're not all thoughtless men;
We have as much (perhaps more) good sense as have the Upper
    Ten;
And if some proof they wish to have that my remarks are true,
Let them come here and see this club, that has been built by
    you.
We've asked no guineas from the rich, nor patronage from
    peers;
We're independent of them all, and have been so for years.
To build their churches and their schools, the parson often
    begs;
The 'scum' pay for their clubs themselves, as also do the 'dregs.'
We have toil'd hard, been oft cast down, depressed, yet not lost
    heart;
We felt success would crown the end, though humble was the
    start.
So now tonight we welcome friends of clubs both far and near,
To share the pleasure that we feel in what we're doing here.

Many of the early records of the club movement were destroyed by a fire at Club Union House, the headquarters of the CIU, in 1978, which makes John Taylor's work on the 'collection of papers and journals in a forgotten basement corner' of the building so valuable. Apart from Taylor's pamphlet, most of what we have left is the work of people like Solly and reformers like Charles Booth and Walter Besant. Rarely do we get to hear the working men's side of the story. The line 'if we drink we also think' in particular challenges the binary view that men were either drunkards or had been 'reformed.' The radical clubs of the East End were notoriously beer-sodden, but they were part of a loose coalition that eventually solidified into the Labour movement. Via Gaston, they had their voice in the *CIJ*, whose reporting became increasingly atheist, secular, and critical of the orthodoxies of the State. The voices of people like Hodgson Pratt, committed to holding the CIU together and keeping it functioning, were pointedly absent from this discourse. The Union itself remained resolutely apolitical – a difficult path at this time, but one that would ultimately see it outlive the radical clubs that dominated it at the close of the nineteenth century.

* * *

The Mildmay Radical Club and Institute was founded in August 1888 at 36 Newington Green Road. One of the earliest records we have of it is a letter sent by the club secretary to Hypatia Bradlaugh Bonner, Charles Bradlaugh's daughter, on the occasion of his death, expressing the view of the majority of members who saw the event as a 'national loss.'

It seems that the Mildmay wasn't the only radical club at number 36. Another letter to Hypatia Bradlaugh Bonner, this one from the Balls Pond Secular Road Society at the same address, also detailed a resolution expressing their condolences for a loss which most members took as personal. What's odd about this is that in 1951, one ancient member of the Mildmay told the *CIJ* that the Balls Pond Secular Society saw their club 'go on the rocks,' and the Mildmay Radical Club formed from its ashes, with sixteen members subscribing ten shilling each towards the first month's rent.

The letters to Hypatia Bradlaugh Bonner were uncovered by Andrew Whitehead, a local historian and, after years of trying, now a fellow Mildmay member. 'It's actually quite mysterious,' he tells me over a pint in the club bar. 'By 1900 there's a Bradlaugh Club & Institute listed at – wait for it – 36 Newington Green Road. But by that time the Mildmay is long gone from there.'

Whether the Mildmay was a rival or a successor to any of these other groups, in 1894 it moved to a new site on the north side of Newington Green, just a few hundred yards from St Matthias church. This must have delighted the vicar there, who had previously railed against the Mildmay Club's 'pernicious influence among the young.'

Newington Green was a symbolic place for a radical club to make its new home. Straddling the border between Hackney and Islington, it was once one of Henry VIII's many hunting grounds. In the seventeenth century, it became a magnet for radical and non-conformist thinkers. Religious non-conformists were not allowed to gather inside the walls of the City of London, and Newington Green was an agricultural village two-and-a-half miles up the Great Cambridge Road, now better known as the A10. Educational academies were set up all around the Green by progressive thinkers, with Daniel Defoe being one of their early pupils. In 1758, Richard Price, the Welsh philosopher and non-conformist minister, took over the Newington Green Meeting House, now Newington Green Unitarian Church, still standing a few doors away from the Mildmay Club. Radical thinkers flocked to hear his sermons and to exchange ideas. When John Adams, one of the Founding Fathers of the United States, was ambassador to Britain in 1785, he stayed with Price to escape George III's hostile courtiers. He may well have bumped into Mary Wollstonecraft there, who moved her fledgling school for girls – itself a radical idea for the time – to Newington Green in 1784. Wollstonecraft would write her books, *A Vindication of the Rights of Men* and *A Vindication of the Rights of Women* while living on Newington Green, and is regarded as one of the founding thinkers of feminism.

With radical thought bleeding deep into the very soil of the place, it's no surprise that the Mildmay Radical Club & Institute quickly established a reputation as one of the largest and most politically active of the capital's working men's clubs, supporting Home Rule in Ireland, strongly opposing the Second Boer War, raising money for striking miners, and calling for the abolition of the House of Lords.

'Here's another opaque part,' says Andrew. 'The 1951 article says that when it moved, the club bought "an old mansion at 34 Newington Green comprising 12 rooms and with spacious grounds." But the Historic England website, where the club is listed, says the site was gifted in the will of two sisters. Either way, what we know for sure is that in 1900, a new building was designed by the architect Alfred Allen, who was a member and trustee of the club, and the foundation stone, which you can still see, was laid by A. A. Smith, the club president.'

If the Mildmay had bought an old mansion with spacious grounds, that suggests an unlikely level of affluence for a club that had started with a whip-round to pay the room hire down the road, in a place it seemingly had to share with at least one rival club. So perhaps the story of the will is more likely. But either way, 1900's new clubhouse presents a confounding twist to the story of what was, by all accounts, a radical political organisation.

The Mildmay's website states that the 'Radical' tag was dropped in 1930, 'and it became the Mildmay Club and Institute … establishing its non-political credentials.' But the fabric of the building suggests this name change was long overdue: in 1900, it was purpose-built, from scratch, as a massive, opulent pleasure palace. The new Mildmay sported two concert theatres, a billiards room big enough to comfortably accommodate nine full-size tables, and a bar bigger than most pubs, plus libraries, reading rooms and accommodation. Even before this new building was begun, an ad for the Mildmay in *Club Life* from January 1900 boasts six consecutive nights of entertainment, including a production of *Othello* on Sunday evening, a 'Plain and Fancy Dress Ball' on Tuesday with a 'Full Quadrille Band,' and a 'Lyric Pantomime' on Thursday evening, complete with 'New scenery and effects.' If there were any political speeches or meetings that week, they weren't deemed worthy of advertising.

The new building was clearly designed with entertainment and relaxation front-of-mind. It also suggests that at the time, the Mildmay Club was incredibly rich. In 1900, most working men's clubs met in rented halls like the one back on Newington Green Road, or rooms above shops. Where clubhouses were purpose-built, they were little more than sheds.

The new Mildmay clearly became as important in the world of entertainment as it had been in politics. During the 1907 Music Hall strike, Marie Lloyd used the club as a base to give out food and drink to performers campaigning for better pay and conditions, allowing them to campaign for longer, until their demands were met.

By 1910, an ad in the *Tottenham and Wood Green Advertiser*, boasts that the Mildmay is 'The largest and best appointed Working Men's

Club in London,' with a 'Lending Library, Reading Room, Smoking Rooms, Theatre, Ball Room, Billiards, Bagatelle, Card Rooms, Rifle Range, and Grounds for Garden Parties, Cricket and Quoits; Benevolent, Sick and Loan Societies.' In 1894, when the CIU was broke, and again in 1912, they pleaded with member clubs for funds to help bail out their struggling convalescent homes on the coast in Kent and Yorkshire. Each time, the Mildmay Club was one of the top three donors.

'The rifle range was added in 1907, and again in 1921,' says Andrew, 'which suggests the membership was relatively affluent, because shooting was an expensive pastime.'

Maybe the gentrification of the Mildmay, which some older members are so unhappy about today, goes back much further than we think.

The Mildmay would go on to be a noted venue for what was becoming known as variety entertainment. Vera Lynn sang in working men's clubs because her father was a lifelong clubman. She started in 1924 when she was just 7 years old, later insisting that 'there's nothing strange about it all really, with the club life practically in my blood.' She described the clubs as 'part of a network of entertainment of which, unless you grew up in it, you could be completely unaware.' She was billed as a 'descriptive child vocalist' and of all the clubs she played between 1924 and 1930, when she came to write her autobiography in 2009, she remembered 'the old Mildmay Club at Newington Green' most vividly:

I appeared many times at the Mildmay, with its large hall where the rows of chairs had ledges on the backs of them to hold glasses of beer, and where the chairman and committee of the club sat in front of the stage at a long table. That was the standard practice and, very much as in an old-fashioned music hall, the chairman could quickly gauge the mood of an audience. This was very important, because it was the committee who decided, according to the strength of the applause, whether you were worth an encore or not. That made all the difference to the money you earned: an extra encore meant you earned a shilling and sixpence.

If the Mildmay switched its focus from politics to entertainment more dramatically and on a larger scale than other clubs, it was still illustrating a broader shift of emphasis in clubland at the end of the nineteenth century. Traditionally, London clubs held their political lectures on Sundays: in 1888, 64 per cent of all London clubs claimed to hold them, compared to 50 per cent who held concerts on the same day. By 1913, the positions were emphatically reversed: 70 per cent of London clubs held Sunday concerts, while just 27 per cent persisted with lectures. In 1888, 62 per cent of London's clubs claimed to have a political objective at the core of their charter. By 1913, this had fallen to just 34 per cent. When the Mildmay dropped the 'radical' tag, it was actually one of the last to do so.

So what happened? Did club members en masse lose their interest in radical politics and think, sod it, let's just sing 'Roll Out the Barrel' instead? Not really: it was more a case of the political activity peeling away from the mainstream working men's club and finding its own niche. The clubs that embraced socialism eventually became part of the coalition that created the Labour Party and named themselves Labour Clubs. This buffer to the left allowed the remaining radicals to identify with the Liberals and rename themselves accordingly. Not to be outdone, the Conservative Party founded its own network of working men's clubs, before looking at itself and deciding these should just be 'Conservative Clubs,' with no differentiation according to class. Some of the Labour, Liberal and Conservative clubs saw a benefit in joining the CIU – and all who wanted to were welcomed – while others did not. Some of these clubs remained avowedly political, but they were no longer the places where ideas and campaigns were formulated. In each case, they became foot-soldiers within the bigger party machine, called upon to knock on doors and give out leaflets in elections. Over time, many succumbed to the same gravitational pull that had done for the previous generation of radical clubs, joining the decaying orbit around the idea of a social club where you just went at the end of a hard day to have a pint and a game of dominoes, irrespective of your political allegiance. While the Union did retain some strong links with political bodies such as trades unions, the Cooperative Movement and the Labour Party, the working men's club increasingly became the place where its members left their politics at the door.

This, then, was the great truth of the clubbable man: you might gravitate towards people whose background or beliefs you held in common. In different circumstances and places, you might campaign or even fight alongside those people. But when you met in a club, you relaxed and enjoyed yourselves, safe in the knowledge that you were around good, like-minded people – whatever that meant to you.

When you're dealing with something like the CIU, or any large organisation, often the most seismic events in their history seem like the dullest things to relate. Amid the blood and drama of the radical era, the destiny of the CIU and its member clubs was cemented by a couple of key bits of bureaucracy.

In 1889, without fireworks or conflict, the CIU's third general secretary, J. J. Dent, registered the Union as a 'Society' under the Industrial and Provident Societies Act of 1876. At a stroke, this made every club a shareholder, putting the Union in the direct control of its members, and essentially making the illustrious list of vice-presidents redundant. This would prove to be crucial to the Union's survival, the final seal on the democracy that had taken over twenty years to bring about. The number of clubs, and the membership of those clubs, grew accordingly. In 1887 there were 328 clubs in the Union. Ten years later, this number had risen to 627, and carried on climbing to reach 1,445 by 1911.

B. T. Hall, who succeeded Dent as general secretary, further embedded democracy within the structure of the CIU by working steadily to organise clubs around the country into branches, another level of management between the CIU Council and individual clubs. Club committee men could be elected to run the branch, and from 1910 onwards, those branches, according to their size, sent members to sit on the main CIU Council. Not only were the clubs now democratic, the Union itself was a nationally representative organisation.

The effect of the branches was dramatic. While clubs grew in number across the country, the branch system prompted a sweeping shift in emphasis. The 154 clubs that existed in London in 1889 saw a modest growth to 159 twenty years later. But away from London, with independence and democratic representation codified into the structure of the organisation, and beer providing financial security, working men's clubs could now open and thrive in industrial areas that were far away from sources of wealthy patronage. Over the same time period as the London clubs grew modestly, the new Lancashire and Cheshire branch of the CIU grew from 68 clubs to 211, and in Yorkshire, 26 clubs multiplied to 341. In a matter of years, the story of working men's clubs switched from London to the industrial North.

The original patrons gradually drifted away, and while these rational recreationists may have regarded the club movement as a failure fifty years after it began, the self-improving aspect of the modern club had not disappeared: crucially, as we'll see in the next chapter, it happened in the way working men wanted it to happen rather than how the upper and middle classes thought it should happen. Some remnants of Solly's vision – the libraries, games and reading rooms – would remain for much of the twentieth century. And it turned out he was right that in most clubs, drinking was not the same without the desperate drive for commercial competition. Here was the working men's club, fully formed and grown up: political with a small 'p', self-improving on its own terms, a more moderate alternative to the pub, the true heir of music hall, and the continuation of self-determined working-class leisure.

Without the attention of the spurned reformers and philanthropists, and increasingly distant from London, the story of the club slipped beneath the waves and would be ignored by academia, cultural pundits and all other forms of 'serious' analysis until the 1970s. Unobserved and not interfered with, it was free to shape large parts of the culture and society of the twentieth century.

PART TWO

THE NORTH

6

THE CLUB AND
US (AND THEM)

Greasbrough Club, Rotherham, South Yorkshire

In 1965, the BBC programme *Panorama* ventured into what it called 'the big kitchens of the industrial North,' where two-thirds of Britain's working men's clubs were by then located. Extending a dubious analogy, the narrator talks about how 'the blackened pots and pans of factories burn and bubble above the coal seams.' On 'the smouldering rim of Rotherham,' he finds a strong tradition among the miners: 'get home, get washed, get fed, get out,' the homeward trudge ultimately leading to Greasbrough Social Club. The ten-minute film shows a club packed with a thousand people every night, half of them women. 'It's a far cry from the sawdust covered barns and the spittoons of thirty years ago,' he tells us. 'While some of the old idealism of self-help and community spirit is preserved, the main emphasis now is on pleasure and entertainment.'

I search online to see if Greasbrough club is still going. Greasbrough Working Men's Club has a Facebook page without a single post on it – just one picture and nothing else. Is this the same Greasbrough Club that used to pack them in for people like Bob Monkhouse, Johnny Ray, Dusty Springfield, Sandie Shaw, The Shadows, Matt Munro and the Nolans?

A link to a small Wix site for the club says that it is. Like most clubs, the only other links that aren't to nostalgic stories about the club's illustrious past are entries on directory sites such as Yell. The entry for the club on whatpub.com confirms that this is the club the stars used to play.

The village of Greasbrough crawls up a hill a couple of miles outside Rotherham, overlooking the grounds of the Wentworth Woodhouse estate, former home of the Earls Fitzwilliam, whose vast wealth grew near-incalculable on the back of coal mining. The club is a sprawling affair. The main building facing the street is, I discover later, a former Methodist church, a drab, homely building with a gable roof that, from the side, looks like three terraced houses shunted together. But this original building now forms a small part of an overall complex that has had bits and pieces added to it over the years. Redbrick extensions have newer redbrick extensions of their own, spilling out over the big carpark with views of Wentworth Woodhouse that are prettier now than when I visited as a kid, when the rivers ran ferrous orange.

In a tradition that echoes many northern households, the front door is not the main door. The front door, as you'd expect, faces onto the main road. But the *main* door is round the back, in the car park. The front door opens into a small hallway with doors off for the treasurer's and secretary's offices, a committee room, and another door into the lounge bar. If it's anything like the houses I grew up in, the front door is only used by strangers. So I go around the back, halfway down the car park, and find the main door leading into a concert hall that's bigger than the rest of the sprawling club put together. I think I recognise the room from the *Panorama* film, a big stage at one end, a bar running down one wall.

'I recognise this from the telly!' I say to John Murrie, former club secretary and now president, when he comes out to meet me.

'This in't that club, mate. That was Greasbrough *social* club, at bottom o' t'hill. You know, where the Co-op is now?'

Great, I'm at the wrong club.

It turns out that Greasbrough Social Club, built in 1961, closed down in 1969. This one, which is much older, is, for now at least, still here. But how long it will remain so seems to be in doubt.

We settle down in the smaller lounge bar, carpeted and cosy, and away from the bingo that's about to start in the main bar. Not having Bob Monkhouse and *Panorama* to talk about, I'm a bit lost in terms of where to steer the conversation, but this doesn't slow John down.

'This used to be the whole club,' says John, and I work out that we're sitting in the old Methodist church. 'Started off as a bar for Greasbrough Brass Band. Bar were over there in that corner, and there were a snooker table in the middle of the room, and that were it. They'd cover the snooker table up and use it as a table when it got busy.'

Over the years, each new addition to the club has been built by the members themselves. Steel is the main industry around here, and it comes with many ancillary trades. 'Hot jobs' in front of the furnaces were a boon for clubs like this, with noon till 3pm a key time for thirsty, dehydrated workers between shifts. And when expansion was needed, everyone chipped in. 'We have some very good club members,' says John. 'We needed a new roof doing. Pete's a roofer. Twenty grand we got quoted and he did it for five.'

But just like Sheffield Lane a handful of miles away, this club is still here thanks to other members like John bringing a broader range of skills to the club than building, painting and decorating, vital though those are.

'I used to work in production and then sales, so I know about costs, margins and so on,' John says. 'I know how to read a balance sheet. Brewers come in and they just assume people don't know about business. The CIU is promoting Heineken but there's no special deal or anything, no bulk discount for buying for clubs, so we play the brewers off against each other.'

The day-to-day management of the club throws up issues that would be challenging to people from any background. There's just been an exchange with the Health and Safety Executive over the temperature of the water in the taps. The bar steward has to be auto-enrolled into a pension scheme. There are ongoing issues with the status of clubs regarding VAT. If a committee doesn't know this stuff, a club could quickly find itself in a situation where it is closed down.

Later, when I watch the *Panorama* programme again, it turns out Greasbrough Working Men's Club does feature after all. 'Five minutes' walk up the hill from the social club should be something more nearly approaching the ideas of the Unitarian minister, the Reverend Henry Solly, who founded the club movement a century ago,' says the narrator, 'ironically the little Methodist chapel is another, older, working men's club.' The grey building with its gabled roof and filled-in round window under the eaves is clearly recognisable. Obviously, the BBC enter through the front door, and inside the room where I'm sitting just now, they find a piano where the pulpit once stood, and a packed room full of elderly people singing along to 'If You Were the Only Girl (In the World).' The entire room is joining in. One man, clearly in his eighties, puts down his pint as the camera approaches and belts out the words as if his life depends on it, while the microphone picks up one his neighbours grumbling, "*E* can't sing!'

'The old nostalgia will soon seem out of place,' says the narrator. 'Even here, there'll soon be carpets on the floor, and extensions. The brewery has lent £12,000.'

It's fascinating that *Panorama* came here to film this club as a contrast to the dynamic, glamorous world of the social club just down the road. 'The gulf that separates this from the big club is wider than the five-minute walk between them,' says the narrator. And yet, 'the big club' is long gone, along with any idea that modern working men's clubs, which 'demanded the sophistication of the West End,' would replace television in working-class leisure time. But this place is still here. And if they're not belting out 'If You Were the Only Girl (In the World)' or even 'Human,' the crowd here for the bingo is the same age now as the singers were back then. The youngest committee member is 67, and the club is having trouble attracting new members.

'They'll come in for the band, and when the bingo comes on they'll go across the road to the pub for an hour and drink beer that's a pound a pint dearer. But then, the bingo is a draw to an older crowd,' says John.

What about music?

'Well Motown doesn't do bad, that appeals across the ages. Northern Soul, that does well. But the DJ's having an operation.'

As we're wrapping up our chat in the otherwise deserted lounge bar, a fit-looking man in his late sixties storms in through the front door.

'I couldn't fookin' watch no more o' that.'

'Are they losing?' asks John.

'No, they're winning, two-nil, burr'it's horrible, it's not football.'

'Well gerrin there, I'll come and have a pint wi' thi afore I go home.'

'What tha doin' in 'ere?'

'I'm talking to this gentleman. He's writing a book on working men's clubs.'

The football fan explodes.

'Well what the fookin' 'ell is 'e talking to thee for then?'

'I know, I know fook all about working, do I?'

'No, and tha knows fook all about clubs neither!'

He slams open the door to the main bar. Framed in the doorway, just for a second, he breaks character, turning back to check that we're both laughing, then heads for the bar.

* * *

A century after the rational recreationists, social mobility in the class system had reached a point where if any working people did wish to better themselves in the way the middle classes thought they should, that was just about possible. By the middle of the twentieth century, some of the people looking at the working classes and asking what should be done about or for them were actually of working-class origin themselves.

In 1957, Richard Hoggart's *Uses of Literacy* took us deep into the streets of areas like those where he and I grew up: back-to-back, parallel terraces of redbrick houses, veined with ginnels and snickets, keeping time to the pit sirens. Hoggart based his observations on the time he spent growing up in Leeds from the 1920s to the 1940s, but much of what he writes sounds like the pit village I grew up in forty years later.

When you see the mid-twentieth century working-class from Hoggart's viewpoint, it's much easier to appreciate how and why clubs developed as they did. In the coal-blacked streets, people lived almost on top of each other, everyone knowing everyone else's business. Within these close-knit communities, people felt they belonged in their own private sphere that didn't extend much further than a few streets away. Loyalty was to family first, neighbourhood second. Reality was what was known, what was visible and concrete. What a man was earning at 21 he would likely still be earning at 51, unless accident or injury curtailed him. He looked to marry a woman from his own class, and they aspired to getting a home of their own together and living their lives inside it, no more than a few streets away from where they had grown up. The need for some privacy meant the house was a private sphere, screened off by regularly-washed net curtains and that never-opened front door. Only family and the very closest few friends crossed the threshold. It helped, like the clean nets and the scrubbed front step, to maintain the essential view that you were a respectable family.

Everyone was in the same boat, but in any group of streets there were useful specialists: the chap at number 32 might be a bit of a 'professor' with a full set of encyclopaedias which he'd be happy to consult if there was anything you needed to know. The bachelor at the end of the road might have excellent penmanship and be good at filling in forms. When you needed it, the community helped each other out.

Beyond the home, beyond the community, Hoggart describes the public sphere, the national sphere, as 'strange and unhelpful' with 'most of the counters stacked on its side.' Inside the community is us, and people like us. Outside is the world of 'them,' the bosses, authority figures, and 'people at the top,' and petty clerks and officious people who look down their nose at you: 'They' don't have our best interests at heart: 'There exists, with some reason, a feeling among working-class people that they are often at a disadvantage, that the law is in some things readier against them than against some other groups … they tend to regard the policeman primarily as someone who is watching them, who represents the authority which has its eye on them, rather than as a member of the public services whose job it is to help and protect them.'

Hoggart, like everyone else, doesn't have too much to say directly about working men's clubs, although he does at least address their role, and he absolutely nails club singers for us in the next chapter. But indirectly, he explains for us why clubmen rejected well-meaning altruism, political and religious interventions, and rebuilt their clubs on their own terms:

> This is not a very self-conscious sense of community; it is worlds away from the 'fellowship in service' of some of the socially purposive movements. It does not draw its main strength from – indeed, it precedes, and is more elementary than – the belief in the need to improve each other's lot jointly which gave rise to such organizations as the Co-operative movement. It arises chiefly from a knowledge, born of living close together, that one is inescapably part of a group, from the warmth and security that knowledge can give, from the lack of change in the group, and from the frequent need to 'turn to a neighbour' since services cannot often be bought.

The strength of clubs was in a framework that allowed 'people like us' to get on with each other and, when needed, to help each other out. It wasn't about altruism or paternalism, but solidarity.

One of the most fundamental aspects of this way of life – which was of crucial importance for the clubs – was that it was handed down from generation to generation. Hoggart tugs my heartstrings when he writes, 'On leaving school [a boy] is, probably for the first time, close to his father and finds his father ready to be close to him; they now share the real world of work and men's pleasures.' For millions of men, getting your club cards for your eighteenth birthday and going down to sup with your dad was part of this closeness, a ritual sharing of 'Men's pleasures' that I managed to fail at with my own father.

Ian Clayton has both a deep fondness for working men's clubs and an inside/outside understanding of the working-class experience to rival Richard Hoggart. He still lives in the former mining town of Featherstone, where he grew up. A writer, broadcaster, interviewer and teacher, he is above all else a storyteller, whose books combine the language and outlook of the Yorkshire coalfields with an astonishingly wide range of references and interests.

Ian was brought up by his grandparents, and begins his memoir *It's the Beer Talking* with the story of how, at 4 years old, he accompanied his granddad, Ted Fletcher, to the pit to collect his wages, and then into the miner's welfare club for a pint. Here – when Ted left him to place a bet with a bookie's runner – Ian tasted his first beer from Ted's glass. The story was so vividly told, Ian was the first person I wanted to speak to about the working men's club.

'I adored my grandad, and everything he did, I tried to copy him,' says Ian as we sit in the converted chapel he now lives in in Featherstone. 'Everything. Way he shaved. Way he washed coal dust from his eyes when he got home from work. I thought I'd go down t'pit just like him, but he said, 'If I ever see thee round pit yard I'll kick thee so hard up t'arse tha'll come down wi' snow on thi cap.'

'What shall I do then?'

'Read some books.'

'And I became an avid library user. That's how I got my education. Looking back, those three words … he barely said three words in any sentence. By time he died he'd got it down to one word, he were that clever.'

Ian fell in love with music, and as a teenager he travelled far and wide from Featherstone and came back looking quite different:

By the time I was seventeen I'd grown me hair long and I was hitch-hiking everywhere. He were like 'Tha wants to get thi bloody hair cut,' and that's a working men's club thing too. I was really proud when I first became a member of the Girnhill Lane

WMC, which was always called the Corra, because it was built around the time of Victoria's son, Edward VII. I saw it as a rite of passage, following in me grandad's big footsteps.

When I first became a member there were a man called Shakka Highway, reight old retired miner, sat behind a little desk as you go in through t' front door. And it took me about six month before he stopped asking me 'Is thy a member?' Reight deep voice, and I couldn't get past him. 'Is thy a member?' I say 'Aye, you know who me grandad is, Ted Fletcher.' 'Ted Fletcher's grandson?' I says 'Aye,' 'Oh aye, gerrin then.' Next time – 'Is thy a member?'

I think it were probably because we wore different clothes each time. He might not have recognised me because I didn't look like anyone else who were going in. Anybody that goes in looking different from what they do, they want to know what you're up to. There's almost a uniform, especially at weekends when they all put their best suits on. Me grandad had three suits. One for knocking about house in, one for work and one for t'club. I'd wear different shirts or have me hair different.

Eventually after about six month, I went in ... and he didn't ask me. So I looked round as I was going in, I looked at him and he says, 'I know, Ted Fletcher's grandson.' You've made it! But you're not yourself. You're somebody's lad. It's about continuums. You've got to be somebody's lad or somebody's grandson or daughter. You'd go to join, and the first question would be 'Who's yer dad? What's he do?'

This intimate, generational approach was a crucial difference from works clubs. These proliferated in the early twentieth century as an update on the idea of Mechanics' Institutes: they looked like working men's clubs and offered similar services, perhaps with a bigger emphasis on lectures and lending libraries, but they were owned and run by employers rather than working men themselves. With the primary aim of offering men a 'better' alternative to the pub, a cynic might suggest that it was also a way for bosses to relieve men of the wages they had just paid them. On the whole, they didn't go down well.

'The pit owners opened a miners welfare club in Featherstone,' says Ian, 'and they had strict rules about gambling, bookies runners, snooker chalkers, talking money, foul language. They tried to introduce more cultured things – one of local toffs donated all books he didn't want – they had unusual talks. And the miners hated it. They thought they were being controlled by the bosses. So they bought some land next door and built their own club. Not so they could gamble and swear and be ignorant, but because they didn't want what the pit owners were offering. We have to stand them all day at work, why do we have to stand them afterwards?'

This idea of community and continuity tells us everything about why the paternalistic attempts of the reformers were routinely resisted, about sarcastic clapping and the pie boy and the potboy interrupting lectures by famous thinkers. It also highlights the difficulties for the person who wants to improve themselves, the girl who gets a scholarship or the boy who becomes an autodidact in the local library. Ian Clayton pulled off the balance with seemingly perfect ease – still living in Featherstone and drinking with friends he's known since school, but lecturing all over the world. Although when I mention Tall Poppy Syndrome in a later email, he tells me he knows all about that.

These communities don't automatically reject the ambitious student. But as Richard Hoggart discovered when he won the scholarship that would eventually lead to an academic life, it's an ambiguous situation. On the one hand, there is some respect: 'I remember sitting, not long after I had won a scholarship, next to a middle-aged bachelor miner in a working-men's club. Whenever he paid for his rum-and-hot milk he passed me a half crown from the change. I tried to refuse: "Tek it lad, and use it for thee education," he said. "Ah'm like all miners. Ah only waste t'bluddy stuff."'

But there's also a mistrust of 'book learning' – what good does it actually do you? Does it make you any happier? 'That doubt acquires some of its force from the group-sense itself: for the group seeks to conserve, and may impede an inclination in any of its members to make a change, to leave the group, to be different.'

The group works against the idea of change, and imposes pressure to conform. Those who become different through education can be tolerated, but 'only if the key class assumptions are shared': 'The group does not like to be shocked or attacked from within. There may be little of the competitive urge to keep up with the Joneses, but just as powerful can be the pressure to keep down with the Atkinses … If you want to be one of the group you must not try to "alter people's ways," and you will be disliked if you imply a criticism of their ways by acting differently yourself; if you infringe the taboos you will run into disfavour, condemned as "stuck up," "getting above yourself."'

And of course, looking back now, that's exactly what I did. My dad reached out in his way and took me to the club. But in both the Tin Hat and New Road, I got above myself. I spoke different. I looked different. I actually told them I was of a different class.

I was no longer Us; I had already become one of Them.

* * *

This framework of Us and Them explains everything about the motives and actions of working men's clubs throughout the twentieth century. By 1912, the clubs had had fifty years of various Thems saying, 'This is what you should do'; 'This is how you should do it'; and 'No, you shouldn't be doing that.' Every time, the clubs responded along the lines of 'Yeah, thanks for the input. But we're going to do it this way.'

Some early clubs were little better than Nissen huts or garden sheds, but as membership grew and the beer started flowing, expansion became a constant, with workers using their skills for mutual gain. Eventually a club might inherit a house, like the Mildmay did, or a disused Methodist Chapel, like Greasbrough Club. In 1968, sociologist Brian Jackson published *Working Class Community: Some general notions raised by a series of studies in northern England*. As part of his research, he visited sixteen of the seventy CIU-affiliated clubs that were then in Huddersfield: 'Most commonly the club owns some blackened stone-built house which they have converted, over the years, to their own uses.' Typically it has a bar, a lounge, perhaps a smaller women's room. There may be a games and billiards room, and the upstairs would be turned into one big concert room. Other clubs, such as the Langham in North London, found that the long garden behind the house they had acquired was big enough to build a concert room on the ground floor. Invariably, these conversions and extensions were carried out by the club's members themselves.

Having built their club, members then ran every aspect of it on their own terms. Here was local democracy in action, before the poorest of these men were even eligible to vote in general elections.* To become a member of the club, you had to be proposed and seconded by two existing members. The club was run by a committee that was elected by the members. The committee appointed a president, secretary and treasurer who were legally responsible for the club. These office-holders could then stand for regional branch positions, and from there they could stand for the National Executive and, ultimately, for the positions of president, vice-president and general secretary. In this way, a plumber from Barnsley such as Ken Green can rise to be the current successor to Henry Solly himself.

The only barrier to advancement for these men was that many had left school at fourteen, or even younger, and didn't possess the skills or knowledge needed to run the clubs. This was where the full benefit of being a member of the CIU became apparent. There was the eternal danger that the first time a club might hear about some essential aspect of licensing or employment law was when they unintentionally broke it. The CIU told club committee men everything they needed to know to prevent that. If a club did fall foul of law or regulation, the CIU would step in and help, and then share any new learnings with the rest of its members clubs.

In 1934, this was all codified into the Union's Club Management Diploma (CMD), a six-month correspondence course covering best

---

* Universal suffrage for men over 21 was granted in the 1918 Representation of the People Act. The Representation of the People (Equal Franchise) Act of 1928 finally extended the vote to all women.

practice in areas such as club law, book-keeping, administration and accountancy, followed by an exam which, when passed, resulted in a diploma that allowed you to put the letters CMD after your name – which every successful committee man proudly did.

Of course, when people who are not born to power and influence suddenly attain it, there's always a danger that it might go to their heads. Every club had its stories of the committee men who, with their perks such as free beer tokens and, later, reserved parking spaces, started to enjoy throwing their weight around. By the 1970s, the phrase 'Little Hitler' was shared across clubland, and the character jumped into mainstream popular culture.

The late comedian Normal Collier was a mainstay of the northern club circuit and was named by Jimmy Tarbuck as 'the comedian's comedian.' Much of his complex, detailed act didn't transfer as well to TV, so today he's mainly remembered for his impersonation of a chicken and his routine where he creates the impression of a microphone that keeps cutting out. This latter routine was originally based on an officious club chairman. Between the staccato silences, Collier would interrupt his announcements and his comedically bad crooning to yell 'Give order, please!' at the laughing crowd.

Collier's chairman was a very heavy influence on Colin Crompton's dictatorial concert secretary on *The Wheeltappers and Shunters Social Club*. Crompton's version of the character is best remembered for announcing several times during every show that 'We've had a mee-TING! Of the Committ-EEH! And passed a resolu-SHUUUN!' about some minor by-law or point of order that invariably acts as a stark contrast to the glamour onstage, or punctures the ego of a particular performer. There's an interesting episode where the two comedians, both in character, come face-to-face, with Crompton's bored, slightly glazed secretary talking over Collier, imploring the audience to 'Give him a chance, he's doing his best!'

This officiousness still lurks in clubs today, even if it's less direct. In an essay about the relationship between the band The Fall and working men's clubs, writer and designer Paul Wilson ponders the two different types of notices you see plastered around any working men's club. On the one hand are those advertising live entertainment: 'glossily overcompensating for the performer's relative obscurity, or for whatever quality of musicianship might be on offer, with the use of a broad grammar of stylistic devices that mirror a perceived visual style seen in the wider world, while creating a genre all of their own … never-too-decorative font selection combined with experiments that bravely explore the hinterlands of legibility – all working together to portray a culture that's actively striving for a kind of glamour, fashion and exoticism that belies the humdrum surroundings of your average Club's concert room.'

These contrast with the more formal notices:

> … drawing a visitor's attention to the environment of the Club itself and the institutional rules which must be paid heed to … Mostly home-printed A4 pages, messily nested and clustered together, these notices act as an organisational barometer, telling stories of that Club's shared values, its commonly held needs and the demands which mustn't be ignored … Echoing the announcements and pronouncements of the Wheeltappers' Colin Crompton, the notices to members and associates often speak on behalf of the (faceless, nameless) Club committee and adopt a formal visual and typographic tone, while throwing off any artifice of a designed professionalism or pretence towards positive visual or typographic engagement with their readers.

Once this has been pointed out, it's impossible to ignore. When I was visiting clubs in 2021, Covid-19 had multiplied the need for formal notices and they had exploded from the noticeboards onto walls all around the building, along with more yellow hazard tape, floor markings and plastic screens than I've seen in any pub, a constant reminder that while you're here, you play by the rules, and the Committ-eeh will be watching to see that you do.

But it's too easy to ridicule the officiousness of clubmen. It's not as if they're the only people who let power go to their heads, who exercise their authority overzealously. This is not the class that is told from an early age that it was born to rule. These were people who might be working at a coalface or furnace by day, and then by night running an organisation with a bigger turnover than their employer's. As their clubs thrived and grew, they showed they were capable of far more than physical labour if given a chance, helped only by their peers in the Union.

The club committee was itself a great emancipation for thousands of working men. The fact that the Union remained avowedly apolitical meant it could support people of all political persuasions, but inevitably clubs formed links with other organisations in their communities. Often, the link would come about because having got a taste for committee life, the same men would stand for office in several different organisations. A survey carried out by the Union in 1922 showed that clubmen accounted for 178 Members of Parliament, 474 county councillors, 1497 town councillors, 1242 district councillors, and 1030 magistrates.

George Orwell loved what clubs represented, and what they said about the people who built them. In *The Road to Wigan Pier*, he wrote: 'The English working class ... have a wonderful talent for organisation. The whole trade union movement testifies to this; so too do the excellent working men's clubs – really a sort of glorified co-operative pub, and splendidly organised – which are so common in Yorkshire.'

But this compliment would not have been received kindly by wide swathes of the club movement. In the first decades of the twentieth century, the temperance movement and the licensed victuallers were still working together to denigrate clubs at any opportunity – usually when yet another licensing bill was before parliament. Pub numbers had peaked at the end of the nineteenth century and were now in decline, while the growth of clubs was surging. The victuallers and temperance campaigners still insisted on characterising any and all clubs as 'unlicensed drinking clubs,' so it was essential that CIU-affiliated clubs distanced themselves from such establishments.

Different 'Theys' were also still complaining that the clubs had abandoned the 'improving' principles laid down by Solly and his well-meaning nobles, and had also abandoned their political motive. Did this mean that clubs were just co-operative pubs now, as Orwell claimed?

Such a view – and it's one that has been expressed widely – can only be arrived at if you're not one of 'Us', if you're looking in at clubs from the outside and not really understanding what was going on. Once the clubs were running profitably and autonomously, they began looking outwards. With growing confidence and deepening pockets, they realised they could provide for their members not just in the club itself, but in the community more broadly.

The only slightly awkward issue with celebrating what the clubs went on to achieve was that it was all made possible by the sale of cheap beer – the very thing some people criticised them for. Before the clubs could reach their full potential, the supply of that beer was one of the first items on the agenda for the newly empowered club-men.

* * *

Britain's brewers had an ambivalent relationship with clubs. On the one hand, they were competition for their pubs. On the other, they were a potential new market when the number of those pubs began to decline. The rush to the stock market and the gin palace craze of the late nineteenth century had created a situation where the brewers either owned the pubs they supplied outright or tied them in the form of loans in return for exclusivity. That was fine for the pubs you had, because they could only sell your beers. But that was the extent of your potential market, because the pubs you didn't have were tied to other breweries. So while the beer trade publicly condemned working men's clubs as drinking dens, privately they fought to supply the beer these dreadful people were consuming so irresponsibly.

If the breweries were happy with this arrangement, the clubs were often less so. During the First World War, if supplies were tricky, the clubs were always at the back of the queue, behind the tied pubs. And when they got the beer, it was watered down 'government beer' aimed at reducing drunkenness in munitions factories, but the brewers were still charging clubs the price for full-strength beer.

With their new spirit of independence, clubs around the country decided that if brewers wouldn't deal with them fairly, they would brew their own beer. Even before the war, a group of Leeds Liberal Clubs had come together in 1911 to organise a brewery 'in practical protest against the brewers' profiteering.' It soon collapsed but was revived in 1914. In 1919, wartime restrictions on the issuing of new brewing licenses was lifted. Many breweries had gone out of business, so premises and equipment were readily available to buy.

B. T. Hall, now president of the Union, used the *Club and Institute Journal* to urge club brewers forward. In May 1919, a 'Correspondent' offered some advice to those clubs considering their own brewing ventures, He said the experiment by the Leeds Liberal Clubs had failed because of two factors, 'one technical and the other moral.' The moral side he 'fully understood,' essentially accusing commercial brewers of badmouthing the Leeds beer and bribing clubs not to accept it.*

The articles and analysis continued. Here was the CIU doing what it did so well, learning from any failures or shortcomings, and spreading that learning across all its clubs. All around the country, breweries were being established by cooperatives of clubs. The clubs put the money in and got the beer in return, and also received dividends from any surplus in the accounts.

Of these cooperative breweries, the most famous was the Northern Clubs Federation Brewery in Newcastle. The north east was already emerging as a powerhouse of the club movement. In December 1919, the *CIJ* reported that eighty (probably a misprint for eighteen) CIU clubs in Northumberland and nine in Durham 'have decided to

---

* They were able to do this because of the character of serious beer drinkers, which the correspondent describes in a way that will be familiar to anyone who has experienced the craft beer scene of a century later: 'The childish, fanatical partisanship of beer drinkers, their pretence to omniscient knowledge of the beverage and their unmovable confidence in their judgement of its varieties – all these, as an old committeeman, I have seen.'

purchase jointly a brewery at Alnwick.' This turned out to be a dreadful idea: another piece of learning from the venture, to be shared urgently across clubland, was that if you're spending ten grand on a brewery (about £300,000 today) it might be an idea to get a brewing expert to look at the kit before you buy it rather than after. The brewing equipment was beyond repair, the building having been used as a munitions factory throughout the war.

Undaunted – apart from some sternly worded motions from various committee men – the consortium found another site in Newcastle and finally began brewing in 1921. 'The Fed' became notorious in clubland and would end up selling beer to almost 500 clubs. It's remembered as beer whose main selling point was that it was cheap rather than good, reinforced by the mid-twentieth century trend of dispensing with casks and shipping the beer by tanker to be poured into huge holding tanks in the club cellars. But Fed Bitter can't have been as bad as is commonly remembered: for many years, the Fed was the main supplier of beers to the Houses of Parliament, and in the 1980s several Fed beers won big at the International Brewing Awards.

But the Fed had a wider significance in the club movement. It was a symbol of the power the clubs found in union: if a club couldn't get what it wanted on its own, somewhere in clubland it would find people it could ally with for mutual benefit. If clubs could set up their own breweries as well as putting their own people in parliament, what external forces could stop them now?

* * *

With the cash flowing as well as the beer, the clubs raised their game, prefiguring the welfare state by providing services that made life better for their members, and their families and communities, from cradle to grave.

As we've already seen, education was an important aspect of being a committee member, but at the same time it could be a source of tension where most people didn't have it. In 1944 the CIU secretary stated that: 'The great majority of working men, perhaps because their school education finished at the early age of 14, or possibly before then, are not inclined, having reached manhood, to engage in any form of education which involves study, and the promotion of education by the Union has been an uphill struggle.'

Nevertheless, the Union persisted. One of the first things it did was to introduce a circulating library among the clubs, in the form of boxes of books. Queen Victoria devoted several volumes she'd written herself, and even as noble patronage declined, the library still grew. By 1912, 888 boxes of books were being shared by 110,000 CIU-affiliated club members nationwide. Various exams and courses were held in subjects going way beyond club management. In 1884, William Johnson of Bedworth got top prize in a history exam. He repeated this five years running, and went on to become a Member of Parliament. In many clubs, the reading room remained long after most suggested improving features by the gentry had disappeared.

'On left hand side of the Corra as you went in were the reading room,' says Ian Clayton. 'And all down one side there were these sloped tables, all the day's newspapers, from the *Daily Mail* to the *Morning Star* to the *Daily Telegraph*, on wooden blades. Me grandad, he read every one, religiously. He formed a very strong understanding of how the media worked. He didn't just read them, he wanted to know what it meant. If there's something missing from a working men's club today, it's that sense of educating people as well.'

In 1921, the CIU spent £3000 on special classes for member's children. Additional summer schools allowed parents to get a break from looking after their children. That same year, the CIU also invested in higher education, with the organisation of twelve scholarships for members to Ruskin College, Oxford. This educational aspect had all but disappeared by the 1980s because, according to George Tremlett, 'the growth of the State's role in education has reduced the necessity for this aspect of the Union's work.' That may have been true when Tremlett wrote *Clubmen* in 1988. It feels less so now.

One of the few essential chroniclers of the working men's club movement was himself a product of the Ruskin Scholarship scheme. John Taylor, author of *From Self Help to Glamour: The Working Man's*

Club 1860–1972, was the CIU's sole Ruskin scholar in 1970, a life-long clubman in his hometown of Newport, South Wales who gained the place in his late thirties after working as a house painter and construction worker. His tutor at Oxford encouraged him to write about his own experience of clubs, and together they discovered 'a collection of papers and journals in a forgotten basement corner of the CIU HQ in Islington,' from which Taylor produced his unique and irreplaceable account of club history.

For the less academically minded, clubs provided services people didn't have at home, such as baths and showers for those who lived in houses like the one my parents owned when I was born, with only a kitchen sink and an outside toilet. In the 1960s, the Oakes club in Sheffield advertised 'Baths available Thursday onwards.' About a dozen club members took advantage each week. The Lindley Working Men's Club had four baths, and designated Thursday night as women only, for the families of club members.

Once road travel became widely accessible, clubs would organise coach trips for members. Often these would be to another club ten miles away, just for a change of scene. But as summer rolled round, every club member and their families would be taken on a fleet of coaches to the seaside for the day, with a friendly brewery donating a few crates of ale for the journey. 'We'd write to a club about halfway there,' reminisces one old member interviewed by Neil Anderson for his *Dirty Stop Out's Guide to Working Men's Clubs*, 'and we'd stop there on the way back till we got kicked out.'

The children of club members also got their own seaside trip, usually organised and stewarded by a few wives or, as the clubs referred to them from the 1950s onwards, 'lady members.' The kids would be labelled with name tags, given pop, crisps and a few shillings spending money, and let loose on Cleethorpes or Bridlington while back home their parents could spend a relaxing day – where else? – at the club.

The annual Christmas dinners laid on for the elderly would sell out weeks in advance and seem to be a particular point of pride for many clubs. At several places I visit, committee members get out piles of old photographs to show me how successful these events were.

The CIU was even prouder of its convalescent homes. The first of these was opened in Pegwell Bay, Kent, in 1894. Various other sites around the country followed, and on the CIU's centenary in 1962, the homes had 4000 residents between them. Less well celebrated, but noted by Jackson in his study of Huddersfield clubs, 'Many of the coalfield clubs build bungalows for retired miners and rent them out at 7/6d a week.'

Along with hardship funds for members who were injured or sick and couldn't work, free meeting rooms for local societies and groups, and the games, sports and entertainment we'll be looking at later, the cradle-to-grave community support provided by the clubs elevated them far beyond mere drinking dens. And yet, each time a licensing bill came before parliament, they had to defend themselves against that charge. At one debate in 1933, Lord Astor insisted: 'The club movement brings relaxation and education in a large number of towns and villages up and down the country. There is not a word to be said against the movement. In fact, it is deserving of the greatest support.'

The clubs had gone from being the plaything of peers, to independent entities receiving objective admiration from them. But even the Union itself didn't always seem convinced of its worth. In 1944, the Trades Union Congress explored the issue of 'active citizenship,' a widespread look at what leisure meant for working men, with a wartime throwback to the idea of rational recreation to make sure British men were doing proper British leisure in a way that wouldn't leave them vulnerable to the lure of fascism or communism. A memo from the then secretary of the CIU made the earlier point about education being an uphill struggle, before giving a less than convincing account of the Union's worth. According to the TUC report's author:

The Secretary went on to point out that games and sports, both indoor and outdoor, along with concerts, flower shows and dances, aroused the greatest interest among members. It is significant that he expressed all this in a defensive, almost apologetic tone, making every effort to draw out the 'improving' side of the CIU mission. 'Every endeavour is made to develop the spirit of sportsmanship and tolerance, and a right sense of neighbourliness and civic duty and responsibility.' For all this, the CIU's was perhaps the most authentic of all the responses received by the TUC in revealing what 'leisure' really meant to working men.

Some external observers remained blind to the broader role of the club in the community. In 1956, *Coal is our Life: An Analysis of a Yorkshire Mining Community* recounted the findings of a bunch of sociologists who spent time in a place they anonymised as 'Ashton,' but was in fact Featherstone. When they visited the clubs Ian Clayton and his grandad went to, they looked at the original aims of the club movement drawn up Henry Solly almost a century before, and used these as a benchmark for evaluation – despite the clubs having rejected Solly's vision seventy years previously. While acknowledging that 'there is a certain amount of mutual helpfulness,' this is dismissed as being 'not at all impressive,' just the odd bloke buying a pint for his mate when he was a bit short. The researchers complain that 'the clubs can scarcely be said to be seriously concerned with either "mental and moral improvement" or "rational recreation."' Instead, the men drink with people they have known all their lives, talk about work and sport, about 'concrete cases, whether of actual incidents at the colliery, or actual incidents on the field of play,' and there is 'little provision for "intellectual" interests.'

It's all about as useful as criticising a sports car for its lack of luggage space, or slagging off *Star Wars* for its over-reliance on special effects. External observers rarely attempted to look at the working classes on their own terms. And when they began doing so in the 1960s and 1970s, they often failed to understand what they were seeing. Their first mistake was that when they examined the clubs, they only saw men drinking beer and talking. Their second mistake was concluding that this, in itself, was a bad thing. They were so obsessed with beer being drunk in clubs, they didn't look close enough at the members themselves, and why they were drinking beer there rather than in a pub.

* * *

The working men's club had become two different things. On the one hand, the movement had grown to become a vital service that affected not just the club's members and their families but the whole communities in which they were based. On the other, the club remained a private space where men went to be in the company of their male neighbours and male workmates. The contradiction between these two roles would eventually prove unsustainable, and the club movement's struggle to accept women on equal terms is arguably the darkest stain on its history. We'll come to that later, but before we do, it's worth digging a little deeper into the importance of having these male spaces in the first place, and why sometimes, 'us' meant men while 'they' were women.

Throughout the First World War, the growth of clubs slowed, but didn't stop. After they returned home, tens of thousands of men struggled to adjust and come to terms with what they'd experienced. While many psychologically damaged men were saved by wives who showed patience and compassion, others could no longer relate to normal life, and to the women who they had, in some cases, married just days before leaving for the front. In *Forgotten Voices of the Great War*, historian Max Arthur reveals what it was like for both sides, quoting people who recorded their memories for the Imperial War Museum.

Mabel Lethbridge remembers: 'When my father and brothers, uncles, relatives and friends came home on leave and were staying at or visiting our house, I noticed a strange lack of ability to communicate with us. They couldn't tell us what it was really like. They would perhaps make a joke, but you'd feel it sounded hollow, as there was nothing to laugh about.'

Captain Charles Carrington of the 1/5 Battalion, Royal Warwickshire Regiment, explained why:

This world of the trenches, which had built up for so long and which seemed to be going on forever ... was entirely a man's world. Women had no part in it, and when one went on leave one escaped out of the man's world into the women's world. But one found that however pleased one was to see one's girlfriend, one could never somehow get through, however nice they were. If the girl didn't quite say the right thing one was curiously upset. One got annoyed by the attempts of well-meaning people to sympathise, which only reflected the fact that they didn't really understand at all. So there was almost a sense of relief when one went back into the man's world ...

It's no surprise then that after the war, men sought out male-only spaces, particularly those shared by men who had been through the same ordeal. Whether it was discussed openly or not, the important thing was that you were around people who understood. Post-Traumatic Stress Disorder hadn't been diagnosed, and the northern version of the British stiff upper lip was just shuttin' up and gerrin on wi' it. British Legion clubs and ex-servicemen's clubs formed in over a thousand towns, cities and villages, and many of them affiliated to the CIU. On the Armistice in November 1918, there were 1666 CIU clubs with 688,972 members. Four years later, when the CIU celebrated its 60th anniversary, this had grown to 2269 clubs with 1,150,000 men.

There were similar issues in 1945, with men coming home and being expected to resume roles within their communities as reliable breadwinners and good husbands and fathers – roles which were still considered masculine, but in a very different way from the action, terror and heroism of war. Working men's clubs were all-male spaces where these new roles could be worked out – or avoided. Some new clubs were even built using physical remnants from the war like military huts, tank repair kits and air raid shelters. More than pubs, the relaxed, homely nature of clubs gave men an alternative domestic space where they could just go and be themselves. Women were welcomed on Friday and Saturday nights for the turns and the bingo, but the rest of the time, men would often go most days to simply be with other men.

As one Huddersfield clubman told Brian Jackson, 'I always feel that when you are in a pub, and your glass gets down, they all start looking at you.' Whereas in the club, 'Y'not compelled to have a drink. You can come in and read the paper or have a game of dominoes and no one pesters you ... You can sit with a gill* in y'hand all night in a club; y'couldn't do it in a pub.'

A major survey carried out for Guinness by Mass Observation in 1947–48, found that, of people who used both pubs and clubs, 68 per cent preferred the club and only 22 per cent the pub. The price of drink was a factor, but not the only one. The pub was seen as having better quality beer and a more varied clientele, but this was outweighed by the stability, conviviality and superior recreational facilities of the club: 'Drink, as so often before, is an incidental, and the clubgoer in particular regards it as of far less importance than the social activities. For the clubgoer is on the whole the casual drinker, and the serious drinker who appreciates his beer on its own merits alone is content in his pub and his home without bothering about clubs.'

Clubs had a different kind of atmosphere. You knew everyone there, and strangers couldn't walk in and cause trouble.

The preference for the club experience over that of the pub soon began to show up in statistics. In 1939 there were over 18,000 clubs in total in the UK, making up about 20 per cent of total on-licensed premises. Less than half of these were affiliated to the CIU, but the affiliated working men's club defined what clubs meant to people. Between 1945 and 1960 the number of clubs grew modestly, but over the same period the number of pubs fell, until there were around 75,000 pubs compared to 25,000 licensed clubs. The Federation Brewery was at its peak, supplying cheap beer to thousands of clubs, and Britain's breweries started to take notice of the threat to their business.

Some pubs responded by turning parts of their premises into quasi-clubs offering exclusivity and a range of social activities such as games, raffles, outings. Clubs may have always had a small market share over-all (70 per cent of club members also went to pubs) but they were

---

* In this context, he's probably referring to the imperial measurement of four fluid ounces rather than part of a fish.

instrumental in forcing brewers to think more seriously about improving pubs.

As working men's clubs approached the peak of their popularity, the nature of domestic life for the communities they served was about to undergo a profound change.

Between 1955 and 1980, a great programme of house building got under way across Britain. While no one missed the bomb sites that were common in most industrial cities, there was more ambivalence about the clearance of Richard Hoggart's tight back-to-backs with their ginnels and snickets. An average of 67,000 homes were demolished each year. People were moved to council houses on new suburban estates, and later to inner city high-rises. These new homes may have had bathrooms and electricity, but those close-knit communities were uprooted and displaced, and would never reappear with that same intensity. For people who were suspicious of change and revelled in continuity, the effects were devastating – for one of Brian Jackson's Huddersfield informants, they could even be fatal:

> I'll tell you what, I've noticed this with old folk that's been moved away – they don't seem to have reigned long … that woman over there, her sister and her husband they were moved from Brow Road. Well, he were a big mate o' mine, used to go about a lot, and they were moved up Crosland Moor. Well, nothing wrong with Crosland Moor, up top end it's a nice district, but do you know they were both dead within twelve month. Somehow it seemed to knock all t'stuffing out of them, down here you know everything and everybody, I know Millbank stone by stone as you might say.

Those who survived the upheaval took their fondness for the club with them, even though on the new estates, with warmer, more comfortable homes, they had more free time and more options of how to spend it, than ever before. Unemployment was low, wages were improving, and many women were entering the workplace for the first time, gaining a new sense of independence and engagement with the world beyond the well-scrubbed doorstep and the garden fence. In 1960, 25 per cent of homes had a TV set. By 1970, that figure exceeded 80 per cent. And those TVs brought glossy advertising into the home, for items working families could now afford: as well as new TVs, they bought new ovens, fridges and accessories that made the housework much easier.

While watching telly became the dominant working-class pastime, it doesn't seem to have dulled the desire to get out of the house: if anything, the images of an aspirational lifestyle and a world beyond the terraces that this new working class had grown up in fired their appetites to do more. A car became an essential rather than a luxury, and young couples could drive out to decent country pubs, or cinemas and clubs in town, rather than just socialising in the streets where they lived.

Rather than kill off the working men's clubs, this affluent new lifestyle pushed them to greater heights. With many clubmen having graduated to local government, the councils in charge of planning the new estates like those I visited in the north of Sheffield left space on those estates for new clubs to be built. With so many chimney pots in such close proximity, brewers were happy to lend the money for ever more ambitious new purpose-built clubs to be erected. Gone were the days when members had to be confined by their own skills and budgets: these new clubs, with spacious concert halls, a number of bars and a good-sized car park, were on a far grander scale than the old converted houses and rooms above shops.

Stories about expansion schemes to existing clubs costing £70,000 became routine on the *CIJ*, with the new, purpose-built estate clubs costing £250,000 to £300,000. These stories ran alongside a blizzard of ads for furniture, fixtures and fittings. Now people's homes were more comfortable, the clubs had to offer them something extra in return for leaving the house. In July 1973, CIU Secretary Gen Ding observed: 'When one walks into the "foyer" of the Brun Grove Club, Blackpool, you might well think you were in the entrance of a first-class hotel. The design of the reception area is something to be proud of, light and airy, mahogany lined with pleasant lighting AND plenty of room for people to gather. Brun Grove, like so many other Clubs, started from small beginnings, a "tin hut" to be precise.'

These were the clubs that would witness the peak in the popularity of the whole club movement, their big new concert halls bringing the outside world to their doorsteps, finally dissolving the barriers between Us and Them. Ironically, they would also turn out to be the soil where the seeds of clubland's decline were planted.

7

THE CLUB AND THE TURNS

Batley Variety Club, Batley, West Yorkshire

The first time I ever heard the story about Shirley Bassey and the sink was from Ian Clayton.

In his book *Bringing it All Back Home*, Ian recounts a drunken afternoon he spent with the singer Richard Hawley. Hawley comes from a musical family: his grandfather had an act in the music halls in which he played the violin behind his back while standing on his head. His uncle was blues guitarist Frank White, and his dad Dave was a Teddy Boy and celebrated guitarist on the Sheffield music scene.

As Richard told the story to Ian, Dave Hawley was part of a band who were just about to go on stage at Batley Variety Club: 'Just before the band is announced his dad decides he needs to pee. He asks a man backstage where the nearest toilet is. The man says 'Can't tha piss in that sink?' Richard's dad says, 'Well I'm not sure I can piss in a sink.' The backstage hand says 'What's up with thi? If it's good enough for Shirley Bassey I'm sure it's good enough for thee.' We all laugh like drains and Richard orders another round.'

Google the term 'If it's good enough for Shirley Bassey' and this version of the story doesn't appear. Instead, almost all the results relate to David Bowie, recalling his early days as Ziggy Stardust, playing in a string of 'grotty' clubs where you had 'a rock act, then a stripper – sometimes one and the same':

When we used to play the working men's clubs up north – very rough district – and I first went out as Ziggy Stardust, I was in the dressing room in one club and I said to the manager: 'Could you show me where the lavatory is, please?' And he said: 'Aye, look up that corridor and you see the sink attached to the wall at the end? There you go.' So, I tottered briefly on my stack-heeled boots and said: 'My dear man, I'm not pissing in a sink.' He said: 'Look son, if it's good enough for Shirley Bassey, it's good enough for you.' Them were the days, I guess.

When I'm deep into my research into clubs, I mention the subject to my friend Richard Thomas. Richard used to be New Order's tour promoter, and he has a few contacts I'm interested in speaking to.

'Ah!' says Richard. 'I've got a great story about working men's clubs for you. Back in the late seventies, my friend John used to roadie for The Damned, and they were up North playing a club, Batley Variety Club I think, and –'

'Is this the one about Shirley Bassey and the sink?'

'Yes! Did he already tell it to you?'

'Not as such, no …'

I doubt any version of the story is true, and Shirley Bassey's people never responded to my request for an interview. True or not, it's a meme that sustains, because it illustrates a deeper truth about the matter-of-fact nature of working men's club entertainment: no star is bigger than the club, and anyone who does play the clubs does so on the club's terms, not theirs.

But if it does tell this deeper truth, might one version of the story actually be true?

I suspect not. Partly, because Shirley Bassey didn't actually come up through the club circuit. She rose to stardom via theatres and was already famous when the clubs started booking acts of her calibre. She *did* play Batley Variety Club, and this is why people often claim the sink incident happened there. It also sounds right: onomatopoeically, Batley just sounds like the kind of place you might be told to piss in a sink.

But as soon as someone claims it happened in Batley, that's how you can tell it's definitely *not* true. Batley Variety was a purpose-built theatre club with no rival. Rather than a corridor with a sink in it backstage, there were purpose-built facilities that were superior to pretty much any theatre in the country. During her frequent residencies at Batley in the 1960s and 1970s, Shirley Bassey had a suite with a shower and bathroom, a dressing room with well-lit mirrors, and a sitting room with a sofa, coffee table and chairs. She even had bespoke hooks fitted in the suite to accommodate her lavish costumes. Other acts on the bill had their own dressing rooms along the corridor.

This was the real joke about Batley: from an artiste's point of view, this club in a small mill town just outside Wakefield was the least likely venue in the country where any artiste caught short would end up having to piss in a sink.

* * *

James Lord Corrigan was born into a poor travelling fairground family. He grew up working the stalls until the fair arrived in Batley in 1949, where he fell in love with a local girl, Betty Wimpenny, married her, and left the travelling life. When bingo was legalised in the early 1960s, he rented a room above Batley Conservative Club and ran a bingo hall. This was so successful it attracted the attention of Derek Ford, an accountant and travel agent who suggested they work together to build a chain of bingo halls. Corrigan Ford Enterprises eventually acquired twenty-two bingo halls and three cinemas. The fairground boy had become a wealthy businessman.

As all kinds of clubs proliferated across Britain, supper clubs became popular. The Kon-Tiki Club in Wakefield had a small stage in the corner where cabaret acts entertained diners. When James and Betty dined there in 1966, he mulled the idea of executing a similar concept on a large scale. The Corrigans flew to Las Vegas, studied the show bars on the strip, and decided to build something similar in Batley.

It was an outrageous idea, and a brilliant one. There was nothing on a similar scale – well, maybe Greasbrough, which James visited often – but this would be bigger and more glamorous. Motorways were linking up the North, and Batley was less than an hour's drive from Leeds, Manchester, Sheffield, and scores of smaller towns where 3 million people sat at home watching *Sunday Night at the London Palladium*. These viewers might not have been able to afford to go out in the West End in person, but surely they'd come and see the stars of the show if they were on their doorstep?

The audacity of the plan was underlined when James decided to build his club on the site of a disused sewerage works. As Michael Parkinson observed in a 1982 documentary, 'The locals are familiar with the saying, "where there's muck there's brass," but this was ridiculous.' The club was designed to seat 1,750 people with no pillars to block the view. Guests were to be seated at tables for eating and drinking, in a horseshoe formation, with five tiers descending to a stage at the bottom, and bars stretching the entire length of the room. There was no orchestra pit, and the low stage brought the performers closer to the audience than they ever were in a theatre. The food menu stretched to chicken in a basket, fish and chips and scampi and chips. The business model was to keep admission prices low and boost drink sales to create a profit. The Corrigans may have been thinking Vegas, but in many ways, the concept was closer to Victorian music hall.

Batley was never strictly a working men's club – it was never a member of the CIU, and existed only as an entertainment venue. But the Corrigans realised they needed extra drinking hours for the numbers to work. At the time, pubs had to close at 10.30pm on a week night, 11pm on Saturday and 10pm on Sunday. The venue needed to be open and serving drinks until midnight so, echoing the working men's clubs of the 1880s, Batley was conceived as a private member's club, with a club licence and the requirement for membership.

James Corrigan had inherited his family's gift for showmanship. He offered popular singing group The Bachelors double what they made in theatres to headline the opening week in March 1967 and had them parade through Batley in an open-topped limousine when they came to ceremonially lay the foundation stone, just fourteen weeks before they were due to play. Much of the public thought Corrigan's scheme was insane, but stunts like this brought people out onto the streets to stare. Before the club had even opened, it had 70,000 members. That number would eventually top 300,000 – for a club in a town of less than 50,000 people.

As soon as the club opened, it was packed seven nights a week. In 1968, Corrigan flew to New York to persuade Louis Armstrong to play a two-week residency. Word spread in showbusiness circles that while it might sound like a joke, Batley was a great gig, the pay was good, the facilities excellent, the audience generous. Shirley Bassey, Roy Orbison, Tina Turner, Tom Jones, Morecambe and Wise, Cliff Richard, Gracie Fields, Dusty Springfield, Johnny Mathis, the Four Tops, the Bee Gees and Cilla Black were soon queuing up to have their names light up the marquee. When the Bee Gees played, Maurice Gibb met and subsequently married one of the waitresses. Roy Orbison met his second wife there.

It would probably be quicker to list the famous names of the late 1960s who didn't play Batley. Corrigan's number one target was his personal idol, Dean Martin, He got on a plane to Vegas to go and see Martin's management. The first question they asked was how much money Corrigan was offering. When Corrigan replied £45,000 – double what he'd paid for Satchmo, and approximately £800,000 today – Martin's manager said, 'My boy wouldn't get out of bed to piss for that,' sink or no sink.

As well as bringing the biggest stars in the world to Batley, Corrigan's club also created its own. When I was a kid, I adored watching Bernie Clifton romping through BBC's *Crackerjack* in his Oscar the Ostridge costume (and like all kids, I'm secretly ashamed at how long it took me to figure out how it worked – was he riding a very strong child?) I had no idea then that he had made his name just fifteen miles up the road from where I was watching.

'Batley Variety Club changed my life,' he tells me almost fifty years later. 'As a promising young turn on the lower levels of the Yorkshire Club circuit, in 1971 I made it to the "Clubland Command Show" at

Batley. Barney Colehan, who produced and directed the *Good Old Days*, saw me there – at my best – and booked me for the show. That's where I met Les Dawson, who urged me to be different. "Plough your own furrow," were his words. I told him I loved being visual and he said, "Off you go then, become a 'prop' comic, none of the others can be arsed." So I did, and over the years we became good friends. He'd wink and say "I put you right there, didn't I?"'

'Yes, Batley was a landmark for me, and I'm sure for many more up and coming "turns" of the day. After years in the lower leagues, here was a sign that we were on our way. Jimmy Corrigan even took me to London in his Rolls Royce and introduced me to a major West End agent, a huge step away from the street corner Clubs I'd been used to for the previous ten to fifteen years.'

Even as he became a regular on TV, Bernie remained a constant at Batley. 'I did month-long sessions as compere working with Bassey, Sedaka and many of the biggest stars of the day,' he says.

These stars were usually booked for a week's residency (apart from Shirley Bassey, who could sell out a three-week run) playing every night with little to do during the day. The stark difference between Batley and London became apparent to anyone who went into town looking for something to do. There's a piece of grainy black-and-white video footage which encapsulates the entire absurdity and brilliance of the Batley Variety story into a couple of minutes. When Eartha Kitt played her week in 1969, by the Friday she was understandably bored, and decided to have a wander around Batley Market. Stunningly beautiful, fully made-up and wearing furs and an elaborate headscarf, she soon attracted an audience of less elaborately head-scarved house-wives, and young men who had clearly left their shops and offices to come and gawp at her. She visited a tripe stall, because – understand-ably again – the American megastar whom Orson Welles once called 'the most exciting woman on earth' had never encountered tripe before. In the video, Eartha Kitt fails to completely hide her disgust at both the tripe itself, and the serving suggestion of smothering it in industrial quantities of salt and vinegar. She eats a small piece and retches just about visibly, looks like she's about to vomit, and finally swallows. Then – unbelievably – she reaches for the salt and vinegar, hammers both, and goes in again. Somehow she recovers, says she's been singing all week, and asks her rapt audience what they like to sing themselves. A minute later, the multi-award-winning TV, movie and Broadway icon is leading the whole of Batley market in a hearty rendition of 'On Ilkley Moor 'Baht 'At.'

The scene features in the 1982 Parkinson documentary about Batley, which is available on YouTube, which I'm adding here because if I were you reading this, I wouldn't believe me, and because you just don't see anything that good on Graham Norton these days.

* * *

When Gracie Fields played Batley Variety Club, she was delighted to find that it reminded her of the old variety theatres which had by now all but disappeared, converted into cinemas or bingo halls. Variety in the form of shows like *Sunday Night at the London Palladium* drove the most popular programmes on TV. The sanitisation of music hall into variety theatre and then into light entertainment meant that it was perfect viewing for all the family and appealed to all social classes. As cinema and variety theatre declined, clubs continued to prosper, because they managed to offer something that you couldn't get on TV – the continuity of self-determined working-class entertainment. A club was a blank canvas on which its members could collectively determine their perfect night rather than have it sold to them by a commercial business.

The Free and Easy itself was enduringly popular. To people like Ian Clayton's grandparents, it was far better than t'rubbish on telly.

'There was Betty Wheatley, a Welsh woman down at Corra, and she had a heaven-sent voice, but she would never have thought to be a singer,' says Ian. 'But at the end of the night, she'd had a few, and they'd all encourage her.

"Betty, sing T'Owd rugged cross,"

"Oh no I don't feel like it."

"Oh go on, sing T'Owd Rugged Cross."

'Her husband would be on at er, "Go on Betty, sing it for 'em, you know you like to."

'She'd be there wi t' glass and t'fag:
ON A HILL FAR AWAYYYYY
STOOD AN OOOOOOLD RUGGED CROSS …

'They're all dabbing their eyes. And they'd take the story home with 'em. I'd be sat watching some bloody late-night Hammer Horror film on Saturday night television and they'd come in, me gran would still be having the conversation as she came through t'door, "Ooh, Betty Wheatley, have you ever heard anyone sing T'Owd Rugged Cross like Betty Wheatley? Eddie, in't it beautiful? Ooh she's fetched tears to my eyes each time she sings it."

'Me grandad: "Well she will do, she's Welsh."

'Exactly the same conversation the following week.'

While the Free and Easy never went away, in a different room in the club, or on a different night of the week, the new, purpose-built stages with their professional lighting and sound would play host to professional entertainers, or at least people who fancied themselves as such. It wasn't always like *Sunday Night at the London Palladium*, but this was the point: why would you go out to a club to see something you could watch on the telly?

'Most working men's club entertainment was vulgar and brash,' says Ian Clayton, 'and it had to be. It had to be loud because there's a lot of people talking, smoking, clinking glasses, laughing, joking among themselves, entertaining each other.'

This reminds me of something else Bernie Clifton told me: 'Someone once said, "In comedy, timing is everything." But they probably never stood on stage performing to a queue of people buying their bingo tickets.'

'And it all goes back to that tradition of music hall,' continues Ian. 'The great music hall stars had quite a surreal humour that somehow managed to transfer to the audience that they were performing to. So when you hear somebody like George Formby's dad – quite surreal ditties and songs. Marie Lloyd as well – she uses popular culture references but puts them in in a weird way. She's reflecting their society back to them but in a clever, wordy way. That's what working men's club entertainment comes from.'

The 1965 *Panorama* film about Greasbrough Social Club was based on the premise that this new breed of ambitious club offered an alternative to what people could watch on TV, a point put robustly by the star of that night's show, a youthful Bob Monkhouse. We see him run on stage before the film cuts to the stuff about the other Greasbrough club, and then return to a visibly buzzing yet exhausted Monkhouse, skipping towards the camera as the stage curtains close behind him.

In his clipped tones, the off-screen presenter says, 'A lot of the material here seems to be very robust to say the least. Very bawdy. Why is this?'

Monkhouse becomes defensive and starts to choose his words carefully, but he delivers them with a force and honesty that's quite different from the oily smarm I remember from 1970s and early 1980s TV.

'I don't think it's bawdy, I think it's adult. I think this audience is extremely quick-witted – the club audience I'm talking about – I think they've had a load of disinfected pap from television for a long time, which they like very well in their own homes, but when they get together in the community, they want to hear something stronger, brighter, gayer and a little bit more engaging to the adult taste.'

'It is a bit *rough* though, wouldn't you agree?'

'No, I wouldn't agree it's rough. What I think is it's grown up, as distinct from children's hour entertainment.'

'But would you agree with me that none of the material that you and other comedians have prepared for viewers in a place like this could be used on television?'

'No, it couldn't be used on television because television couldn't stomach it, and I can quite imagine that every one of these people here in the audience would be offended if they heard certain jokes in their own home which they can thoroughly enjoy either in parties or in a place like this. In other words, you will exchange a joke at a party in your own home when you've got a group that you will enjoy, that you would censor out if you were sitting with your children or the vicar or your grandmother. Here, no vicars, no grandmothers, just people.'

This dynamic partially explains the nature, appeal and controversy around clubland's most notorious figure. Bernard Manning was many things. His defenders are right to point out that he was a technically gifted comedian whose timing and delivery were far better than any of his peers. But they're wrong to insist that his virulent racism was simply of its time. His critics are wrong to say he wasn't funny, but right not to attempt to critically rehabilitate him in the way many have reassessed late comic talents such as Bob Monkhouse or Les Dawson.

Bernard John Manning was born in 1930 in the heart of Manchester, and grew up in Harpurhey, a northern district of the city. His father ran a successful greengrocer's business and young Bernard was spoiled as a kid. He began his showbiz career as a singer rather than a comedian, and was singing in pubs and clubs before he was old enough to drink in them. He quickly caught the eye of impresarios, and was fronting big bands in London by the late 1940s. But he missed home – he was never really happy anywhere outside Harpurhey – so he returned to Manchester to sing on the club circuit. He was naturally funny but felt himself to be too young to survive as a comic in the working men's clubs. Instead, he took on the role of compere in Manchester's cabaret clubs, singing a few songs, telling a few gags, and introducing the acts. He had to be quick on his feet, and this sharpened his skills. '"Being a singer was my crutch,"' he explained to his biographer, Jonathan Margolis, '"Do a song, whip in a couple of quips and gags, have a go at a few folk. One thing led to another and I could do two hours, no problem."' He saw his relationship with the audience as a battle that he simply had to win: insulting people and heckling the audience before they could heckle him became his trade mark.

Manning was a workaholic, fiercely ambitious, and obsessed with making money and using it to keep score. But at the same time, he was loath to set foot outside Harpurhey. He became famous in Manchester while remaining unknown outside, and soon harboured a desire to do what he could do for his own benefit rather than some-one else's. In 1959, he borrowed £30,000 from his dad to convert a knackered snooker hall in Harpurhey into the Embassy Club. Every day, he looked after all the business of running a club, and every night he introduced a variety of acts, insulted his audience, and told jokes that were far too offensive for TV. This all made him a very rich man. In 1996, he said, 'It doesn't bother me one iota that they say I'm a fascist. It's money in the bank.'

Reading Manning's interviews with Margolis, he comes across as a narcissist more than anything else. He talks about himself in the same way Donald Trump did when he was president: all the people really liked me, even when I was working in a dead-end job, everyone said I was the best person they'd ever seen do it, and so on. Manning could do the blue, racist stuff at the Embassy, then nip down the road and do a perfectly clean set at the nearby Catholic Club, then head to a gay club at midnight and do a set that went down a storm there. Near the end of his career, and at the peak of his notoriety, he did a set at alternative comedy club Jongleurs and received a standing ovation. Margolis expressed doubts that Manning was truly racist: he was just adept at doing whatever worked in any given situation.

Margolis, like many others, excuses Manning as a product of his time. But the difference between Manning and other comedians is that when the times changed, most comics changed with them, modi-fying their act in line with what was considered acceptable. Instead, Manning leaned into the racism, actually becoming more extreme and offensive than the typical club comic of the early seventies.

I felt like I had to get to the bottom of Bernard Manning – sorry, that's an unpleasant image – because for many people, he came to define the working men's club comedian, and symbolised the club's allure of 'You can't get this on the telly' more than anyone else. While reading and learning about him, I developed a theory that he wasn't actually racist at all but pretended to be because it was a lucrative niche that no one else dare go near. He could own a profitable niche and clean up from it, and money was all he cared about. In a way, this was even worse: at least genuine racists believe what they say. But while I was writing this book, I met a successful Manchester comedian and writer who had worked with Manning when he was a guest on a popular BBC TV programme in the 1990s. I put my theory to him, and in response he told me some of the things Manning had said in the dressing room, when there was no audience to appeal to, and he wasn't being recorded. They were far more offensive, far more steeped in genuine hatred, than anything he said on stage. Bernard Manning was a virulent, hateful racist, as well as a brilliantly gifted comedian. He was not truly representative of the clubland comedian, and the fact that he came to be seen as such would become a significant factor in clubland's decline.

* * *

Behind every great performer stands the list of people they have to thank at awards ceremonies, and clubland is no different. Alongside comperes like Bernie Clifton, the house backing band needed to be versatile enough to accompany any musical style clubland threw at them. For one musician, this was solid training for a career that took him in a radically different direction than the usual tropes of clubland entertainment. Against stiff competition from the direction of Eartha Kitt and, as we'll see shortly, Arthur Scargill, the most improbable sentence I am likely to write in this book is this: the house bassist at Greasbrough Club was Gavin Bryars.

For anyone unaware of his work, Bryars is an English musician and composer who has worked in jazz, free improvisation, minimalism, avant-garde and experimental music, collaborating with other ground-breaking musicians such as Tom Waits to Brian Eno. He has been described as 'arguably the most important British post-minimalist composer.' Outside jazz and avant-garde, he's probably best known for 'Jesus' Blood Never Failed Me Yet,' which is built around a field recording he discovered of a frail, old tramp singing in the street, Bryars put it on a loop, then built washes of warm brass and strings around it, rising to a crescendo that easily moves the unwary listener to floods of hot tears.

The standard biography of Bryars tells how when he was a philosophy student at Sheffield in the mid-1960s, he became a jazz bassist in an improvisatory trio called Joseph Holbrooke. What went unrecorded, until Bryars wrote about it on his website in April 2020, is that between January 1965 and August 1966, he barely took a night off from playing bass at the miners' club he describes as 'The Palladium of the North':

> There were 8 shows a week – 7 nights plus Sunday lunchtime, and seven or eight acts in each show, with the top of the bill, being the most famous, on last and all were rehearsed from 10am to midday on Sunday morning, when the first show started. The band's sight-reading was phenomenal and with some things that we didn't even bother rehearsing, we would glance at the parts or let Terry, the pianist, talk it through. Some comedians included songs, but most were just played on and off and during their time the back curtains were drawn so we could slip off for a drink. We would be back in place for the last gag followed by a high-speed version of 'When You're Smiling …'

Bryars played for Freddie and the Dreamers, Dusty Springfield, Des O' Connor, Kathy Kirby, Val Doonican, Vera Lynn, Little and Large and Arthur Askey. He played for conjurers, mind-readers, ventriloquists, and a man who strapped a xylophone to his waist and played it while spinning in circles on roller skates under strobe lights. He reckons he took just one night off in eighteen months.

In a way, his subsequent career makes sense: after that kind of boot camp, not only would you be able to play in any musical style you fancied; nothing would be off-limits creatively. It took Gavin Bryars just five years from appearing briefly behind Bob Monkhouse on the *Panorama* clip to premiering 'Jesus' Blood' at the Queen Elizabeth Hall on the South Bank.

The orchestrator of this wonderful and frightening world of entertainment was the concert secretary, by the 1960s, the most powerful figure in clubland. He was a direct continuation of the music hall and singing saloon chairman, a curiously British bureaucratic office-holder rather than a slick, Vegas-style compere trying to whip up the audience between acts. In club lore he was constantly calling for 'order all around the room please,' and bigging up acts in a uniquely down-to-earth way, mangling performers' names and at times deflating them with well-intentioned appeals for quiet such as 'come on, give the poor cow a chance.'

The concert secretary at Greasbrough Social Club, whom Gavin Bryars remembers fondly, was Les Booth. *Panorama* introduces Les on screen while he's on the phone, asking 'Any news about Shirley Bassey? Well do your best. And follow Sammy Davis through.' He's described as 'a printer in the daytime who has growing power in the variety world, and is spoken of as an impresario.'

With the perfect blend of vision and practicality, Les explains that he went to see his favourite comedy act at a theatre in Sheffield and there were twelve people in the audience. 'So I thought, why can't these people come to Greasbrough?'

'What made you think they would come to a place like Greasbrough, which hardly anyone's ever heard of?' ask the presenter.

'Well why shouldn't they come to Greasbrough?' Les responds.

As if he's talking to a child (or, perhaps, a thick northerner) the presenter explains that the top acts cost a thousand pounds. 'Where's the money going to come from?'

'Well, the sale of beer!' says Les. 'We've taken £118,000 over the bars so far this year!'

When they weren't on the phone asking about Shirley Bassey, concert secretaries would gather at 'shop window' audition days and watch act after act, most of them from the local area, their grinning faces on headshot postcards ready to hand out. An act on the way up could fill their diaries for months at a day like this, and the concert secretary would fill his schedule with comedians, singers and variety acts.

Being such power brokers obviously went to a few heads, and concert secretaries often developed fearsome reputations for 'paying up' acts that weren't working – giving them some or all of their fee and telling them to leave, or even not letting them into the club in the first place. As the sixties turned into – well the sixties, older northern men who had fought in the Second World War and otherwise never been outside their tightly-knit communities came into contact with the world outside, the world of Them. People who would go on to be huge stars could be sent packing with 'You're not coming into my club dressed like that.' Ronnie Lane was the bassist for a then little-known group called the Small Faces, who came up from London to play a Sheffield Working Men's club. In the *Dirty Stop Out's Guide to Working Men's Clubs* he relates: 'After playing a couple of numbers we were asked to leave. We decided to drive around a bit and see if we could find somewhere else to play. We saw all these mods going into a club. This was our first big break as the club was being run by two young brothers, the Stringfellows. It was a bit like *Ready Steady Go*, full of mods. After we played the Mojo, mods adopted us as their own band. We always received an enthusiastic welcome from the crowds of mods when we played the Mojo.'

This lack of worldly knowledge went further than the latest trends in music and fashion. Ian Clayton remembers Tiger Gascoigne, concert secretary at the Corra in Featherstone. One Saturday, a young female singer who was the turn that night arrived in the afternoon, at about 3.25, just as the club was closing. As Ian tells it, Tiger was somewhat taken aback.

'We're just putting t'bolts across love, what do you want?'

'Oh, I'm t' turn tonight.'

'Turn? Well, they don't normally turn up while about half past six. You're a bit early.'

'Well I live at Derbyshire and I didn't know how long it would take me and I'm here.'

'Well, what we gonna do with thi? I can't leave thi in t' club, I've to lock up and go home.'

'Oh, right.'

'As'll have to tek thi home wi me. Tha'll have to sit on me sofa.'

'Oh, that's alright, I can do that till I come back and do me sound-check.'

'I live across road.'

'Right.'

Tiger takes the singer across the road to his house and sits her on the sofa in the front room. 'Do you want a pot of tea?' he asks.

'Ooh, that'll be lovely I haven't had anything since I set off this morning.'

So he goes into the kitchen. About five minutes later he come back he says 'Does tha know owt about gas ovens?'

'What?'

'Only, our lass normally makes tea and puts kettle on. I don't know how to turn t'gas on.'

'There he is,' says Ian, 'Concert secretary, organising turns, shouting for order, doesn't know how to put a kettle on!'

Another of Ian's stories involves his own interaction with a concert secretary and could happily take its place in the tradition of the culture-laden surrealism from the music halls we were discussing earlier.

Ian had written a play about the Featherstone Massacre of 1893 to mark its centenary. In 1893, the plummeting price of coal led to miners' wages being slashed by 25 per cent. The miners came out on strike, and the pit owners hired blackleg labour to move coal from the pits. Each time it was rumoured this was happening, miners would gather at the pit to protest. At this time, the town of Featherstone had a total of three police officers. On 7 September, two of them had been sent to cover the St Leger race at Doncaster, so when it became apparent that there was going to be conflict at Ackton Hall pit, which neighboured Featherstone, the army was drafted in to keep the peace. Instead of doing that, when the protestors refused to disperse, the army opened fire on them, murdering two men and injuring another six. The incident spurred the growth of the Labour movement and is still bitterly remembered in the former coal fields.

'It was at the Central Club in Featherstone,' Ian remembers. In 1993 it was on its arse, with fourth rate turns using backing tapes, terrible beer and a useless committee. I invited Arthur Scargill to come and speak at the launch of a seven-night run of the play. I decided to have the speech made in The Central because Arthur had given a very memorable speech there during the [1984–85] strike. He did a wonderful launch speech from the main stage in front of a golden streamer curtain, using the bingo caller's rostrum to rest his papers on. He went home straight after. I walked him to his car. When I came back in, one of the committee men said, 'Has he gone?' I nodded. He said, 'Well it dun't matter, we were going to give him a meat tray to say thank you, but I'll put it in t' pigeon club raffle instead nar.' I left shortly after. As I went through the door, the same committee man shouted after me. 'Next time tha sees him, thee tell him he's best fookin' turn we've had on here for years.'

What makes this story even better is that it's not even the best one Ian has about the infamous former leader of the National Union of Mineworkers and the concert secretary of a Yorkshire Working Men's Club. When he tells me the next one, I suspect Ian of winding me up, so he refers me to the relevant passage of the memoir written by Ann Scargill, Arthur's wife.

American singer Harry Belafonte had written to Arthur Scargill to say that he was coming to England and would like to meet up. Arthur invited Harry and his wife to come and stay with him and Ann in Barnsley. Before he arrived, Arthur went to the Swaithe Working Men's Club in Monkspring, near Barnsley, to ask if the concert secretary there would like to have Harry Belafonte sing a few songs. The concert secretary thought for a bit and said, 'Ooh! I'm not sure about that Arthur. I've got plenty of top turns booked up well in advance. I can't just make exceptions at the drop of a hat. Arabella who, did tha say?'

I have so many questions the first time Ian tells me this story. But the one that barges to the front and demands to be asked immediately is, 'How the hell did Harry Belafonte know Arthur Scargill and why did he want to come and stay with him?'

'The Scargills were guests of Fidel Castro at the 11th World Festival of Youth and Students in Cuba in 1978,' answers Ian. 'While they were there, Arthur sat with the dignitaries; Joshua Nkomo, Yasser Arafat, who was carrying a silver pistol, and Harry Belafonte, who was there as some sort of cultural ambassador. Ann went swimming with Belafonte and his wife every morning. Arthur tells a brilliant story about how at the closing ceremony they were all sat close together on a podium. He leaned over to Belafonte and said "It's to be hoped if any snipers are thinking of having a pot at Fidel today, that they're a good shot!'"

Belafonte's trip to Yorkshire never happened in the end. Would history have been different if the gig at Swaithe Working Men's Club had been booked in? I guess we'll never know.

*   *   *

I peeped into the concert hall and amid the cigarette smoke, that was festooned in spirals above the heads of the audience, I saw a scene that reminded me of a Cecil B. de Mille version of a Pagan temple. Glowering razor-lipped miners drinking from dark pots in sullen silence; small chattering women in heavy cosmetics; darting waiters with swilling trays, minnow-like in their exper- tise. I wasn't encouraged by what I saw; it was an altogether familiar pattern that sent despair surging into my guts.

There are many passages like this in *A Card for the Clubs*, Les Dawson's debut novel, which was published in 1974. Read today, it is in many ways a deeply unpleasant book: the narrator is a racist, sexist, homo- phobic, anti-semitic, violent alcoholic who blunders his way up and down a career as a stand-up comedian on the clubland circuit. There are elements here that are autobiographical, clearly taken from Dawson's own experience. But after reading Louis Barfe's biography of him, it's clear Dawson shared none of his narrator's prejudices. Early in the novel the narrator, 'Joe King,' steals another comic's material and performs it, going down a storm. In real life Les Dawson never did this, but Bernard Manning did, performing the act just before the other comedian came on. Dawson and Manning didn't get on, so I suspect some of the aspects of Joe King are based partially on Manning.

While the misanthropic attitude may be someone else's, the language in which it is expressed is all Dawson:

To any reader who may contemplate a career in the wastes of clubland, allow me to paint you a portrait of what you can expect. First impression, you have entered a Londonderry training camp for the IRA. The main preoccupation is to swill as much ale into your system as Mother Nature will allow and the IQ is minus two. You will then walk on to a stage that is a replica of a Yukon gallows platform, bow to an unfeeling sea of pallid faces, and commence to entertain that ocean of indifference. You may be lucky and one or two of the audience will raise their heads from a frothy pot and actually listen to what you are trying to say. All the time you are stood in the glare of two hundred-watt bulbs, there will be a constant crocodile lurching to the loos, and as they pass by you they'll probably look up and tell you that you are 'Fucking awful.' The one thing to remember is that, wherever you are or whatever you play, be it a Soho haunt for debutantes, or a weaver's club in Paisley … they're all the same.

Joe King hates his audience because he fears them. Every club performer did, because the club audience was different from a theatre audience. In a theatre, the audience paid for tickets specifically to come and see you. In the club, you were an outsider intruding on their space, and you had to come to it on their terms.

Another Les, Leslie Dennis Heseltine, was twenty years younger than many of the acts he shared the working men's club circuit with. Shortening his name to Les Dennis, he did his first stand-up gig aged sixteen at a social club in Liverpool, where his mum knew the concert secretary. He did his first paid gig while he was still at school, and turned professional at nineteen, quickly becoming established in clubs around Liverpool, Manchester and North Wales.

'I was lucky I was so young,' Les tells me over the phone. 'The audience were like, 'Aw, he's alright, let's give him a chance.' But it was a real baptism by fire. You had to compete with the bingo, the raffle, the meat pies. 'Pies have come' – that really happened. You'd find yourself playing to a queue at the back of the room.'

This story is corroborated by the late Bobby Knutt, a comedian who was a huge draw on the South Yorkshire club circuit. He spoke to Neil Anderson, author of the Sheffield-themed *Dirty Stop Out's Guide to Working Men's Clubs*, shortly before he died, and in true Yorkshire style, if he were still around today, he would probably have responded to Les Dennis with 'You were lucky to have a queue at the back of the room.'

I got to the club and the chairman came into the room. You're on at 8.15pm and then about 10.20pm after the bingo. And he said, 'How long's your first spot' and I said 'about 45 minutes. He said 'okay.' So about five past eight I got up an switched my gear on and got changed.

In between me going back into the dressing room and being announced onto the stage two women had set up this big table in front of the stage with pies, a big cauldron of mushy peas, chips and sandwiches.

I walked on stage to be greeted by a massive queue – they're queuing for the pies! I was speechless. I couldn't believe what was happening.

I shouted, 'what are you doing'? And she replied, 'selling pies, does tha want one?'

'I said "no" and I said I'd come back on when they finished selling them.

Well the chairman marched into the dressing room and said, 'what's tha walking off for'? And I said 'I can't perform to a f**king pie queue.' And he begrudgingly said, 'alreet.'

And that was their norm – they normally sold pies when the act was on.

I asked why on earth they put them bang in front of the stage? And he replied, 'well they won't know they've arrived if we put them in the corridor.'

'Also, I learned very quickly that if you're a turn, you don't play bingo,' says Les Dennis. 'If you did, and you won, your second spot was an absolute nightmare.'

Comedians like Les would share the bill with 'a "girl vocalist" or "female voc" as they called them.' Each act would play two spots, with the vocalist going on last. 'The singer would be top of the bill, when everyone had finished eating. The comic had to compete with the clatter of chicken in a basket or pies being eaten as well.

'By your second spot, they were all half-cut. There's an apocryphal story about this but it's actually true, it really happened. Mick Miller was once doing so badly on stage that when he came off, he really didn't want to go back on for his second spot. In his dressing room there was one of those old-style bingo machines that they were just about to take on stage for the interval. He stole three balls out of it so the game went on all night.'

Of course, if you were really bad, there was always the threat of being 'paid up.'

'Oh, I had that happen to me a few times,' says Les. 'The committees were a law unto themselves. In some places you got a compere but in others it would be the concert secretary, sitting in his booth at the side of the stage in his flat cap, calling for order. The rest of the committee would all be there, all wearing badges – chairman, concert sec, head of pies, whatever. Sometimes you'd see them having a committee meeting at the back of the room, deciding whether to pay you off. They'd come to a decision, look at you, and sometimes these big curtains would just roll closed in front of you. I always used to try and stay on. Don't walk off, you'll get paid off. Stay on and you've won. That was my rule.

'It was harder in the north east than anywhere else. You'd do Sunday lunchtime shows there. The White House in Washington, I'll never forget that. All you can hear is the sound of your own feet as you walk on stage, and all you can see is a sea of *News of the Worlds*. They put them down, looked at you, and put them back up again. I'd try and stay on, and there would be the concert sec, the curtains closing on me, going, "Come off, bonny lad, don't punish yourself."'

In *A Card for the Clubs*, Joe King has a weekly residency at a club in Leeds, and he 'dies' on stage on the first night. On the second night, drunk and back on stage: '… it dawned on me just what a fraud and a failure I had been in my life and without any set routine I just started talking: "Mind you I don't have to do this for a living; I could always starve to death. To give you some idea of my act, last night a fisherman stood up in the front and fired off a distress signal. My agent said to me never mind Joe, one day your ship will come in … after the week I've had at this club it must have been the Titanic."'

Where he had died the night before, he now kills it.

This part is based absolutely on Dawson's own big break. He used to get drunk before he went on stage, and in a story he retold many times, he did a gig in Hull at a venue he described as a 'renovated fish crate.' As Louis Barfe relates, he took the piss out of Hull and then 'looked that audience firmly in the eye and told them tales of woe firmly based in the reality of his everyday life.' While he may be best remembered for his mother-in-law jokes (which were always more surreal than sexist) the main target of his comedy was himself, and this is how it began, with jokes about poverty and failure, and lines like 'I'm the only one on this bill that I've never heard of.' Worried initially that it was a fluke, Dawson tried this droll, resigned, fatalistic approach again, and it worked every time. He managed to share with the audience the hardships of life in a way that they recognised, but also make it funny by seasoning it with some good old music-hall-style surrealism: 'The house is so cold we put the milk in the fridge to stop it freezing.'

Whereas many comedians saw the club audience like Joe King did, looking in from the outside at 'flat-capped Woodbine puffing, horny handed cretins, with eyes that mirrored souls bludgeoned with harsh survival,' Dawson pulled off the trick of being one of them, or rather, one of *Us*. It's an approach that was later adopted by comedians like Alan Carr, Lily Savage and of course, Peter Kay, an antidote to Hello-Liverpool-what-a-wonderful-audience-type smarm and insincerity. It was perfect for the clubs and couldn't have happened without the clubs. As Barfe writes, it made Les Dawson, 'A comedian who, perhaps more than any other, spoke for the phlegmatic, resigned, sarcastic, glorious British attitude to life.'

* * *

The club audience was funny in its own right – jokes are the bar room currency of the North – but it was a bold bar-stool comic who would consider getting up on stage to entertain their peers. It's different for singers – every club has a Betty Wheatley, or a 'too good' karaoke singer.

Like Les Dawson's comedy, there was a knack to club singing. It became a style of its own, mercilessly lampooned on *Shooting Stars* by Vic Reeves, who would sing a popular song 'in the club style,' mangling it so badly that the contestants had to try to guess what song it was. But this style, like Reeves and Mortimer's surrealism, came from music hall, and from the Free and Easies before it.

Richard Hoggart goes into great detail about club singing. He regards it as part of the 'full rich life' of working-class communities, something that is 'ours' and ours alone, the unmediated popular culture that outsiders can't even recognise as culture. It remains in contact with older traditions of folk song at the same time as 'assimilating and modifying new material to their established interests.' Hoggart describes it as a style that has to deliver intense personal feeling without ever being egocentric. It conveys deeply felt emotion such as grief over the treachery of a loved one, but rather than the histrionics of 'the crooners,' who have to make it larger than (anyone else's) life, it assumes, crucially, that everyone in the room has felt these same deep emotions in the same way, via a style Hoggart calls the 'big dipper':

Here the voice takes enormous lifts and dips to fill out the lines of a lush emotional journey … Each emotional phrase is pulled out and stretched; it is the verbal equivalent of rock-making, where the sweet and sticky mass is pulled to surprising lengths and pounded; there is a pause as each emotional phrase is completed, before the great rise to the next and over the top. The whole effect is increased by a nasal quality, though one slighter than that used by the crooners. The most immediately recognisable characteristic is the 'ēr' extension to emotionally important work, which I take to be the result partly of the need to draw every ounce of sentiment from the swing of the rhythm, and partly of the wish to underline the pattern of the emotional statement. The result is something like this:

You are-ēr the only one-ēr for me-ēr,
No one else-ēr can share a dream-ēr with me-ēr
(pause with trills from the piano leading to the next great
    sweep)
Some folks-ēr may say-ēr …

For the singers who inhabited what Hoggart describes as 'a great shadow-world of semi-professional entertainers,' who hadn't given up the day job but worked the club circuit, these vocal stylings were complemented by a performance full of tics that established familiarity with the audience: a nod here, a wink here, a pointing of the finger in real or feigned recognition of someone sitting at a table halfway back – all moves taken straight from the Marie Lloyd playbook. It looks to entertain the audience, but at the same time to erase the gap separating audience and performer, to be seen not so much as a 'star' but more like your mum's glamorous friend.

Jane McDonald began her singing career in working men's clubs, and quickly grasped how to make it work. In her autobiography *Riding the Waves*, she describes the club circuit of the mid-1980s as 'Yorkshire RADA.' Saturday nights were when communities came together to 'have a drink and a right good laugh,' and it 'was irrelevant what was on that stage' – 'It was a battle every time. I'd look out into the audience and think, "Right what do you want?" It was up to you to create the atmosphere and it wasn't always easy. If you showed any weakness in a club, they would kill you. They'd be "Nah, not for me," and go back to what they were doing. I had to learn the hard way; I had to die onstage a few times.'

McDonald learned quickly how to relate to the audience on their own terms. She started with the women, asking them between songs if they'd seen *Emmerdale* that week, or saying how difficult it had been to find the club, 'Flipping heck, if there's ever another war, I'm coming here, the Russians will never find us!' She gained people's attention by establishing a common bond with them, and 'Once I had something in common with everybody, boom, I'd give them a big song so that they'd think, "Wow!"' She was soon being billed as a 'personality vocalist.' Following encounters with house musicians who weren't quite up to the standard of Gavin Bryars, she bought her own PA, even her own lights, and had her pick of club bookings until she moved onto cruise ships.

Among both comedians and singers who came up via the club circuit, there's a universal acknowledgement that while it may have been tough, it was valuable experience. 'For people who wanted to get into the business, it was great training,' says Les Dennis. 'I know I've made it sound quite antagonistic, but the thing is, if you did well, you came out feeling so good, because you knew you'd had to compete with all that.'

This apprenticeship was useful for a surprising range of acts, not just the stereotypical club singers. Noddy Holder began his career in Walsall Labour Club, saying 'I started singing in working men's clubs when I was 7 years old and so I grew up on stage.'

Paul Weller grew up in a house next door to Woking working men's club, where his dad John was a member. In 1972, a fourteen-year-old Paul and his friend Steve Brooks played their first ever gig as The Jam to an indifferent audience of local drinkers. 'We did about eight songs, mostly Beatle songs,' recalled Steve in a Weller biography. 'We had this idea of wearing the same gear ... We both had a black-and-white Elvis Presley shirt along with the orange loon pants with training shoes!' The club closed on Sunday afternoons, and John, later the group's manager, got them inside to use it as a rehearsal space. One of John's regular drinking buddies in the club was Rick Parfitt of Status

Quo, who gave Paul what advice he could about the music business. The Jam ended up getting a regular slot in the club, which became, as it did for everyone, a great training ground, but also an increasing source of frustration. The band would try to play as much of their own material as possible, but as Weller told *Melody Maker's* Brian Harrigan in 1977: 'We just had to play other people's music in these little working men's clubs ... people coming up to you and asking if you could do "The Last Waltz" or mainly just people telling you to turn it down!' The money from the club gigs subsidised the proper gigs the band were trying to get in London, and when they started getting coverage in the music press, The Jam abandoned the club circuit and its songs, worried about how it might affect their growing credibility.

Mark E. Smith had no such concerns around image – indeed, it's surprising how much of working men's club culture is in The Fall's output when you know how to spot it. In a 1992 interview, Smith made the 'training ground' point in his inimitable way: 'We were doing cabaret circuits at the time, just to earn money. Working Men's Clubs and all that. Fuckin' godawful! Fuckin' terrible! Good though. It toughened you up. They'd be throwing glasses – proper glasses, like – and spitting at you. I see a lot of groups today, and they don't know they're born. But touch wood nobody ever walks out of a Fall concert. You've got to keep the fuckers in there. That's how we got half our following. You fuckin' win them over and get their respect. They still come now. Miners from Wakefield and Newcastle.'

On the sleeve of The Fall's first live album, *Totale's Turns*, Smith explains 'turns' in the Working Men's Club context, and creates the character of Roman Totale, an honorary member of the 'Wakefield Young-Drinker's Club.' Some of the album was recorded at working men's club gigs, and Smith clearly relishes the antagonistic relationship with the audience, spitting lyrical riffs such as 'The difference between you and us is that we have brains-er/Because we're northern white crap/But we-er talk-er back-er.' And what's this? Had Mark E. Smith had been reading Richard Hoggart? It's possible – he was very well-read. Is his trademark vocal styling a parody of the authentic, unmediated voice of the club singer? In another twist, one of the many twenty-first century bands owing a heavy stylistic influence to The Fall decided to call themselves … Working Men's Club. It all adds up.

* * *

In 1955, the Independent Television network was launched to provide an alternative to the BBC, which had enjoyed a monopoly on TV airtime since its launch in 1932. In line with its brief to create competition in TV broadcasting, ITV was to be made up of various regional licences rather than one national broadcaster.

From its launch night, ITV was different from the BBC. The Beeb was still bound by its Reithian mission to educate, entertain and inform, whereas ITV had one simple job: entertainment, punctuated by the novelty of Britain's first ever TV advertising. Depending on your point of view, ITV was either the people's TV station in contrast to the stuffy BBC, or the low-rent, tabloid version of TV offering cheap thrills rather than worthwhile programming. In northern, three-channel TV households such as mine, BBC2 may as well not have existed – I don't even think we had it tuned on our TV set. As kids, we were allowed to watch BBC1 for the children's programmes when we got home from school, and then as soon as it was time for the news at 5.45 it had to be changed to Yorkshire TV, the local ITV franchise, where it remained for the rest of the evening, no matter what was on either side. By contrast, in the posher households further up the hill, where the teachers, bank managers and clergymen lived, there was often a blanket ban on ITV. My mate Chris, whose dad was a Methodist minister, doesn't remember his parents ever watching ITV, because the BBC was considered more aspirational.

The best comics of their generation, people like Les Dawson and Morecambe and Wise, would move from ITV to BBC and back again. But beyond the exceptional talents, a pattern quickly emerged.

For the light entertainment part of its remit, the BBC mined London's variety theatres until there was nothing left in them. In addition, there was a steady flow from Oxford and Cambridge into

Broadcasting House. Peter Cook, various Goodies and Pythons all came from the Cambridge Footlights to the BBC, creating comedy that was often clever and satirical.

ITV offered something brasher. Granada TV in Manchester and, later, Yorkshire TV in Leeds, were right in the heart of clubland and had remits to make programming that would work locally, with the occasional hit making it onto the national network.

Jimmy Tarbuck was the first club comic to go from playing the circuit to national stardom. His cheeky take on the club comic persona made him the perfect host for ITV's flagship programme, *Sunday Night at the London Palladium*. Others would soon follow. In 1964, ITV revived *Opportunity Knocks*, a format that ran briefly on the radio on the BBC's Light Programme and then Radio Luxembourg, and for one series on ITV in 1956. The 1964 revival saw it become a prime time hit that ran until 1978.

It's no coincidence that this time period was the peak of clubland entertainment. The clubs provided a bottomless reservoir of seasoned talent who knew their chops, with established club acts such as Les Dawson, Paul Daniels, Frank Carson and Little and Large getting their TV break via *Opportunity Knocks*. (In a nice twist, Dawson would go on to present the show's revival in 1990).

So successful was '*Opp Knocks*,' produced by London ITV franchise ABC Weekend Television and later its successor Thames Television, that a rival ITV franchise – Associated TeleVision (ATV) in the Midlands – launched a rival show, *New Faces*, which also became a nationwide ITV hit. *New Faces* gave big breaks to club acts such as Lenny Henry, Roy Walker and Mick Miller. Les Dennis made it to the grand final in 1974, and this kickstarted his successful TV career. 'I still did the clubs well into the eighties,' he says. 'A week at the London Palladium, and then back to do a show at a British Legion. That brings you back down to earth with a bump. I'd try to big myself up, say to the concert secretary, "Tell them I've done telly." "Ooh no," they'd say. "They'll have yer for that."'

In this way, working men's clubs provided yet another escape route from everyday working-class life for those who wanted it. For some, this wasn't a matter of getting too big for your boots – it was a means of survival.

Lynne Denise Shepherd was born in Sheffield and endured a terrible childhood. Her father died of cancer when she was 7 years old, after which her mother sought solace in drink and drugs, and her paternal grandfather sexually abused her. She escaped aged seventeen by marrying a local butcher's boy, working variously as a model, croupier and petrol pump attendant. Two years later, her mother died, and she was unable to afford the funeral expenses. In desperation, she auditioned to sing at Chapeltown WMC, got the gig, and soon became a regular on the Yorkshire circuit, going through several stage names before settling on Marti Caine.

Privately, Lynne Shepherd remained desperately insecure and anxious. The more successful she became, the more she worried that it might all disappear. Publicly, Marti Caine had everything she needed to become the Queen of Clubland. She was glamorous and sexy, but gawky and clownish at the same time. She could sing beautifully but was nervous about doing so, claiming her voice was so shaky at that first audition that she sounded like 'Edith Piaf with Parkinson's disease.' Standing in front of the club audiences that so terrified hard-bitten male comics, she 'just started talking' when she was nervous and began doing comedy between songs. Clubland had seen many curiosities on stage, but nothing quite like a glamorous woman in a tight-fitting sparkly dress doing comedy so filthy it could make Bernard Manning blush, then ripping into a sentimental ballad that brought tears to their eyes. In 1975 she won the Grand Final of series three of *New Faces*, beating both Lenny Henry and Victoria Wood, and went on to host TV series and record a number of successful albums before dying of cancer aged just 50 in 1995.

It was obvious that clubland was a rich seam of talent, and that enough artists within it were willing to tone down their material to get on TV. Johnnie Hamp had worked for Granada since it was just a chain of theatres and cinemas, but in 1954 it won the bid to become the Manchester-based broadcaster in the ITV network. In 1962 Hamp was moved to Manchester to produce light entertainment. He knew just where to look. 'There were literally hundreds of clubs in the surrounding area,' he wrote in his memoirs. 'Clubs of all types from the beer and darts working men's clubs to the gigantic theatre restaurant and posh night clubs in the city centre. They all presented cabaret of some sort, from the resident singer backed up by organ and drums, to the top American superstars of the day.' Johnnie Hamp subsequently made his career by giving TV debuts to the Beatles – and Bernard Manning.

Visiting working men's clubs became a regular part of Hamp's professional routine. Although initially he was looking for singers because they were always top of the bill – and therefore presumably the brightest talents – it was the supporting comedians who ended up catching his eye. He was struck by their versatility and tenacity, holding down hour-long spots compared to the five-minute acts he'd seen in variety theatres, and changing their material completely depending on what kind of venue they were playing. He loved comics like Manning and Charlie Williams most of all, and realised that beyond the club circuit, they were completely unknown.

'The format for *The Comedians* was a simple idea,' he wrote. 'I invited thirty of these unknown comedians into the studio, ten a night for three consecutive nights, and recorded ten-minute spots for each of them … from nine hours of non-stop gags I edited up the first half hour pilot show, cutting from comic to comic, matching up the jokes so it would appear that the comedians were standing in a line trying to top each other with their material.'

There were concerns that the format would burn through material too quickly, that people wouldn't be able to understand Charlie Williams's thick Barnsley accent, even that some of Manning's material might be a bit blue. Showing his versatility, Manning is one of the cleanest, most inoffensive acts on their collective TV debut, following anti-Semitic jokes from Williams and racist jokes by a comic called Mike Coyne with a gag about seagulls at Blackpool.

Within a few weeks of this first episode being broadcast in June 1971, *The Comedians* was second only to *Coronation Street* in the ratings. By the end of the first series, Manning and Williams were nationally famous. Over the next few years, they were joined by people like Frank Carson, Mike Reid and Mick Miller, and the image of the frilly-shirted and bow-tied comic holding a microphone in one hand and a fag in the other became the defining image of mainstream stand-up comedy.

Les Dennis became the youngest ever act to appear on *The Comedians* when he was just nineteen. 'I had jokes about me mam and dad. Nothing about mothers-in-law or anything like that. They filmed it really quickly because the other comics had to get off and go and do clubs shows after, so I ended up going on last, after Jim Bowen, after Bernard Manning doing jokes about an air crash.'

Each show of *The Comedians* finished with a song and dance act with a big chorus and all the comics performing together on screen. These spots had different themes, such as an old-time music hall or a circus with the comics all dressed as clowns. One set was a northern working men's club, with the comedians doing well-rehearsed, intentionally lousy acts. This proved so popular that Hamp took the format and made it into another series.

The Wheeltappers and Shunters Social Club ran for six series between 1974 and 1977. Built as a studio set at Granada, the designers did such a good job that viewers would phone the broadcaster asking where the club was so they could make reservations for the following Saturday. It's all there: officious notices warning that 'Hats will not be tolerated in this room,' Colin Crompton's MC interrupting acts to announce the arrival of the pies, waitresses (including Liz Dawn, who went on to become *Coronation Street's* Vera Duckworth) carrying pint-filled trays to the thirsty two-hundred strong audience, seated cabaret-style around the stage, and Bernard Manning as MC.

Watched today, *Wheeltappers and Shunters* both confirms and challenges the prevailing stereotype of working men's clubs that it helped solidify into popular culture. The mix of acts is astonishing: yes, there's another roll-call of clubland stars who would find TV fame afterwards – Cannon and Ball, the Krankies, Paul Daniels again – but there were also legendary names from the past, from Bill Hayley and His Comets and Lonnie Donegan to variety stars Winnifred

Atwell and Tessie O' Shea, as well as popular music acts of the day. You can virtually smell the fag smoke and spilled beer, but editorially it feels quite contemporary. There's no showiness in the presentation, no editorialising as such: most programmes start with something like a singalong fading in half way through, as if you've just got to the club late. There's no concession to the fact that this is a TV show, with even commercial breaks being advertised as 'bingo breaks.' Some acts feel very much of their time, while others are quite ahead of it. Whether you come to critically rehabilitate *Wheeltappers and Shunters* or to bury it forever, you'll find evidence in most shows to help build your case.

The biggest star clubland has ever produced didn't need any of these shows on his way to becoming a global phenomenon. There are various clubs in South Wales that claim to be the one where Tommy Woodward made his stage debut, with the owners of one contender in Treforest telling a newspaper interviewer in 2019 that they think it was there, but there are conflicting rumours as to what exactly happened. If only there was some way of finding out the truth – such as reading the star's 2015 autobiography, which I did after his management ignored my requests for an interview.

By the time he was seventeen, Tommy Woodward was married with a baby son, going out drinking with his mates in Treforest and spending Sunday evenings with his dad, uncles and cousins at Wood Road Club. Sundays were a blend of free-and-easy and paid singers. Young Tommy was in thrall to rock and rollers like Elvis Presley and Jerry Lee Lewis, and would occasionally sing something himself around the piano in his local pub. One night at Wood Road, he was struck by the sheer power of a local man, Glynog Evans, who had the piss taken out of him by his mates for taking singing so seriously, but had to stand well back when the club finally got a proper microphone because his voice was so powerful. Glynog gets up amid the ribbing and sings 'My Mother's Eyes,' an old song from 1929: 'And by the end of it, some of these guys who have mocked him are crying. There's an experience there, and a power, and by the end, you cannot dispute the fact that this man can get through to people. This affects me … That singing speaks directly to me … "My Mother's Eyes" feels as real to me as "Whole Lotta Shakin" or "Rip It Up."'

Sometime later, Tommy was back at Wood Road Club one Sunday night when the paid turn hadn't shown up. The flustered entertainment secretary collared Tommy, as he'd heard he could sing and play guitar, and could he fill in? Tommy ran home for his cheap Spanish guitar, and treated the club to a set of songs like 'Blue Suede Shoes' and Tennessee Ernie Ford's 'Sixteen Tons.' He went down well and got paid £1 for his efforts.

Off this back of his stage debut, Tommy was approached by a local fishmonger, Bryn the Fish, who ran a variety revue package along the lines of the old concert parties, which he took around working men's clubs as a one-stop full night of variety entertainment. Tommy joined this group, known as the Misfits, as the young rock and roll singer to appeal to the more youthful end of the audience:

> The younger guys liked me because I was the thing they could connect to. The older guys were more of a problem. Rock'n'roll wasn't always what a working man's club wanted to hear. In fact there was enormous resistance to it and suspicion of it. It wasn't 'proper singing'; it was 'just a racket,' 'a bloody noise.' I pretty quickly learned that just the sight of a bloke with a quiff and a guitar moving towards the microphone would be enough to trigger shouts of 'Pay him off!' So I made sure I had some ballads up my sleeve for when they weren't into the rockier stuff and might need some calming down.

In the early sixties, Tommy became the frontman for beat group Tommy Scott and the Senators. The group played dance halls in South Wales, but Tommy persuaded them to do the club circuit as well and got Bryn the Fish in to help. He claimed to be the first person ever to take an electric guitar onto a working men's club stage:

We had our first working men's club booking on a Saturday night in one of the local places where I was known. But even so we attracted immediate suspicion, on sight, just walking in with the gear. 'Oh, Christ – electric guitars, is it? Rock'n'roll now, eh, Tommy?' As we were setting up, some of the fellas were already shouting, 'Pay 'em off.' But I asked the old fellas to just give us a chance and a listen. The audience was, as usual, seated at tables around the room and more than ready to be appalled. But we kept the volume down. I said, 'Let's do "I Believe"' – a ballad that I knew would go over. We eased into it, played the sparkier stuff later, when everyone was onside. At the end of the night, the secretary of the club said he was going to move the chairs and tables aside and asked if we would play a few extra songs so they could have a dance. At which point we knew we had won. That was it. We were in business.

At one of these gigs, Tommy was spotted by Gordon Mills, a Welsh manager now based in London. He took Tommy back to the capital and changed his name to Tom Jones. The first single they did together flopped. The second – 'It's Not Unusual' – made Tom a global star.

Three years later, Tommy from Treforest was playing the Vegas strip and becoming mates with his idol, Elvis Presley. It was an experience his clubland origins had prepared him for. In the same year James Corrigan brought Vegas-style glamour to Batley, Tom Jones took his working men's club chops to Vegas: 'Vegas feels other-worldly, and yet not. What I see in these big hotel and casino venues in Las Vegas is, essentially, bigger versions of the working men's clubs I have grown up with in Wales. That's what they feel like to me.'

* * *

'It's a shame the clubs have gone now,' says Les Dennis. 'You could work fifty-two weeks a year if you wanted to. People like Bobby Thompson could fill the north east clubs, same with Jackie Hamilton in Liverpool. They might not have broken through nationally, but when you were that good you could work off your local area. *The Stage* had all the clubs listed in the back. Not anymore.'

Greasbrough Social Club closed suddenly in 1969. In a retrospective phone-in programme on BBC Radio Sheffield recently, some of the people who were there blamed the introduction of the breathalyser: the club had a huge car park, sat in a tiny village, and paid for its big names out of the bar takings. It was a formula that couldn't survive changing attitudes around drunk driving.

Batley Variety Club, with its denser concentration of chimney pots, kept going until 1978. It, too, was highly geared: the magic formula of low entry prices and top names – again, paid for by the bar take – meant the club's bars needed to be busy seven nights a week, or the numbers didn't add up. After ten years of seeing everyone they wanted on their doorstep, the audience were taking it for granted, and becoming choosier about who they were prepared to leave the house for. On top of that, the big sums James Corrigan was prepared to pay for the performers he really wanted became known around the variety world, and acts started asking for fees he couldn't really afford. He was also now at war with his wife Betty, after a string of infidelities on both sides, and was trying to save his fortune by embarking on other ill-thought-out schemes that only drained his accounts faster. After one final almighty fight, James was charged with assault against Betty. He pleaded guilty and was bound over to keep the peace. He did so by walking out of both his marriage and the club. Betty and their son James closed the club, reopened it briefly as a disco, renamed 'Crumpets,' and then that, too, closed.

Following the closure of the club, Corrigan was declared bankrupt. He worked for a while buying used tyres from Germany and trying to sell them in the UK for a small profit, and then got a job as a road sweeper. After thirteen years of hardship his second marriage failed, and he found himself living alone in a tiny house in York, eking out a living selling old coins on a market stall at 67 years old. In 1997, at the age of 72, he was diagnosed with terminal cancer.

Maureen Prest, formerly the promotions and PR manager at Batley club, remained a lifelong friend of James, and tried to help by getting media interest in his rags-to-riches-to-rags story. James gave many interviews, and in her book *King of Clubs*, Maureen recounts the story of the final TV interview, which was conducted by Ian Clayton. Ian got him to open up like no one else had, telling his entire story. Maureen writes 'It was the best interview he ever gave and it was to be his last.'

At the end of the book, Maureen Prest reveals a magical twist in the tale. In May 1999, Maureen saw in the newspaper that James's second wife, Elaine, from whom he was now also divorced, had won £2.2 million on the National Lottery. Something about the timing of events didn't add up, and she pressed James on it. It had been his lottery win, but as he was now terminally ill, he wanted to present it as Elaine's. The man who had gone from fairground barker to multi-millionaire club impresario to road sweeper died in December 2000, a secret millionaire.

The peak of James Corrigan's fortunes was also the peak of working men's clubs. Music and comedy had put them at the heart of popular culture, but both music and comedy were changing.

'There was a shift in music in the 1970s,' says Ian Clayton when I ask him what changed. 'The popular music in the early seventies was glam rock. In the late seventies it was punk. You're never going to translate those forms of music into a working men's club. Up to then, popular music was everybody's music. In the 1940s and 1950s, everybody had to listen to Frank Sinatra or the Beverley Sisters or whoever it was that was popular at the time. Even in the sixties, the pop bands were amenable for copying without making such a mess of it. You could easily do a Beatles song in a working men's club, could probably even get away with a Rolling Stones song. By the time it gets to T-Rex and Slade, you're struggling. I did once see, in the Corra, a band try and do a T-Rex song, 'Ride a White Swan'. Well, with all the best will in the world yer can't do that in a working men's club, can yer? Yer can do Michelle my belle, or she loves you, but you can't start on about wizards. And certainly when it gets to punk, you're not going to be able to replicate a punk record with an organ and drums.'

Meanwhile, the frilly-shirted *Comedians* were now the establishment, and they gave a new wave of alternative comedians, partly inspired by punk, a target to rail against. While I'm researching this book, I find myself at a literary festival, in a pub, with Stewart Lee and Alexei Sayle deep in conversation at the next table. My friend Travis Elborough, who I've just done an event with, starts talking about a Satanic album that Daryl Hall and John Oates once made, which attracts Stewart Lee's attention, so we start talking together. I ask Alexei Sayle if he ever played working men's clubs, and realise almost immediately what a colossally stupid question that is. His entire face becomes a wide, thin-lipped grin, baring his teeth, and he says, very slowly, 'I don't think acts like ours would have gone down very well there,' and we leave it at that.

I was 3 years old when *The Comedians* debuted on ITV. I was 14 when Alexei Sayle, along with Rik Mayall, Ade Edmonson and the rest of the punkish young comics from the Comedy Store and the Comic Strip, exploded onto BBC2 with *The Young Ones*, doing for comedy what the Sex Pistols had to music a few years earlier. So here's a huge part of the answer to the question I posed myself at the start of this book: why was my generation the first in clubland's heartland to turn our backs on it?

By the time I was 13, I had managed to acquire an ancient black-and-white TV which allowed me, if it was in the right mood, to watch *The Young Ones* in my bedroom through a snowstorm of static interference and join in with the ritualistic recitation of every line we could remember at school the following day.

It would be pushing it to try to claim *The Young Ones* as a natural evolution of music hall, but it did share some common characteristics. The humour mixed surrealism and slapstick. It was gleefully anarchic, flicking V-signs at the establishment. And the presence of a live band in each show meant that the BBC classified it as 'variety' rather than straight 'comedy.' As its stars and writers spread their influence, we shared their disdain for the sexist, racist dinosaurs of the seventies. Alternative comedy did the same for us that the club comics had done for our parents' and grandparents' generations – we didn't need them anymore.

Many of those clubland acts evolved and adapted. And as always happens with any group of revolutionaries, the alternative comics eventually merged into the new establishment. Some would eventually admit that performers like Bob Monkhouse and Les Dawson were huge influences, and Rik Mayall would appear in primetime TV sketches with Cannon and Ball.

But while individuals could change and evolve, in the popular imagination, clubland could not. When acts from the clubs dominated *The Comedians*, *New Faces*, *Opportunity Knocks* and *Wheeltappers and Shunters*, they were an accurate representation of popular entertainment and popular culture at the time. But as these shows didn't really outlive the 1970s, they are remembered as *being* the 1970s. As entertainment moved on, and clubland's biggest stars were given their own TV shows with new formats, the club once again slipped out of public consciousness, remaining frozen at its peak, increasingly out of step with the modern world. In this way, Clubland's phenomenal success gave birth to its decline.

* * *

There's not much in the centre of Batley. And this isn't even the centre of Batley.

Bradford Road is a busy main road full of small redbrick buildings, the kind of place where you find used car lots and MOT centres. Walls sport faded signs for defunct brands like Ever Ready, and graffiti reading 'Palestinian Lives Matter.' There are ten times as many car parking spaces as there are cars to use them. Months after the 2021 Batley and Spen by-election, fifty yards up the road from JD Gym there are still signs outside George Galloway's former campaign HQ, his fedoraed face leering over the pavement where people used to queue to get into Shirley Bassey gigs.

More recently, big, lounge-style restaurants have appeared here and there, as if some of the Vegas glamour of Batley Variety Club stuck around in the water table. An Italian restaurant called Zucchini's has been built onto the side of the massive gym, like a cheeky attempt to cancel it out.

Batley Variety Club reopened in the early 1980s as The Frontier. The big-name stars were long gone, but the Frontier continued as a live music venue and nightclub for far longer than Batley Variety had managed, hanging on until 2016, when the venue announced its closure. Citing changes in entertainment technology, transport links, drinking laws and the smoking ban as factors, general manager Nick Westwell said, 'Since the turn of the century, the commercial entertainment landscape has changed and the demands for larger arenas, as opposed to smaller style concert halls, has been prevalent.'

In 2017, the building reopened as the massive JD Gym that still dominates the road. Today, there are turnstiles at the entrance admitting members only. Beyond them, Chris and I can see a vast space, filled with cross-fits and treadmills, far bigger than it needs to be for its function, but with great acoustics that give a mighty boom to the eternal, rhythmic pounding of the music and the members alike.

On one side of the foyer is a reception window and a bag-drop. Above this is an old black and white photo of Batley Variety Club in its prime, its marquee now photoshopped to read 'FITNESS JUST GOT SERIOUS.' On the opposite wall is a collage of photographs and show bills. Chris and I start taking photos of it.

'Are we alright there, lads?'

A tall man in his early twenties wearing a gym-branded polo shirt comes through the turnstile to see what we're up to. I explain, and he tries to sell us gym memberships. After a while, it becomes clear that this wall is the only part of the gym we're interested in, and Gym Guy looks at it with us.

The biggest photo shows Louis Armstrong grinning, arms held wide, in the centre of Batley. One bill announces upcoming acts, week by week: Ken Dodd, Roy Orbison, Buddy Greco, then Shirley Bassey for three weeks.

'I'm only twenty-five so I don't know any of 'em,' says Gym Guy. 'Me grandparents came here in the sixties. Saw people like Roy Orbison.'

After Shirley Bassey there was Johnny Mathis, then Neil Sedaka, the Everly Brothers, then right at the bottom, the Four Tops. One photo shows the Four Tops on stage, shot from behind so you can see the packed audience in front of them.

'It's nice they kept it though,' says Gym Guy.

James Corrigan stands with smartly uniformed waiting staff. Below, a grinning Harry Secombe poses with someone's mum. Princess Michael of Kent says hello to Charlie Williams.

'Funny innit?' says Gym Guy. 'People went from getting pissed 'ere to getting fit 'ere.'

We move on.

8

THE CLUB
AND GAMES

The Langham Club, Green Lanes, North London

My dad had a very fatalistic approach to life. I think he was happiest when he was at work with his mates, or when he was alone. His temper was short. Whenever something broke at home, or there was a problem, he'd look to the ceiling and shout 'Nothing ever goes right in this bloody house!' When we were in the car, waiting to pull out onto the main road at a junction, without fail he'd say, 'Huh, they come from miles around as soon as it's us trying to get out.'

He had a reputation in the village, something born deep in the past in a community where grudges could outlive people. More than once, a new friend I'd made at school came in one day and told me they weren't allowed to play with me anymore, and I never understood why. I was shy and quiet, crap at sport, crap at fighting, but good in the classroom, at anything apart from maths. And yet, whenever the group of kids on our street got a little over-excited and smashed a window with a football or bounced it hard enough against someone's front door to make it rattle and force the people inside to come out and tell us off, it was always me that got the blame. I was still being identified as the culprit months after I'd stopped playing out on the street altogether thanks to all the revision I had to do for my O-levels. Just a few weeks before my exams, and probably at least six months after my last ever game of three-and-in, hot rice or hide-and-seek, a bloke from down the street came to the door and said he'd seen me with his own eyes (well how else would you see anything, my inner-teenage-smart-arse now wants to shout) smash his car window, not ten minutes before. My dad got angry, saying 'Ow the bloody 'ell does tha think he's done that when I've been watching him sitting theer at that table doin' his homework since t'minute he came home from school!'

And then, one day, I realised it was my dad, rather than me, whom they didn't trust. Once, when we were being told off for kicking a ball into a garden and going over the wall to get it (I had neither kicked the ball, nor scaled the wall) and I was once again identified as the culprit by the angry couple who had been trespassed against, I pointed out that I couldn't even kick a football without falling over, that every-one else in the gang regularly took the piss out of me whenever I tried. The woman, in her sixties, her white hair permed to invulnerability, turned to her husband and said, 'Tha can't trust owt *he* says. *That's* Ronnie Brown's son.'

Whatever my dad had supposedly done, it pre-dated our life together as a family. For the whole of my childhood, he went to work, came home, went to bed, got up again, and occasionally went fishing. That was it. Looking back, perhaps it explained why he constantly felt persecuted by the traffic, the weather and the fates. I was starting to feel like that myself, for the crime of being his son. And maybe that was his only crime too: his older sister, my Auntie Nellie who had lived in Canada since the war, had been born out of wedlock, and was in fact dad's half-sister. Obviously, being born fifteen years later to the same mother, now married, my dad had to carry some of the judge-ment and blame for the scandal. You couldn't trust owt *he* said. *That* was Sally Brown's son.

Fishing was his great escape; the only time, I think, he was ever truly happy. He used to try to get the whole family to go with him, but my brother and I got bored easily and ruined that for him too. There were various reservoirs and canals around Barnsley, but freshwa-ter angling was popular in the North and they were overfished. The common greeting between men arriving with their big wicker baskets and rod bags or leaving their pitch to stretch their legs behind the line of men on the shore, would be 'Caught owt?' The reply to which was invariably 'Nah, they're not biting today' – yet more fuel for dad's fatalism.

Then, when I was ten or eleven, he joined the fishing club at the Tin Hat, the ex-servicemen's club at the bottom of the village(s). The men at the Tin Hat didn't fish the local spots; they organised coach trips to go sea fishing at Bridlington, Whitby and Staithes on the Yorkshire coast. 'Sea fishing' was a phrase that had to be uttered with reverence in our house: at Newmillerdam or Ryhill, the greatest danger you might encounter was pissing off a bad-tempered duck. If you were sea fishing, you might get caught in a storm, or accidentally get Jaws the Shark on your line. Also, the coach left really early on a Saturday morning: best for dad to go on his own.

He'd get back around 6pm, euphoric and giddy, usually carrying something *heavy*. One time, his bag contained a couple of live crabs. We'd never had crab meat before, and we never had it again after my mum tried to boil them in a pan that was too small, and they kept knocking the pan lid off and waving their claws in the air as if signalling for help, with me and my brother stood in the kitchen doorway in tears, snot dripping onto our chests, crying 'STOP! LET THEM GO!' and mum and dad laughing at us fondly and saying 'Go where?'*

The fish were OK, because they were already dead by the time dad got them home. Over the summer months each year they got bigger, and we still have the stereotypical angler's photos of dad standing against the wall outside the back door, grinning beatifically while cradling some three-foot-long monster in his arms.

Soon, he wasn't just bringing fish home on a Saturday: on a Sunday, he was coming back from the club with trophies too. Most of them were small, cheap and mass-produced, plastic made to look like silver or gold. But shit, that didn't matter: they were *trophies*, and the little plaques on the front had my dad's name on them. After a couple of

---

* "We can dig a POND!"

years, there were so many of them that they began to crowd out the shitty ornaments Stuart and I bought on Barnsley market for my mum as last-minute Christmas presents, much to the relief of the entire family.

My interior narrative of my life hinges around the fact that I was the first person in my family ever to go on to higher education and get a degree. That's not an unusual story for someone of my generation. Now, as I sit here at my desk, I often try to come up with ways not to sound like an utter cock when I catch myself thinking, 'I'm going to need more space for my writing awards.' But years before I achieved any of this, my dad had built up a sizeable trophy cabinet of his own. He was the first person in our family to do that. And he did so because his working men's club made it possible. He was happy – or as happy as he could be – with his routine of work, cheap, pulp Westerns and roll-up fags. But the Tin Hat gave him pride and purpose.

* * *

Games in clubs started off on a small scale, with cards and dominoes. The upper classes, who also played card games and billiards in gentlemen's clubs, saw sport and games as encouraging healthy competition and good sportsmanship. Some club patrons disagreed, seeing games as a waste of time because they weren't educational or improving. But by the time games were really taking off in clubs, the influence of these patrons was waning.

As clubs expanded, a games room with a billiards table rivalled a concert hall at the top of the wish list, and usually won. A decent billiards table was a serious investment, but one that soon paid back. When clubs managed to attain both, the quality of a turn or lecture could be judged on whether or not it was good enough to get people out of the billiards room.

The organisation and administration of clubs by the CIU provided a framework that allowed any popular sport or game to thrive. The national Union, with its regional branches, meant that the best players in a club had a ready-made structure through which to progress. The

CIU created a National Team Billiards Championship in 1907, which was followed by an individual Billiards Championship in 1919. Their popularity encouraged the clubs and the Union to create similar competitions for snooker (1925 for the team event, 1927 for individual), darts (1957) and angling (1948). These became so popular that between branch and national level, Northern, Southern and Midland Championships were introduced. By 1933 there were 400 different CIU trophies being awarded across a mind-boggling array of games and sports including darts, angling, dominoes, cribbage, whist, bowls, skittles, don, bagatelle, horticulture, shove-ha'penny, pigeon-racing, football, cricket, shooting, golf, dancing, quizzes, athletics, first-aid, euchre, chess, singing, table-tennis, tippet, draughts, walking, beauty contests, table bowls, tug-of-war, and cage-bird breeding. The club movement had become the largest issuer of sports and games trophies in the country and remains so even today.

But in the 1960s, one game emerged to rule them all. It became so popular it would redefine the entire culture of the working men' club.

* * *

It's Sunday night in the Langham, just before 9pm.

In the main hall, electricity crackles in the air. Outside, dogs howl, and the ghosts of the cows that were here when this was farmland all lie down. Inside, elderly couples alight on banquettes like crows on a fence, glittering eyes watching, waiting. Be quiet. Be respectful. The bingo is approaching, like a gathering storm.

A slim, grey-haired man wearing a white shirt stands on stage with a guitar, PA and mixing desk all within reach, belting out hits from the fifties to the eighties to a dancefloor that's empty apart from mirrorball lights playing cross it like lime and purple sprites. Coloured fairy lights flash behind him, giving the scene a slow-motion, haunted fairground feel. He's on borrowed time, and he seems at peace with this.

Gambling has been a feature of life for ever, and bingo, or games very similar to it, are a longstanding part of that. The modern version is thought to have originated in Italy around 1530 as Lotto, before becoming popular with the French aristocracy and making it to Britain by the eighteenth century. Also known as tombola, housey-housey, beano, lucky radio, fortune, keno, kino or po-keno, different variants were popular around the world by the time working men's clubs were established. In the Second World War, 'Housie' was the only form of gambling permitted in the British army and navy, and many enlisted men came back to the clubs with a taste for it once they demobbed. While it's likely that some games went on behind the closed doors of some clubs – because gambling of various forms often did – bingo was technically illegal until the Small Lotteries and Gaming Act of 1956 sort of made it legal for clubs, depending on whether it was classed as an 'entertainment' or a 'lottery,' and on what happened to the prize money. But gambling laws were a mess, and well-meaning clubs still ended up being sued.

Gambling had always been tolerated, even celebrated, behind the closed doors of gentlemen's clubs. But like everything else, it was seen as problematic among the lower orders. Apart from the very real dangers of gambling addiction, the problem for the new industrial middle classes was that it undermined the credo of hard work, discipline and rational recreation, in that it gave sometimes huge rewards on the basis of chance. As with drink, this had led to laws that were illogical, unfair, and full of loopholes.

The Betting and Gaming Act 1960 was an attempt to tidy up messy legislation. Among other measures, it clarified that bingo could legally be played in any members-only club. This was perfect timing for companies like Granada and Mecca, whose variety halls and cinemas were seeing dwindling numbers. These large chains swiftly converted their empty buildings into bingo halls, and the game became a phenomenon.

By 1963 a national opinion poll showed that 12 per cent of the adult population was involved in commercially organised bingo. By 1966, that figure was one in four British adults. Many of these were playing in the new bingo halls, which peaked at 1600 across the UK.

But bingo was also quickly picked up by twice as many working men's clubs.*

'Women, Leisure and Bingo,' a research project written by Rachael Dixey and Margaret Talbot in 1982, found that 60 to 70 per cent of bingo players were working class, and the vast majority of them were women. While men over 45 showed some enthusiasm, women of all ages couldn't get enough of it. Immediately, then, bingo was declared another moral panic by the police and some sectors of the press. Dixey and Talbot quote an earlier study, *Gambling: Hazard and Reward* by Otto Newman, when they explain why bingo was seen as having all the downsides, but none of the glamour of other forms of gambling: 'Within gambling, bingo is seen as a "low" form. According to Newman, bingo and lotteries are "despised and derided as mechanical and mindless" by those who bet on horses, as the former do not require the skill of the latter. Other games of chance, such as roulette, are not treated in the same way, probably due to the social class of those who play such games and their association with sophistication and wealth.'

Whereas social observers recognised the need for a man to operate in a wider sphere outside the home, it was widely felt that 'A woman is expected to find sufficient interest and satisfaction in her home and family.' The Police Superintendents' Association warned that bingo was leading to children being abandoned at home while the father was at the pub and the mother was at the bingo club. Naturally, it was the mother, not the father, who was to blame for this apparent neglect. She was also blowing the family budget on gambling, risking penury. On top of all that, she was taking part in activity that had 'no benefit.' To outsiders, bingo was boring, repetitive, monotonous, and therefore mindless.

None of these accusations bore much resemblance to what Dixey and Talbot found when they did research among women who played

---

* It should go without saying by now, but despite having double the number of establishments playing the game compared to bespoke bingo halls, working men's clubs aren't mentioned once in any history of bingo I consulted for this research.

bingo. Only a small proportion of them had children young enough to need 'minding' in the evenings, and among those, their husbands were generally happy to look after the kids because this was the one opportunity the woman had for getting out of the house. This trip out was soon seen as vital for the many women who felt isolated and lonely, with little agency of their own, as their husbands both worked and relaxed somewhere else.

As for the supposedly boring game, it fitted in perfectly with the close-knit, us-and-them communities described by Richard Hoggart. According to Dixey and Talbot, the 'constant repetition' of bingo was 'consolidating the world they know rather than expanding it,' and making people secure in their old, established roles rather than having to confront the alien world of 'them' on this rare trip out of the house. Played within such cohesive communities: 'It can be suggested that the popularity of a game of pure chance is that, as it requires no skill, there can be no criticism for failing to win and neither can one's confidence be undermined, as the result has nothing to do with one's own efforts. The absence of competition or the opportunity to show skill minimises the possibility of conflict and the game proceeds (usually) in an amiable manner. It is important that individuals get along with each other and therefore that all players are equal before fate; no-one can use skill to get ahead of the others.'

If Dixey and Talbot had thought to look at working men's clubs in their research, they would have seen that all these elements of the game made it a perfect addition to the remit of the club, a place that was already seen as safe for women, and where women were increasingly being accepted. Clubs saw a massive increase in female membership after bingo arrived. The truth for many working-class families was that instead of the man being in the pub and the woman in the bingo hall, both went to the club together – even if they were in separate rooms while the bingo was on.

Bingo became at least as much a social and cultural activity as a game of chance, developing its own language and customs, many of which would bleed out into everyday use. From legs eleven to two fat ladies, a call and response relationship between the caller and the audience emphasized bingo as yet another form of participative leisure rather than lean-back, passive consumption. The audience reaction to 'Maggie's/Tony's/Boris's Den, number ten' is a more reliable indicator of the political mood in some working-class communities than any opinion poll.

All of this made bingo, at the peak of clubland, the most hallowed aspect of club culture. Every turn knew the frustration of being made to wait until the bingo had finished before setting up their gear or having to finish early themselves for it to start. In *The Dirty Stop Out's Guide to Working Mens' Clubs*, Neil Anderson quotes club-goers who remembered spare pairs of specs as well as pens being stashed behind the bar for players who had come unprepared; a bingo caller insisting that if people wanted to talk, they should show some respect and wait until the turn came on; and the universal threat to the wellbeing of any non-regular clubgoers who might dare to win the jackpot. Mark Sanderson jokes (except it's not really a joke) 'How do you get fifty sweet old ladies to shout "bastard"? Get one to shout "house."' Elaine Siddall's husband played in a Sheffield club band that was waiting to set up while the bingo was on. 'The lead guitarist shouted "mouse" as a joke. They stopped the bingo, paid the band off and banned them for life. They nearly got lynched.'

Bingo, then, is a deadly serious business wrapped in a thin veneer of quite specific humour.

I really hope I don't win.

'You've really never played bingo before?' asks Ruth.

'I definitely have,' I reply. 'But the last time was over twenty years ago.'

When I was an advertising wanker and a group of us went to play it ironically and then I felt bad for taking the piss, I don't add.

Ruth Cherrington is the only other living person on the planet to have written a full-length book about the history of the working men's club movement. It turns out she only lives a couple of miles up the road from me. She goes to the Mildmay every now and then, but the Langham is her main club, and Sunday night is 'the best night' according to the various people who pop over to say hello to Ruth and to see what I'm all about, as the silver fox on stage performs his duty as the musical warm-up act for the main event.

Ruth grew up in Coventry, on one of those big new estates built after the Second World War. The Canley Club was the centre of estate life, and Ruth pretty much spent her childhood in it. In the early 1980s, Ruth was teaching sociology while still spending her free time in working men's clubs. She realised that they were in decline, and that this was linked to changes in industry and changes in working class culture. She also felt that clubs weren't changing quickly enough with regard to their treatment of women. She saw this as fertile ground for an academic project.

'I thought about that one club I grew up in, because it encapsulated changes in working-class culture, changes in society in general, and gender issues,' she says. And then, Ruth went to China, and that became the focus of her studies for two decades. The club project was forgotten. In 2003, the death of her father acted as a wake-up call. 'It gave me a sense of urgency. I realised that this story I wanted to tell, the generation it concerned was disappearing. So many of the men he used to sit around the bagatelle table with – all gone. I thought, who's writing about this? I needed to capture the voices of that generation.'

No one else was interested in the project. She did it in her spare time, and after failing to find a publisher who wanted to engage with working men's clubs (an experience I'm familiar with) she self-published her work in the book *Not Just Beer and Bingo*, in time for the 150th anniversary of the CIU in 2012. It covers a lot of the same ground as this book but is told mainly in the voices of clubgoers themselves, many of whom are no longer around.

We swap stories of the research process, the difficulty in trying to get the CIU interested, the few bits of great source material we've discovered. And then, it's time.

I realise this is the first time I've really looked at a bingo card properly. There are six tickets, each one containing a grid that's three rows by nine columns. That gives a total of 162 squares, 90 of which contain a number between 1 and 90. These are distributed so that each line on the card has five numbers and four blank spaces. I hadn't realised this before, but every number is on there somewhere, on every card. This gives the game a different dynamic than I thought: in a lottery, you pick your numbers and you hope they'll come up. When people joke about various versions of Buzzword Bingo, they invariably ask if you've got, say, 'going forward,' 'hard-working families' or 'I can't comment until the investigation is completed' on your card. But that misrepresents true bingo: here, every time a number is called, *everyone* gets to tick it off at the same time. This gives bingo a unique flavour of tension: it's not just the number that matters; it's where it lies on your card. No one is sitting there thinking it's not fair the machine hasn't called my numbers yet, because every number called is on your card somewhere. The chance is embedded in where, not if.

The house lights go up, making me realise that until now, for the first time on this journey, I've been sitting in a working men's club where the lights were not so bright I could see through my skin. An immaculately dressed woman in her late sixties or early seventies, who, according to Ruth, served on the committee here for a long time, takes her seat behind the bingo machine. I think it's a shame that the old machines with the bouncing balls, like you still see on TV for the National Lottery, have been replaced by electronic random number generators. There's less theatre about it. A red LED number sits alone on a screen, with nothing to do until a button is pushed and it gets replaced by the next one. But it's less fallible, with no room for human error, or tampering by Mick Miller.

'Quiet please. One and five, fifteen.'

I've got it. Of course I do, everyone does.

'Two and seven, twenty-seven.'

Later, I learn that every number on the card has its own 'bingo lingo' if you can learn them all, from 'Kelly's Eye' to 'Top of the Shop.' Most callers will acknowledge thirteen as 'unlucky for some,' but I wonder how many would recognize sixty-four as 'red raw'?

Our caller tonight plays it fairly straight (er … forty-eight?), the audience looking for efficiency rather than call-and-response. I can just about keep up with the numbers being called, tracing up and down the columns. I dab them in an emerging neat pattern, perfectly spaced around my card. If there was a prize for getting one number on every line, for perfectly even distribution with no clusters, I'd be in. But we're playing for a full line, two lines, and house, with cash prizes up to thirty quid for the latter.

I think I've got one line with three out of five numbers on it when the first line is called. The room sags in defeat. The winner knows the score and has the sense to look slightly embarrassed.

'Back home in Coventry I once won the line, two lines and house, all on the same card,' says Ruth. 'I'll never forget it. I've got nothing here tonight though. You?'

I feel slightly embarrassed about sharing my card and then wonder why. What can I lose by Ruth seeing my own random spread of numbers?

It's a long time until the winner of the two rows is called, and the tension in the room approaches the density of a black hole, bending light.

I see can see now how bingo ties into everything I've learned about close-knit working-class communities. We are all in the same situation, all with equal resources, all wishing for the same result for ourselves. The tension comes from knowing that each time you dab a number, so does everyone else in the room.

I realise I have two lines that only need one more number each and –

'Here!'

Someone's got it.

'The full house will go just like that now,' says Ruth.

We must have dabbed well over half the numbers on the card, and neither of us has anything that looks close to a full house. The caller starts again, for the third and final time, and I will my numbers to rearrange themselves, hear 'On its own …' and pray for a nine, but it's a six. Fucking bastard shit. I only have one other number on the same line as that nasty, unstable six.

As part of the research for my ongoing project of pairing different beers with different styles of music, I've spent years exploring synaesthesia, the condition whereby sensory information can get mixed up as it's processed – so some people might be able to 'hear' colour, or 'smell' different sounds. I was shocked and secretly delighted to discover that I have a mild but rare version of it: it turns out that not everybody thinks different numerals have different personality traits, just people like me.

It's not helping now.

Six sits there, boiling in its own piss as it always does, barely containing its neurotic potential for sudden violence. Nearby number twenty-two, long ago dabbed, sits impassively, exuding its characteristic Prince Charles-like haughty blankness.

If I can't win, then I want it to stop. Surely, house will be called soon. But it isn't. It keeps going, and the longer it keeps going, the more chance there is for hope to reignite as you realise every number that hasn't been called yet is one you need. By now, I've developed an immense hatred of number nine, sly and untrustworthy, its snake's tail coiled in below the sleepy yet somehow arrogant seven that was called ages ago. And I realise that on that card, the fifth on my sheet, apart from poisonous nine (you're damn right, 'doctor's orders') I only need goofy, gawky forty-one ('Time for fun') for the full house! Surely I can't –

'House!'

No. Of course I can't.

Somehow the repetitiveness of defeat makes it easier. Even though the full house is by far the biggest prize, by the time it's called the mood is more one of fatalistic resignation rather than the hot agony of the first line. An official finds the person with the winning ticket and solemnly reads it out to the caller, who repeats each number back in confirmation. I'd like to say the tension builds as we wait for the result to be invalidated thanks to a wrong number being dabbed, but like the lines, it goes straight through and that's it – the end of the bingo.

My immediate thought is that I want to go again, the adrenaline of this sensation entertainment flaring briefly. But it's only the one card here at the Langham. It's probably just as well.

Bingo evolved faster than the clubs that hosted it. Some of the ridicule it used to face quietened down in the 1980s, when newspapers introduced bingo games that proved to be a powerful weapon in circulation wars. Then, in the twenty-first century, it migrated online with the rest of small-scale gambling. Most people who play bingo now do so on their smartphones, alone, with none of the sociability that got housewives out and about in the 1960s. Here, it can rampage unchecked, unsupervised, on apps that also encourage you to play slots and 'big money games.' Gala themes its games around *Coronation Street*, *Emmerdale* and 'Cake Off,' with running totals of the four-figure jackpots tempting you into each one. Tombola, 'Britain's biggest bingo site,' requires a minimum stake of £10 to get started, and encourages you to start with £25, compared to the £2 it costs me to play a card at the Langham.

The big chains do still run live clubs, but it takes me a minute or so to find any mention of them on the Mecca website, which is at pains to make clear just how much quicker I could be playing online. These big halls look cold and impersonal, with big screens and tickertapes of running cash prizes. The bingo card itself is yet another screen, this one embedded into a table which can take your cash for games, food and drink without you having to move. They look more like Las Vegas casinos than clubs.

You can of course play slot machines in clubs, too, but it's not as if someone moves a machine next to you as soon as you sit down for a game of bingo.

Like bingo, slots also became popular in clubs after the relaxation of licensing laws in the 1960s. Initially, the CIU strongly advised clubs against installing them, especially as club machines could tempt you with far bigger cash prizes than pubs. The Union would offer no support to any issues arising from the installation of machines and wanted nothing to do with them. Inevitably, one or two clubs broke ranks and installed slots, and word spread quickly that each machine yielded an average profit of £40 per week. This was a lot of money for clubs that were constantly looking to spend on refurbishment and expansion, and the CIU was forced to drop its opposition.

While the boost to club income was welcome, for some club treasurers and secretaries the temptation to help themselves to a bit of the cash proved too much. There were many cases of people absconding with the takings, ripping up their lives for a few hundred quid. Unsurprisingly, the police began to use new powers granted by yet another Gaming Act in 1968 to start looking into how clubs were managed and investigate the personal backgrounds of their office holders. Club committees were outraged. At Pogmoor West End Club in Barnsley, the entire committee resigned in protest, with one member maintaining that 'This is the first step towards a police state,' and 'against all the principles which we believe in.'

What these clubs didn't know at the time was that the scale of criminal activity surrounding games machines in clubs was much bigger than a greedy secretary doing a midnight flit. Naïvely, the clubs seem not to have suspected that criminal elements would invariably be drawn to so much loose cash. Leading London crime families decided, on the toss of a coin, who between them would get to exploit which part of the country. One firm got the north east. They set up a legitimate front company offering finance to clubs that wished to install fruit machines, offering the machines on HP. The clubs, never having been here before, were also making an income they had never imagined before. They didn't realise the HP terms were far too high for the profits they were likely to make. This could have gone unnoticed, but then the firms got greedy, going around and emptying machines on the pretext of doing necessary maintenance. They started feuding between themselves, which led to several murders, and provided the inspiration for the classic movie *Get Carter*. The police couldn't tell whether or not the club committee men were in on all this, hence their investigation of them.

Suddenly, it all felt a long away from the consequences faced by someone shouting 'mouse' as a joke.

* * *

For Ronnie Brown, it was fishing. For Ruth Cherrington, it was bingo. For Bill Davies (no relation to Joe, the legendary player who supposedly played on the table at Reddish Club – but a big fan of the man's technique) it was snooker.

Snooker wasn't Bill's first choice as a sport. He played darts in the pub, and he was pretty good. Then, he developed dartitis, which is obviously a made-up word, but one that describes a genuine condition that even players of Eric Bristow's calibre have suffered from. When he was at the oche, Bill simply couldn't let go of his last dart. It may sound daft, but it became so serious, he had to give up the game.

Instead, he switched to snooker. Decent tables didn't really exist in pubs, so Bill joined his local working men's club, the Lee Green Club in South London, to play. Sometimes, he took along his young son, Steve, to watch.

'I was very young, and I'd sit in the snooker room, transfixed by the balls,' recalls the six-times world champion, sixty years later. 'At one point, I walked over – I could barely see over the table – and I picked the black ball up in the middle of the game. That would have been 1961. Four years old, my introduction to snooker.'

Working men's clubs were so essential to snooker that they hosted the game's professional tournaments. In 1965, the National Individual Snooker Championship was held at Ruth Cherrington's Canley Social Club in Coventry, and was won by a young policeman called Ray Reardon, a regular at Cheadle Social Club. Reardon had started playing snooker as a boy at the Tredegar Workmen's Institute in South Wales, before honing his talent in inter-club competitions in the valleys. When he won the World Professional Snooker Championship for the first time in 1970, he was still representing Cheadle in the club leagues.

At the time there were only eight professional snooker players in the UK. Snooker may have been popular in the smoky rooms of working men's clubs and bespoke snooker clubs, but it didn't capture the popular imagination.

Then, in 1967, BBC2 broadcast the Wimbledon tennis championship in colour, a first for British TV. By 1969 it was broadcasting most of its output in colour, but few people had the equipment to appreciate it. The controller of BBC2 – a young man called David Attenborough – decided that brightly coloured snooker balls might be the incentive needed for people to invest in a colour TV set. On 23 July 1969, while most people were watching the denouement of the first moon landing, Attenbrough launched a televised snooker tournament called *Pot Black* on BBC2.*

Three years later, a young snooker player called Alex Higgins made his World Snooker Championship debut. The competition was held at the Selly Park War Memorial Royal British Legion Club, described by the BBC programme *Gods of Snooker* as 'a down-at-heel British Legion on the outskirts of Birmingham.' Higgins won the final, claiming the prize money of £480, in front of an audience whose tiered seating was created by the club stacking up its empty beer crates.

It would take a few more years, but together Alex Higgins and colour television would turn snooker into a national obsession. Steve Davis watched avidly.

'When I was eight, I got a toy table for Christmas. I played on it for a bit, but eventually it got put away. Then, when I was fourteen, we went to a holiday camp. Me and my dad spent all week in the snooker room in the clubhouse. After that he started taking me up to the club at weekends. I started getting the odd doubles game with my dad and a couple of other blokes.'

---

* In his memoir *Life on Air: Memoirs of a Broadcaster*, Attenborough writes that *Pot Black* 'broke our principle that all colour programmes should be as comprehensible in black and white as in colour, but we agreed that the commentators could deal with that problem. So arose the probably apocryphal story that one of them said, "Steve is going for the pink ball – and for those of you who are watching in black and white, the pink is next to the green."' This quote is commonly attributed to long time BBC snooker commentator 'Whispering' Ted Lowe. While it sounds hilarious, snooker pedants online have pointed out that, if the green ball was still on its designated spot, any fan would know which ball it was. As no one – not even Sir David Bloody Attenborough – seems to know when this supposed gaffe was broadcast, and Ted Lowe died in 2011, we may never know.

The Lee Green Club eventually got rid of its snooker table and turned the room into a family room, so Bill Davis was on the move again. He took Steve to the Plumstead Common Working Men's Club, where, 'They had four tables. Dad bought into the team so they let me come and play, even though I was under-age. I played whenever he went up there. Friday night was games night, and then we'd go on Monday too.'

While snooker was clearly the main draw, young Steve Davis quickly fell in love with all aspects of club life, sharing, as Richard Hoggart put it, 'the world of work and men's pleasures' with his dad.

'I remember the committee men being very important,' Steve recalls. 'I never knew what their day jobs were. The club was their life, where they got their status. Of course, some of them were light-fingered – if they had the keys to the fruit machine they'd be nicking out of that. There'd be an old guy, and when he walked past, people would say, "There's number one" – that was his membership number. You'd move up one each time someone died or left. My dad had a pretty low number.'

If you're a natural sportsperson, the opportunity provided by clubs to compete leaps out at you, wherever it arises. Steve Davis excelled at billiards as well as snooker, and also enjoyed a game of skittles. But he reserved special fondness for a game I had to later check was real, suspecting – not for the first time – that someone I was interviewing might be winding me up.

'There was another inter-club game – fucking hilarious. Tippet.'

'Tippet?'

'Yeah, I loved it. There's a wooden ball. Three people on a team, sitting at a table across from each other, so each team has six hands. The opposing team has to guess which hand the ball is in. It's fucking brilliant.'

'And that's it?'

'Yeah, but it's psychological. It gets very tactical, like poker, trying to throw the other team off.'

By the time he was eighteen, Davis wasn't just representing East Plumstead WMC in inter-club tippet – he was also playing on the club's billiards and snooker teams. By this point he was so good, he never lost a match.

'Winning the CIU Snooker Championship was one of the things that sealed the deal for me,' he says. 'It was very well-respected. That and the English Amateurs were what allowed me to turn pro.'

When Davis did turn pro at 21 – making him the youngest professional player on the circuit – he wasn't playing much in the club with his dad anymore.

'The problem with the clubs was, you put your money down on the table. You only got half an hour, and then you got kicked off. So when I got good, I sought out snooker clubs.' It didn't take long for him to come to the attention of promoter Barry Hearn, who took him around the country playing exhibition matches against other, more established players, whom Davis usually beat. Soon, instead of watching *Pot Black*, he was playing in it.

'I still saw the club team when I was professional,' he says. '*Pot Black* was recorded in three days, and I'd tell people who won it. Then I found out this guy had bets with other people in the club, knowing who'd won, so the next year I told him the wrong winners.'

Working men's clubs gave Steve Davis the route into the game that he would dominate for a decade, winning the World Championship six times and becoming famous among an audience much bigger than that which actually watched snooker. I ask him if the clubs had a bigger impact on the game itself.

'Oh, without a doubt,' he replies. 'Snooker clubs weren't very widespread back then. Working men's clubs kept the game going through the sixties and early seventies. They were particularly important in certain parts of the country. All the great Welsh players – they didn't have any snooker clubs. Ray [Riordan], [Terry] Griffiths, [Doug] Mountjoy – they all came through the clubs. Very few were snooker hall players.'

Just before we finish, I ask him if he ever played at the Mildmay, in its magnificent hall with nine full-sized tables.

'No, we were Great Eastern players,' he says, 'We didn't go north of the river, we were north Kent. We played places like Ashford.'

'Ah well, if you're ever in the area you should pop in,' I say. 'The walls of the snooker room are lined with cues in racks. Some of them haven't been touched in years, the people they belong to have obviously died some time ago. It's like a mausoleum to the club's old players.'

'That's how I got the cue I won six world championships with!' he shouts. 'The club had built a collection of cues. There was this old bloke who used to clean the tables and stuff, and one day he offered me this cue, saying the person who had it wouldn't be needing it any more. I said I was OK with the one I had, so he gave it to my dad, said I was obviously a good player and I deserved a good cue. A month later he passed away. I played with that cue for my entire professional career.'

* * *

In *The Lion and the Unicorn*, George Orwell writes: 'We are a nation of flower-lovers, but also a nation of stamp-collectors, pigeon-fanciers, amateur carpenters, coupon-snippers, darts-players, crossword-puzzle fans. All the culture that is most truly native centres round things which even when they are communal are not official – the pub, the football match, the back garden, the fireside and the "nice cup of tea." The liberty of the individual is still believed in [but] it is the liberty to have a home of your own, to do what you like in your spare time, to choose your own amusements instead of having them chosen for you from above.'

Orwell's list of English hobbies reminds me of the litany of leisure pursuits that were methodically stamped out by the authorities in the early nineteenth century, the attitude that if working-class people liked doing it, it must be bad somehow. The idea that we enjoy them in privacy, independently, also recalls the suspicions of religious groups and police commissioners alike who, because they didn't know what working men were getting up to behind the closed doors of their private members clubs, assumed that whatever it was, it must be evil.

Choosing our own amusements, rather than having them chosen for us from above, is pretty much what the entire story of the working men's club is all about. So what do working-class people really get up to when they succeed in getting a place where they can do what they like, where no one else can see them? Yes, some drink to excess. Others gamble. Many more play dominoes, or snooker, or darts.

On my trip around Newcastle and Gateshead clubs that began in the Labour Club with karaoke, we gradually drifted further out of town. We went to a couple of clubs that were still male-only spaces – technically, now against the law. The casual defence that was offered was 'Well, women wouldn't want to come here anyway,' which immediately made me think of rooms full of pissed, boorish lads swilling lager and swearing at the football.

The reality was quite different.

In one room, about a hundred men sat in a brightly lit space with the remains of a beige buffet in the middle. The lights were once again turned up full, leaving no dark corners, nowhere to hide or scheme. Three big TV screens were showing Friday night football with the sound turned down. No one watched. The atmosphere took me by surprise. It wasn't boorish or lairy. It wasn't the kind of place where women would feel uncomfortable, just somewhere most women genuinely wouldn't have been interested in spending any time. Men in jeans and short-sleeved shirts sat in pairs, sometimes with an odd table of six or eight. The loudest sound was the clack of dominoes.

Throughout the twentieth century, the working men's club movement provided more sports and games than any other organisation in the world. We could choose impressive figures from any year, but let's go with 1988, by which time the movement was in decline. If the number of trophies awarded within the CIU is an indicator of the popularity of a sport or game, the top of the charts ranks as follows:

Darts – 424
Dominoes – 399
Snooker – 270
Cribbage – 252
Angling – 158
Bowls – 132
Pool – 110

Trophies were also presented – and wouldn't Orwell have loved this – for Don, All Fours, whippet-racing, Euchre and Phat.

Any half-decent working men's club has a crowded trophy cabinet, and these cabinets take on a greater significance than the sport itself. A photograph of a club trophy cabinet is the image on the cover of Ruth Cherrington's book. The trophy cabinet at the Mildmay is in the main bar, dominating the wall by the small stage in the corner of the room. It's hardly Wembley or the Crucible. But for fatalistic, working-class men like my dad, these trophies are a lifebelt, a constant reminder that we can do something, we're good at something. We can succeed. Sometimes, we can win.

9

THE CLUB
AND WOMEN

The Red Shed, Wakefield, West Yorkshire

If Blackpool Tower began life as a grifter's attempt to cash in on the astonishing wonder of the Eiffel, then the Winter Gardens was Blackpool's answer to Versailles. Opened in 1878, sixteen years before the tower, it was described by its owners as 'a concert room, promenades, conservatories and other accessories calculated to convert the estate into a pleasant lounge, especially desirous during inclement days.' In the following decades, further opera houses, ballrooms and exhibition spaces were added to create an ambitious, expansive, northern People's Palace.

There are plenty of inclement days in Blackpool, but most holidaymakers tend to shelter from the weather in the pubs, fish and chip shops and amusement arcades that make up the bulk of Blackpool's Golden Mile, and are not much given to promenading through conservatories. The Winter Gardens became another white elephant showcasing the perils of the Victorian middle-class belief in the powers of rational recreation.

But this particular folly was built in Blackpool, and in Blackpool, you never give up: you adapt, and hustle, and survive. The stages in the complex have hosted everything from Gilbert & Sullivan productions to George Formby revues, from the first Royal Variety Performance outside London to the last speech given to a Conservative party conference by Winston Churchill as prime minister. Both Labour and the Conservatives held their annual conferences here for many years, before relocating to what the local MP described in 2015 as 'places like Manchester, Liverpool and Birmingham [that] have dedicated, modern, purpose-built conference centres, which surpass what Blackpool is now able to offer.' That year, the only political party to hold its conference in Blackpool was the Monster Raving Loony Party.

As political parties have moved to glitzier, more modern venues, the CIU's annual conference has remained in Blackpool and down-sized to something less glamorous. At its peak, 2,500 delegates used to file into the Winter Gardens. Now, a few hundred pack into the Norbreck Castle Hotel, three miles up the Prom. In the 1970s, the CIU conference could attract national press coverage to rival any parliamentary party conference. But sometimes, it was coverage the CIU didn't want, and still barely acknowledges, over an issue that would harden the image of the working men's club movement as being outdated and out of touch.

* * *

Wakefield Labour Club is infamous. In an age where the Overton Window has shifted so far right that admitting to being a socialist can cause offence, it remains unapologetically and happily marooned on the proper left. It feels out of place physically as well as politically. Vicarage Street is a short cul-de-sac that ends at the back of the massive edifice of the Trinity Walk Shopping Centre. There, just outside the fire exit and staff car park for Debenhams, is a massive red shed.

Comedian Mark Thomas attended Bretton Hall College, an art school in the middle of Yorkshire Sculpture Park, about halfway between Wakefield and Mapplewell. Given the choice between the two, students like Mark sensibly headed into Wakefield for a night out. 'The first thing that struck me about The Red Shed,' he writes in the foreword of *The Red Shed* – a book celebrating the Red Shed's fiftieth birthday – 'is that this is a wooden shed, possibly the most significant aspect of the club.' I'd take issue with him on this point. I'd argue that the most significant aspect of the club is that it is really, really red. Like, fucking RED. The fact that it is a massive shed is also, I will grant you, significant. These two factors about the club's appearance are probably – I'm guessing – why Wakefield Labour Club is known to everyone as the Red Shed.

The Labour Club used to meet in various rooms belonging to trades clubs and cooperatives, until the rising cost of rents in the 1960s prompted them to seek their own premises. Wakefield Council was undertaking a programme of slum clearances at the time, and the club still has the floorplans for what the site was like before it was cleared. The space this 47-foot-long wooden shed takes up used to have eight houses on it, one-up, one-down dwellings with shared lavatories in the yard out back. Sitting in the cosy shed now, watching a band set up for later, this brings home the reality of industrial slums more vividly than any written description can. Just trying to imagine how small each house must have been for eight of them to fit on this site is a distressing exercise.

Wakefield Council bought the houses between 1961 and 1963, when electoral records showed that there were sixteen adults living in them. These people were relocated, the houses demolished, and the Council leased the land to the club. The shed was originally built for the army, and when the club bought it, it was originally intended as a temporary solution. It was just four walls and a roof, but the members fitted it out, put doors on it, installed partitions, lined the inside, plumbed in toilets, installed the electrics, and declared it open in 1966. They did such a good job, it's still here.

Steve Wiltshire is one of the volunteers who run the club. He talks us through its history between serving a steady stream of customers at the bar. Apart from its politics, and the fact that it's a massive bright red wooden shed, the club is also famous for the quality of its real ales – a rarity in any club. Unsurprisingly, there are no big brewers' brands here, with most beers being sourced from local breweries, so the serving of them often involves some conversation and appraisal.

'There were still quite a lot of houses around here when we opened,' says Steve as he returns from another stint behind the bar. 'But a lot were demolished to make way for the city centre bypass, and then about fifteen years ago a lot more went when they started building this shopping centre. Originally it was going to be a few yards further this way which would have meant we would have had to go, and there were some tense discussions with the Council. If that had gone ahead this street would now be completely dead, but we're still here.'

It is still here, and unlike many Labour, Liberal and Conservative clubs across the country, it's still unashamedly political. 'We do have other strings to our bow, which have helped us keep going over the years,' says Steve, 'But there's always been a determined band of people who want to keep it very much a Labour club. Other clubs might have "Labour" or "Trades" as part of their name, and that might tell you something about their history, where they come from, but they've morphed into just social clubs.'

In our email correspondence setting up this meeting, Steve told me the club has never been a member of the CIU, without going into any reasons why. I ask him about it now.

'It was considered for a time, sometime before I became involved, and I've been around since the early 1980s,' Steve says, 'but the main reason for not joining, as far as I can gather, is the CIU's attitude towards women. We've hosted a lot of campaigns here. One of them, going back to the early 1980s now, it had an acronym – ERICCA. They were fighting for equal rights in clubs. I still remember the pamphlets they put out. So there may have been other reasons we didn't join, but in the recorded history of the club, what's passed down, that was definitely the main one.'

* * *

It was a grey early morning in Blackpool. The coach pulled to a halt outside the Winter Gardens and the doors hissed open. Sheila Capstick descended the stairs and found herself confronted by a media scrum. Beyond the pack there stood the police, ready to use force if necessary to prevent her from entering the building. For a second, Sheila felt the usual panic rising, but she fought it down and pressed forward in her Edwardian dress, clutching a sign reading '1981 Suffragette.'

After the questions from reporters came the abuse from the delegates.

'Get back home to the sink!'

'There's only one thing women are good for and we all know what that is!'

Sheila was shoved and jostled, but as she took in the scene, she realised this was bigger than she had dared hope. As well as the buses she'd organised from Leeds and Wakefield, there were more from Birmingham, Manchester, even Kent. Altogether, she reckoned there were over two hundred protestors – mostly women, but some men, including her husband Ken – facing off against the 2,500 angry men filing into the hall.

'We gave as good as we got,' remembered Sheila, years later. Out came the placards, badges, leaflets and balloons. And then, the jeers and abuse were met with a roaring chant:

'What do we want?'

'Votes for women!'

'When do we want it?'

'Now!'

As a man, Sheila's husband Ken Capstick was able to approach the doors to the conference hall unchallenged. When he reached the entrance, he stopped theatrically and said, 'No, that's it. I can't go in. These women are right – I'm joining them.'

A cheer rose from behind the barrier where the women were corralled. A journalist – not realising that Ken was one of the organisers of the protest – rushed over to him to ask him what had changed his mind. As he took his place behind the crowd barriers, one conference delegate shouted over to him, 'What's up with thee? Is thy a poof?'

'It's thee at that side o' t'barrier wi' all t'men, owd love,' fired back, Ken, 'I'm at this side wi' all t'women.'

Some of the delegates looked embarrassed. Though none followed Ken's example of joining the protestors, one man bought a badge … and then pinned it to his jacket, inside the lapel where none of his brothers would see it.

'I've found a way in!'

David Hinchcliffe – who would later be the Labour MP for Wakefield for eighteen years – appeared at Sheila's side and beckoned her and a few others down a side street. Once inside he led Sheila, her friend and co-conspirator Brenda Haywood, and the rest of their small party up and up, to the top of the building. 'We were like the SAS creeping up in ambush, except we were scared stiff in case anyone copped us,' recalled Sheila. David Hinchcliffe led them to a door, and then waited outside it – 'he knew that was for the women' – as the protestors entered the gods of the great hall.

They were spotted quickly, and shouts rose from around the room.

'We have intruders!'

'There are women in here!'

'Remove them!'

As the organisers called the police, one of the women found a microphone and yelled 'What about giving women equal rights? CIU pass cards for women! Equal rights now!' And then the protestors, triumphant, left the building.

'It was a good day, that,' Sheila wrote in her memoir. 'We right enjoyed ourselves.'

* * *

Out of all the new information I learned while researching this book, one fact stands alone as my favourite trivia question should I ever need to write a quiz: what year did women finally gain equal rights in working men's clubs?

When I ask people, the most common answer is, 'Ooh, I dunno, was it as late as the 1980s?

The correct answer is 2007.

The CIU still seems reluctant to acknowledge the campaign for equal rights for women or talk much about the issue. George Tremlett, in his definitive history of the Union, limits his discussion of female membership to an account of a debate at the 1977 AGM. Derek Dormer, who was vice-president of the Union through the 1970s and president from 1980 to 2000, wrote a memoir crammed with detail about the licensing of games machines, the perils of VAT and the electoral machinations of the National Executive, but limits himself to a single anecdote about the issue of female membership, recounting how he told a meeting in 1955 that he believed women should not be allowed in a working men's club bar: 'I was given the bird in no uncertain terms and I have to confess it did not take long for me to change my view.' Of the subsequent fierce debates and dramatic campaign that happened on his watch, there is no word.

So was the CIU a sexist organisation? Is it still? Are working men's clubs generally? As many have commented, is the clue in the name? If, as some members argued, women were free to set up their own clubs and institutes – the Women's Institute being an obvious example – why did they have to come into a club that was just for men?

The answers to these questions are far more convoluted than a simple kneejerk attack on good old-fashioned male chauvinism. They stretch back to the founding of the CIU – and even further than that.

As we touched on earlier, the second Reform Act of 1867 doubled the number of men eligible to vote from 1 million to 2 million, and the third Reform Act of 1884 extended the franchise to 60 per cent of all men in the United Kingdom. These Acts came as no surprise – there was an inevitable, if slow, momentum towards the principle of 'one man, one vote.' But the suggestion of extending votes to women was still a long way off – the idea that men who didn't own property should be eligible to vote was hard enough for many to swallow. At the same time as the Reform Acts extended democracy and improved the rights of the working class overall, they cemented in law the superiority of men over women, codifying inequality in one space as they took it away in another.

As a result, when reformers decided to look at the leisure habits of working men to see how they could convert brutes into right-minded citizens, they pretty much ignored whatever it was that women chose to do in their free time – there was no urgent need to go there. In 1884, Walter Besant wrote a long and detailed essay entitled 'The Amusements of The People' for the *Contemporary Review*. It remains one of the most important records we have of the leisure habits of the working class in late Victorian Britain, shedding light on areas few people were interested in looking at, and giving us insight into the early years of working men's clubs as well as much more. But it soon becomes clear that by 'people' Besant means 'men.' He deals with women in one line, saying that he has 'never been able to find out anything at all concerning their amusements.' At a time when men generally weren't that interested in finding out what gave a woman pleasure, one suspects he didn't try very hard.

By the late nineteenth century, leisure time for men was quite clearly delineated – it was the time between the end of a working shift and sleep. These times were fixed and working men in towns and cities could usually be found in either music halls or public houses during them. By contrast, the domestic duties that occupied most working-class women were both more fluid and less visible, and to reformers of all stripes, less important. They only mattered when they got in the way of men's precious leisure, and then they were to be shoved back under the carpet once again. Men had toiled all day – they shouldn't have to put up with women cooking, cleaning, or looking after their children while they were trying to relax.

So the thinking behind *working men's* clubs was never that women should be deliberately excluded. It was more that the aims and objectives of the working men's club movement simply weren't seen as being relevant to women. Women weren't getting drunk in the pub and going home to beat their families. Married women weren't habitués of music hall and therefore didn't need to be saved from the political extremism, apathy, degeneracy, or any of the other dangers that 'low' entertainment supposedly fomented among its audience. Sure, a few young shop assistants or milliners started to attend music halls, but they were soon snapped up and whisked into married life. The few social reformers who thought a little bit harder about it than Besant simply assumed that as most women who worked outside their own homes did so in domestic service, they were already being exposed to the 'civilising' values of their betters and would eventually inculcate these values into their own families.

Working men's clubs were conceived to fix a problem, and that problem was with men, not women. But even if women were not seen as part of the problem, they were never entirely absent from the thinking behind the club movement. When Henry Solly expressed his desire to help working men 'throw off the wretched and degrading bondage of the public house,' this was as much, if not more, for the welfare of those men's wives and families as it was for themselves. Wife-beating was not only common, it was socially acceptable among working-class communities,* and was generally seen as being the result of having had too much to drink. Even before the foundation of the CIU, some working men's clubs were actually founded by women. In 1860, Miss Adeline Cooper opened the Westminster WMC in Duck Lane, and a Mrs Bayly opened the Notting Hill Workmen's Hall. Both women did so because they believed the wives and children of working men were suffering because of the amount of time the men spent in pubs, and they saw clubs as the way to alleviate that suffering. Henry Solly was full of praise for these two 'excellent ladies.'

---

* As late as 1981, Yorkshire comedian Tony Capstick (no relation) was able to get to number three in the UK pop charts with a spoof monologue based on the nostalgic Hovis bread adverts of the time. Carrying a heavy debt to Monty Python's 'Four Yorkshiremen' sketch, he jokingly relates how his dad, upon finding out his mum has prepared brown bread and butter for tea, 'reached out and gently pulled mi mam towards 'im by t'throat. "You big fat, idle ugly wart", he said. "You gret useless spawny-eyed parrot-faced wazzock,"' accusing 'mi poor, little, purple-faced mam' of going out and playing bingo instead of getting some 'proper snap' ready for her family. As the story continues, dad gives young Tony half-a-crown to fetch some fish and chips, 'An' then he threw mi mam on t'fire.' This was genuinely considered hilarious at the time, and the single received heavy airplay.

From the start, Solly felt women should have access to the best of the facilities he imagined clubs would have to offer, stating that, 'Women should have the privilege, on a small payment, of taking books out of the library, and of admission to the lectures and concerts of the Institute, also to classes,' but only 'when efficient female superintendence could be procured.'

Working men's clubs were never just about working men: it was more a case of them not being prepared to entertain women on equal terms. In that, once again, they were very much a product of their time: no worse than most institutions of the day, and better than some. As I write this, I'm reminded that even when I was a child in the 1970s and 1980s, most educational books I took out of the library would talk about 'Man and His World,' as if women didn't exist. The problem was, when Man and His World finally did begin to notice women in their own right, and finally acknowledged that His World was in fact Their World, working men's clubs fell increasingly off the pace, until they were no longer 'of their time' at all, but increasingly behind the times.

* * *

Sheila Capstick didn't hate working men's clubs or the CIU – far from it. She enjoyed the cheap beer and free entertainment, the games, trips for kids and events for old people, and the fact that children were allowed in at least some rooms, so entire families could get out of the house together. 'At their best, clubs are socialism in practice,' she said.

As good socialists, Sheila and Ken were both members at the Red Shed, but their main club was the Wakefield City Club. There, as well as sitting and having a beer, Sheila enjoyed a game of snooker, sometimes with Ken, and sometimes with her dad. After her mum died, she would get her dad to come to the club and play a few games with him, to keep him active and ward off his loneliness.

'She wasn't a brilliant snooker player – some people seem to think she should have been professional – she just liked a game with her dad,' recalls Ken when I speak to him in 2021. If Sheila hadn't passed away in 2018, she may have pushed back a little on this point. 'I liked a game and I wasn't a bad player,' she wrote. 'I could beat Ken, my dad and a few of the other blokes.'

One Wednesday in 1978, Sheila and Ken were playing their usual game. As is the custom in many clubs with tables, there was a chalk board where people wanting a game would write their names. Bert Beer, president of the City Club's Committee, didn't have his name there, but he and his sons were deep into practicing to compete in the Club League, and he was frustrated that Sheila and Ken stood between him and his game.

'I'll have this bloody stopped, women playing snooker,' he grumbled as he left the room.

The following Sunday, the snooker room had a new sign up: 'SORRY, LADIES ARE NOT ALLOWED TO PLAY SNOOKER.'

Immediately, Sheila searched out the Committee members. 'What's going on? I haven't done owt wrong.'

'The cloths on those tables cost £120 to replace. It's too big a risk to let women play on them,' replied one Committee Man.

This was nonsense, of course. It's pretty much impossible to tear the felt on a snooker table unless the cue has no tip, and Sheila was a good player. To emphasise the absurdity, women were still perfectly free to play on the pool table in the next room, on the same kind of cloth. It was obvious that Bert Beer had simply found a way to prevent Sheila making him wait for a game.

It quickly became apparent that he'd messed with the wrong woman.

'Sheila was a gritty woman who took no nonsense,' remembers Brenda Haywood. Sheila grew up in a poor family and consistently fought against every challenge this threw at her, working job after job to make ends meet from the age of thirteen, variously as a debt collector, shop assistant, cab driver, and factory worker. By the late 1970s she was also bringing up three children and supporting Ken, who was active in the National Union of Mineworkers and would go on to become vice-president under Arthur Scargill during the 1984–5 miners' strike. Ken was politically engaged some time before Sheila, but he had been gently encouraging her to take a more active interest. When she began to dig more deeply into the snooker ban, her own political engagement ignited.

Sheila was already keenly aware that she didn't have the same rights in clubs that men did. As private members' organisations, clubs were exempt from some regulations covering commercial and public spaces, and each club was free to decide whether it admitted women, and if it did, what privileges they should enjoy. The rules were drawn up by the club committee, and only men were allowed to serve on that committee. Wakefield City Club was, for its time, quite liberal: women were allowed to become members in their own right rather than being signed in as guests, and Sheila was even permitted to go to the bar and buy her own drinks. In some clubs, women were allowed in some rooms, but not others (the City Club magnanimously allowed Sheila to enter the snooker room whenever she wanted, even after she was banned from playing). 'Not all clubs were the same,' Brenda Haywood tells me. 'In some, there'd be a white line across the floor that women were not allowed to cross.'

As Sheila explored her own situation, she learned more about this apartheid of the sexes. Even in the clubs where a woman could become a member, 'she still can't sign visitors in, nominate for the Club Committee or take part in the running of the club in any way … Until I was banned from the snooker table I'd never realised I was only a half-member. About the only right my membership gave me was the right to buy a drink.'

This was no longer about snooker. Sheila simply couldn't understand why an organisation that was, at its best, 'socialism in action,' could behave in this way. 'They were supposed to be about working people and democracy, and yet they denied half their members their rights,' she wrote.

'I think about it this way,' says Ken Capstick. 'The suffragettes managed to win the vote for women, and obviously that was incredibly important. But this was about a day-to-day issue for women, something that happens every day, not just once every four years. It was about a woman's right to a social life.'

*   *   *

To some, there was a kind of logic to not allowing women into clubs. One outside observer visiting clubs in the North was told, 'Miners in these parts will not allow women working in or about mines, neither will they have them in clubs.'

Mines were dangerous, unhealthy spaces. Many miners pleaded with their male children to find an alternative career – or in the case of Ian Clayton's grandfather, threaten to kick his arse if he considered it – so it's no surprise that they wouldn't want the women they loved to be anywhere near such horrible spaces. But the logic of the comment above suggests that clubs were just as bad, just as unwholesome for the 'fairer sex.'

That's probably pushing it a little, but there was a genuine belief that clubs were not suitable for a respectable woman. They were often characterised by heavy smoking as well as drinking, by open gambling among men who swore profusely. There was often a sort of chivalrous code among men that while they had the right – even the need – to let off steam by being coarse, vulgar and debauched, women should not have to hear it. Men and women were different and needed separate spaces sometimes. Some clubs revelled in their shabbiness.

These were all broader cultural norms, not just applying to clubs but to leisure in general, and many women were complicit in it. In Victorian times, most people subscribed to the 'separate spheres' theory that men and women were fundamentally different, and that it was right that they should pursue separate leisure interests. This was one belief that transcended the classes: in upper-class dining rooms, men withdrew from the table to a separate room to smoke cigars and drink port after dinner. In working-class communities, the man went out to the pub or club while the woman stayed in.

This separation was still strong in northern working-class communities in the middle of the twentieth century. Richard Hoggart describes the social life of working-class communities being strictly defined by gender: 'The wife's social life outside her immediate family is found over the washing-line, at the corner shop, visiting relatives at a moderate distance occasionally, and perhaps now and again going with her husband to his pub or club. He has his pub or club, his work, his football matches. The man is the head of the home, brings money into the house – neither want it to change.'

On the very first episode of *The Wheeltappers and Shunters Social Club* in 1974, the Three Degrees perform. In the middle of their song, lead singer Sheila Ferguson breaks off into a monologue saying that while 'Women's Lib is cool,' women should defer to their men, loving and supporting them above all else.

Being just about old enough to remember both *Wheeltappers and Shunters* and the phrase 'Women's Lib,' mine was the first generation to grow up in Britain with the notion of equal rights for women built into us. I always had female friends, female teachers and lecturers, female work contemporaries and female bosses, and believed this was normal.

I'm not asking for a medal, because it *is* normal. But it took me a while to realise just how different my version of normal was from that of my parents' generation. About two years after my dad died, my mum and I had a rare – in fact, unique – heart-to-heart conversation, in which she opened up about her feelings and told me that she simply felt very lonely without him. We talked halfway through the night, and then she gathered herself, sat up and said, 'Oh, I really shouldn't be talking to you about all this.'

'Why not?' I asked gently. 'Because I'm your son?'

'No. Because you're a man.'

The attitudes around women in clubs also applied to pubs. In the 1930s, the Mass Observation study found that it was still unusual for women to go to the pub without a male partner. It was seen as more 'ladylike' for women to drink bottled beer rather than draught. Draught beer was cheaper, however, so it was noted that women might get a half-pint 'when their courting days are over.'

Clubs were actually considered a safer, more appropriate environment for women than pubs, because there was less heavy drinking, and because they were owned and run by people they knew. Policies varied from club to club, but by the 1950s the majority of clubs had 'lady members.' Often they couldn't go to the bar themselves, and it was common for them to arrive with their husbands and then go into a different room. The Mass Observation study suggested that because women generally didn't buy or drink in rounds, it made sense for them to be somewhere else while the men did.

Photos and video footage from the mid-twentieth century show that by then, there were as many women in clubs as men. A German documentary about the Dial Club in Sheffield, filmed in 1964, specifically states that half the members were women. After the introduction of bingo, women's attendance at clubs dramatically increased. By the 1960s, drinks manufacturers were recognising women as a target audience in their own right, with their own money to spend as they entered the workplace. Drinks such as Babycham were launched specifically to appeal to women having a night out, and the first big advertising push for lager in the UK was to position it as a feminine drink, because it was bright and sparkling, with taglines such as 'A blonde for a blonde.'*

Many men actually wanted women to come to clubs, because they wanted the option of taking their entire families for a night out, especially when there was a good turn on. So for the last seventy years, working men's clubs have on the whole catered for women as well as men. The problem was, even where women were accepted, they were not equal. We still see the benefit in sometimes having separate social occasions for men and women – the 'girls' night out,' or stag or hen weekend. The point is, women now have the right to do so on their own terms. In the clubs, women were there entirely on the whim of their male partners and the male committee. They had no voting

---

* In the 1970s, lager marketers had to spend at least double this budget on ads trying to convince men that lager was not effeminate, wondering where on earth men had got such an idea. Every few years, someone in the drinks industry will still have the bright idea of launching 'a beer for girls.' Not one of these launches ever, ever works. Would you try selling coffee for women, or laptops for ladies?

rights and couldn't stand for office. They couldn't visit any other clubs apart from the one of which they were a member unless their husbands took them. If he was barred for bad behaviour, she and her children were excluded as well. If a male member died, grieving widows were told they were no longer welcome.

While the battle for equality was fought on various fronts, most of the arguments used against women being full and equal members fell apart in any club that actually admitted them in the first place: the fact that they had fewer rights didn't make any difference to the club being a male-only space, or the danger of women being exposed to gambling, nudity or foul language. If you didn't want female members, that was one thing. If you decided to admit them, where was the logic in them being second-class members? This everyday discrimination was what Sheila Capstick's campaign was really about. Being banned from the snooker table was simply the last straw.

* * *

The campaign that would culminate in storming the CIU Annual General Meeting in Blackpool began with a letter to *Cosmopolitan*.

Sheila Capstick wasn't normally one for magazines. She dismissed those aimed at women as 'full of adverts and knitting patterns.' When Ken was reading political tracts in bed, Sheila would rather read the *Beano* or *Dandy*. She never worked out how this particular issue of *Cosmo* came into her possession, but she found the letters page 'right interesting,' and thought they might be keen to hear about what had happened to her. She wrote to them:

> During the past few years my husband has taught me to play snooker in the club's snooker table and I have become a reasonably good player. On numerous occasions I have won matches against my husband and other male members of the club, all of whom have been good sports, readily accepting me as an equal.
>
> However, a few weeks ago the committee held a meeting at which it was decided, due to pressure from one member, to stop

all women playing on the snooker table. My husband, myself and other club members have been unable to reverse this decision. In these days of so-called equality, should we have to stand for this?

'The letter got picked up and got some attention,' remembers Brenda Haywood. 'Germaine Greer wrote Sheila a letter of support. I was a local reporter and was asked to go and talk to her, and we got in like a house on fire. The issue was very close to my heart – both sets of my grandparents had been members of working men's clubs. Her stance really struck a chord with me.'

Emboldened by a sack of mail from *Cosmopolitan*, Sheila organised a petition against banning women from playing snooker in clubs. Standing in a precinct by Wakefield Cathedral, her small group gathered 2,000 signatures in an afternoon. They decided to hand the petition to the committee of Wakefield City Club at their next meeting, and picket the club while they were at it.

Fifty people turned up for the picket: some of them club members, some like Brenda Haywood and Pete Lazenby from the local press, others from unions. On a miserable, rainy night, Sheila knocked on the door of the meeting room and was told to go away. Meanwhile, the committee phoned the police and informed them there was a 'riotous mob' causing trouble outside the building.

The police looked bemused when they turned up to find a peaceful protest consisting mainly of women.

'Where's this riotous mob then?'

After Sheila explained the purpose of the demonstration, the policeman asked, 'If you get them to accept this petition, will you all disperse?'

'Yes, that's all I want,' said Sheila.

The police duly escorted her to the committee room and forced the meeting to accept the petition. The Club secretary snatched it from Sheila's grasp, slammed the door, and immediately instructed the Club Steward to burn it.

A group of the protestors, including Brenda Haywood and Pete Lazenby who were by now acting as campaigners rather than journalists, adjourned to a local pub. 'A few of us decided we could help Sheila,' recalls Brenda. 'We were a group of young activists – several of us were involved in other campaigns around women's rights – and we had lots of ideas.'

Collectively, the group decided on an official campaign, with Sheila as president and Brenda on the committee. They landed upon the name ERICCA, which stood for Equal Rights in Clubs Campaign for Action. They had difficulty remembering it at first. Far more memorable was their campaign slogan: 'A Woman's Right to Cues.' Frustratingly for the CIU, this was exactly the same campaigning spirit that had seen them prosper so often against those who dismissed them as clueless, uneducated beer drinkers. Now, they would find out what it was like to have this fire turned back on themselves.

The campaign took off to an extent no one could have foreseen. Brenda Haywood, as an experienced journalist, gained blanket press coverage, and Sheila was asked to give interviews and talks across the country. She devoured an earlier edition of George Tremlett's history of the CIU, learned about its workings, and formulated a list of demands. While snooker always remained the headline, the campaign became about much more. Her focus shifted from the actions of individual clubs to the CIU itself. She realised that the key issue was the associate and pass card. If women were allowed to carry one, then by the CIU's rules they would have equal rights in clubs, able to visit any club in the union whenever they liked and with whomever they wanted.

All this time, Sheila continued to drink at Wakefield City Club, as a matter of principle. 'We were always welcomed,' says Ken. 'The Club enjoyed it in a way – there were coach trips from other clubs! To see the club where all the trouble went on. They still wanted her to go in because it was bringing custom into the club, which they sorely needed.'

TV appearances followed. In 1982, the 120th anniversary of the CIU, Tyne Tees Television made a programme about clubs and invited Sheila to be on it. In the hotel bar afterwards, she found herself standing next to Colin Crompton, Concert Chair of the

Wheeltappers and Shunters Social Club. She overheard him saying to his companion, 'People who go to working men's clubs are nothing but peasants.'

'And people like you are nothing but parasites, living off our backs!' She exploded back at him.

'He had a real go at me,' she wrote, 'Said I was making a spectacle of myself, that I was doing it to be recognised.'

Sheila Capstick didn't want to be recognised. She received death threats, rape threats, threats against her daughter's life. But she pressed on, picketing the conference in Blackpool three times. And then, the colliery where Ken worked was closed down, and he was transferred to Selby in North Yorkshire. 'It died a bit of a death after four years,' says Brenda Haywood. 'Sheila would still get letters about it, but I got less active. It kind of fizzled out.'

For Sheila, it was a relief. 'I was sorry when ERICCA died,' she wrote. 'But if ERICCA hadn't died, I would have done.'

In 1984, the Miners' Strike thrust Ken into the national spotlight instead, and suddenly Sheila was campaigning again. 'She got really involved in the Women's Support Group for striking miners. That came from the snooker campaign,' says Ken. 'There was a meeting upstairs at Oddfellow's pub. Sheila leafleted the area, 'If you're a miner's wife, come to the meeting.' Sheila chaired it. Went around the room asking who you are and what you do. Some of these women had never been involved in anything before. Some found it hard to say their name. One woman – Ann Richards – said she was 'just a house-wife,' and Sheila told her there was no such thing as 'just' a housewife. After that, Ann went on to speak on platforms all around the country alongside politicians and union leaders. She went to college after the strike. Another woman, Pat Thomas, said 'I never knew there was such a thing as life after marriage.' Women enjoyed the strike much more than the men did. It gave them a new lease of life. 'We're not behind our men' they'd say, 'We're shoulder to shoulder with them.'

* * *

It would take another twenty-three years after the end of ERICCA in 1984 before women finally gained equal rights in clubs. Frustratingly, the CIU had already been discussing the issue in smoke-filled meeting rooms for twenty-three years before Sheila Capstick began the campaign in 1978.

In 1955, members of the CIU's National Executive Committee proposed changing the name of the organisation from The Working Men's Club and Institute Union to the National Club and Institute Union. There were two reasons for this. The first was to reflect that over a third of clubs now admitted women, who accounted for 200,000 club memberships. In light of this, the proposal suggested that 'such lady members' should be entitled to associate and pass cards.

The second reason for the proposed name change was that the club movement was part of a long-term struggle to eradicate the glaring inequalities between the working class and those who were better off. The idea was that eventually, improvements in general prosperity should do away with the concept of class for good. But many in industrial areas disagreed and saw the idea of working-class identity as something to be valued. Even today, many still do.

So it was a dumb idea to conflate two complex issues into one vote. When that vote was taken, only four people out of 1,008 delegates voted in favour, meaning even some of those responsible for bringing it to the meeting must have changed their minds.

But the momentum on the question of women had been started, even if its forward motion was barely perceptible for several decades. In 1975 the issue of female membership was debated at a special rules revision conference, and then again at the 1977 AGM. That same year, the Queen became the first reigning monarch to visit a working men's club when she popped into Coventry, one of the oldest and most respected clubs in the country, as part of her Silver Jubilee celebrations. The irony was noted, but the motion was still rejected, with heated speeches on both sides of the debate.

By now, the Executive were openly pushing for change. George Moss, (president of the South Yorkshire Branch) said the rule change could bring in as much as an extra £500,000 a year and urged delegates to 'do away with this prejudice.' A.W. Clifford of Silver Hall Club in Essex said, 'We are not being men if we deny women their rights.'

The same year that Sheila Capstick began her campaign for equal membership for women, the CIU came up with a different solution to the problem she had highlighted, instigating a 'Queen of Clubs' beauty contest. Long-time Executive member Jimmy Cooke felt that beauty contests would 'help in making the ladies more interested in club life.' It had disappeared a decade later.

In many clubs, on a Sunday lunchtime, the only women allowed in were those who took their clothes off onstage. The laws on theatrical nudity were archaic and bizarre. Performers were allowed to appear naked but were not allowed to move of their own volition if they were. This led to models appearing in static *tableaux vivants*, maybe with a rotating stage to provide some movement. Fan dancing was fine, in that the naked body was concealed by fans until they were dropped, at which point the dancer would freeze until the lights were dropped or the curtain closed. In the 1960s the law was changed so that nudity and movement were permitted in private members' clubs. This led to the creation of strip clubs and lap-dancing clubs that covered their modesty by borrowing the name 'gentlemen's club.' It also created a boom in 'exotic dancers' entertaining working-class men while their wives cooked dinner at home. It all contributed to the growing sense that working men's clubs were out of touch and out of time.

In 1985, equal membership for women became the official policy of the CIU. The problem was, for them to pass such a fundamental rule change, they needed a two-thirds majority at the AGM. That was going to take time. Writing in 1988, George Tremlett argues the case very carefully. The CIU was the largest democratic organisation in the country and had a long tradition of balancing different interests against each other. That's why it had survived so long. With 'nearly 4000 clubs and a total membership of maybe 2,500,000 people, with the officials of every club accountable to members of that club; with branch officials accountable to each club; with National Executive members accountable to the branches, and the president, vice-president and general secretary all elected by national ballot,' change in such an organisation was always going to be slow, and Tremlett, writing a CIU-sponsored book under the watchful eye of President Derek Dormer, thought this was 'appropriate.'

A survey commissioned by the CIU in 1986 showed that 70 per cent of the public supported equal rights for women in clubs, with just 12 per cent against. The argument against was becoming increasingly indefensible on all fronts.

Part of the problem was that clubs had become too successful. You couldn't boast that you were a vital pillar of the community, providing coach trips, excursions for kids, dinners for the elderly and elements of social care, and still claim that you were a place for men to drink without their women. Even if you tried, the uncomfortable truth in many clubs was that, increasingly, it was the 'lady members' who were doing all the work in organising these activities, making it more absurd that they were doing so without having an equal voice. Slowly, the issue started to look like pragmatism rather than principle: if women were to be admitted, there was no argument for them not to have equal rights. If they were excluded, the clubs that were beginning to struggle financially would lose a huge chunk of their revenue and most of their organisational capability. Ultimately, the clubs needed women in order to survive.

Coming back again to the key questions I asked myself at the start of this book, I now realise this was where clubs were at when I turned eighteen. Sure, we wanted cheap beer, but by the time we were in our early teens, the 'separate spheres' approach was history. Most of the time, my friends and I socialised in mixed sex groups – we had women as mates as well as men. If we did want to go on a lad's night out, the main priority was to go to places where we could meet single women. If a woman could only enter a club with her spouse, they were no use to seventeen- and eighteen-year-old lads hoping to 'pull.'

At the same time, pubs were changing. As commercial establishments, they figured out a long time before clubs did that alienating half the population didn't make sound business sense. While it certainly took a while for pubs to welcome women and make them feel comfortable, it happened long before clubs eventually did what had to be done. In the 1990s, the Bass brewery commissioned research on why women didn't go to pubs on their own and found several common factors. They didn't feel comfortable if they couldn't see inside before going in. They didn't like queuing at the bar if a bunch of men were sitting on bar stools in their way. And the wine was generally crap. So Bass created All Bar One – a chain of pubs that had big windows onto the streets, no bar stools, a great wine selection, and comfortable sofas. This new breed of high street pub felt both safer and more appealing to women than clubs did. Women flocked to All Bar One and the thousands of other pubs that copied their example. And where women go drinking, as we've just established, men follow.

Perhaps if clubs had passed equality for women in the 1980s, when my pop quiz contestants guess they did, my generation might have joined, and clubs wouldn't be in anywhere near as much trouble as they are now. But it would take until 2007 for the all-important two-thirds majority to pass the resolution.

'I seconded the motion at the conference where it was finally passed,' says Ken Green. 'We knew which side our bread was buttered. We knew it had to come. But the north east were very anti-women, and we had to work around them. The issue was blown out of all proportion by these vociferous females.'

Did I hear that right? Yes I did, because he says it more than once.

'They went about it the wrong way. If you want to change laws that have been laid down for a hundred years, we had to do it our way rather than have it imposed upon us.'

Three years after the vote was finally passed, the whole thing became academic anyway: the 2010 Equalities Act expanded on 'previous obligations on associations not to discriminate because of disability, race and sexual orientation' by 'extending the ban on discrimination to also cover gender reassignment, pregnancy and maternity, religion or belief and sex.' An 'association' was defined as 'an organisation that had rules (not necessarily formal or written) regulating who can be a member and there is a genuine selection process for members,' and included 'private clubs such as golf and other sports clubs, ex-forces clubs, alumni clubs, social clubs, working men's clubs, gaming clubs and drinking clubs.' It was now illegal for a club to ban women, or discriminate against them in any other way.

Some clubs took this better than others. In February 2014, the *Daily Mail* reported that 'Britain's oldest working men's club,' the Anstice Memorial Institute in Shropshire (opened in 1868) was closing its doors and disbanding rather than allowing women to have full membership, in a vote that was passed by 246 of the club's 300 members.

The issue hasn't entirely gone away. In one of the clubs I visit earlier in this book, in 2021, a committee member tells me about how he wrote to the CIU to ask about banning women from the club's snooker tables. 'They told us we weren't allowed to,' he says plaintively, shaking his head at the absurdity of political correctness gone mad.

* * *

Wakefield City Club closed in 2014 and has now been demolished. David Hinchcliffe stepped down as Wakefield's MP in 2005, and was replaced by Mary Creagh, who lost the seat to the Conservatives in 2019 as part of the collapse of the so-called 'Red Wall' of northern constituencies that had until that point been regarded as safe Labour seats. The working class was changing, and finally, people were beginning to notice.

For the first time in its history, the Red Shed sits in a Conservative constituency. It's still politically active. Steve Wiltshire says, 'We're proud to use the s-word here – socialism – and equality is a cornerstone of the place.' He hasn't seen Ken Capstick in the club for a while, but remembers him and Sheila fondly. He remembers that Sheila was involved with ERICCA. When I tell him she founded the campaign, he says solemnly, 'You've told me something I didn't know,' and seems pleased. As we leave, he gives me a small book – pulled together by Ian Clayton – on the history of the club. Mark Thomas writes the introduction, revealing that he did his first ever gigs here. It feels like all the strands are coming together. I linger by the notices in the foyer, advertising the entertainment that's on here under the banner of 'Red Shedonism.' For the first time in a long time, I regret leaving Yorkshire as soon as I could.

When I first told Sheila's story to my wife Liz, she shook her head, and with brimming eyes, asked 'Why isn't there a film of her life?'

'She never liked the media attention,' says Ken on the phone. 'It was something she had to do, and she did it magnificently, but she wasn't comfortable in the spotlight.'

Sheila herself went further in her book, revealing that the BBC wanted to produce a play about her campaign. She was uncomfortable with the idea. She and Brenda negotiated over writers, the BBC suggesting Barry Hines, ERRICA suggesting that given the subject matter, maybe it should be a woman, such as documentary maker Frances Berrigan. The BBC kept increasing the amount of money on the table, from an initial offer of fifty quid to a figure 'in thousands,' but wouldn't give final creative sign-off to the campaign. Sheila, worried that the depiction of her and Ken would damage him publicly, said they could do it if they didn't mention the Capsticks, but for the BBC, the Capsticks were the whole point of it. The play was never made.

Sheila died in 2018, eleven years after women were given equal rights in clubs, and eight years after equality was enshrined in the 2010 Equalities Act. But that wasn't really the point: before either of these events, and alongside them and after them, Sheila lived long enough to see everyday equality for women become the norm.

'Look at women's sport: it's changed massively now,' says Ken. 'A woman like Nicola Adams [born just up the road in Leeds] can get in a boxing ring and win gold medals! Look at women's football, which is now getting so much more attention. There are now women refereeing football matches, and this year, there was a female referee in the World Snooker Championships. Snooker was the tipping point. Sheila would have been delighted to see women playing football, cricket ... why not, for God's sake? Women should be allowed to take part in any sport they like. This is what Sheila's campaign was really about.'

Ken tells me that Wakefield Museum has an exhibit about Sheila, made up mainly of Brenda Haywood's souvenirs of the campaign. The morning after the night in the Red Shed, I cross a deserted Wakefield city centre to go and see it. The museum does what good local museums do: saying 'this place is important, this place matters,' with exhibits about industry, music, culture, botany, and the local origins of the Luddites. In one corner, there's a glass case with a sign reading, 'PROTEST.' Beside it, there's a sign with a photo of Sheila Capstick wearing her 'Snooker for women' T-shirt, holding a placard painted with EQUAL RIGHTS NOW in thick black letters. An identical T-shirt hangs in the middle of the glass case. But I've seen photos of the ERICCA exhibit, and this is not the same: there's less stuff here, the many press cuttings about the campaign have gone. ERICCA now has to share this cramped museum space with exhibits about Wakefield' protests against racism, nuclear arms, the Corn Laws, and Clause 28.

At first, I'm saddened and a little angry that a collection of material that was all about Sheila Capstick's campaign for equality in working men's clubs has been subsumed into this broader exhibit about Wakefield's history of left-wing protest more generally, that she's been downgraded as time has passed. Then, I look again at the placard by the display case, at the photograph of this young working-class woman in her cheap T-shirt and hand-painted sign, standing in front of a garden fence that's one of a row of garden fences, not packed in as tightly as the houses that once stood where the Red Shed is, but not far off. She looks determined, defiant, unsure of whether to smile for this posed photograph or not, a little out of her depth, alone, and strong. And I realise that while she may now be part of a broader exhibit, she's the headline of it. Out of all this city's long history of protest, ERICCA has been chosen as the most important example.

And I think to myself, that really is not bad going for a 'vociferous female.'

10

THE CLUB
AND CHANGE

The White Swan, Highbury Corner, London

If this were a work of fiction, at this stage I might look for some powerful symbol or metaphor for the decline of the working men's club movement. Where do people go to relax now instead of working men's clubs? How could I symbolise the club being pushed aside by the march of progress?

And I'd think, 'J D Wetherspoons.'

Imagine if it were a movie. Visually, how could I show 'Spoons replacing the club? Well, literally, I could have a working men's club close down, and a branch of 'Spoons open in its place. OK, fine. But what if I turned the pathos up to eleven? What if I tried to suggest Wetherspoons hadn't just replaced one club, but the whole club movement? What if I had a 'Spoons open up not just on the site of a closed club, BUT IN THE VERY BUILDING THE CIU HAD BUILT FOR ITS HEADQUARTERS!

Excited, I would show this to my editor, and if my editor were any good, they'd say, 'Pete, don't you think you're laying this metaphor on with a trowel? It's a bit obvious and trite.'

'No, it's brilliant, people will love it,' I'd say.

'No they won't. They'll think you're ridiculous. You're not very good at writing fiction, are you?'

And I would have to admit that I'm not. That's why I write non-fiction, where the stories are already waiting for you if you know where to look and how to unearth them. And in non-fiction, this is exactly what happened.

In 1961, the CIU began work on building a new head office on Highbury Corner, North London, after buying the site in 1960. Eight months later, the Union celebrated is centenary with the formal opening of its new £250,000 headquarters.

It celebrated a century of the emancipation of the working man, and a Working Men's Club and Institute Union that was unparalleled in the world, which oversaw 3,500 clubs, 2,250,000 members, and assets totalling £31 million.

The original idea for the new office building was that it should also contain a hotel and a model working men's club, a shining example of just how good a club can be. There was some opposition to this, and in the end, the plan for the model club was scrapped. But somehow, the concert hall and balcony that were going to be part of the club remained in the plans and were still built. According to Derek Dormer, who was then a member of the Union's executive committee and the centenary committee, various CIU heads of department didn't spot it because they were more concerned with how big their own new offices were going to be. In the end, Dormer redrew the plans himself. As he did so, he left the third floor of the building vacant, so that it could be rented out until the ever-expanding CIU needed more space. No one thought that was going to take very long.

The building was opened on 14 June 1962, a hundred years to the day since Henry Solly convened the first meeting of the Working Men's Club and Institute Union. The Sixth Lord Rosebery, grandson of the CIU's first president who was sworn in that day, was persuaded to give a speech: 'If one casts one's eye back a hundred years one can see how welcome the start of this Union must have been. In those days the working man was housed in badly lit uncomfortable rooms, and the only place where he could be warm and meet his fellow men was in public houses, the majority of which were very different in those days from what they are now.'

The CIU presented Rosebery with an engraved silver salver as thanks, which Rosebery said he would cherish forever.*

The CIU never did grow to the point where it needed to expand onto that vacant third floor. In fact, by 2000, it had shrunk its operations to the extent that the ground floor was also vacant. The National Executive Committee leased it to a property company for 999 years in return for £1 million. A few years later, J D Wetherspoon opened a new pub, The White Swan, on the site. For the past twenty years, anyone visiting Club Union House has had to walk past a massive 'Spoons to get to the door.

The White Swan occupies about two-thirds of the ground floor of Club Union House. Next to it is a cramped-looking reception area for the CIU, and on the other side of that is a McDonalds. What must surely be the balcony Derek Dormer referred to as a 'white elephant' confronts you as soon as you enter the pub. Last time I was here, many years ago, I assumed the place must have been a cinema in a previous life, but now we know it wasn't: it's just an architectural and bureaucratic fuck-up that now affords this particular branch of Wetherspoons a nice mezzanine level.

If the CIU had built a model club here, as some wanted, it would probably still be thriving today. There's certainly the demand for it. The White Swan is busy at four in the afternoon, and its resemblance to many of the clubs I've visited is remarkable. Built from scratch in 2000, the whole place nevertheless has a resolutely 1960s flat-roof estate pub feel about it, from the colour scheme of muted browns and reds to the Sputnik-style light fittings. The carpet isn't up there in the Champions League of garish designs, but it has enough personality to clash and clang with the patterns on various of the mismatched upholstered chairs. The lighting isn't quite fluorescent strip, but it banishes shadow from anywhere in the space as surely as it eradicates any chance of atmosphere. Most tables are occupied by middle-aged or elderly men, sitting on their own. Some stare into space. Others are

---

* Some years later, Dormer's wife found it in a jumble sale at Mentmore Towers, the stately home of the Rosebery family, and bought it back.

waiting for friends. Some sit back, relaxed, reading books. They all look like they're here for a bit of solace and comfort – a need that Henry Solly was one of the first to recognise and articulate. The beer is just as cheap as it is in the clubs too: Pints of bitter start at £2.39, lager at £3.49. On a Monday, the lagers and ciders come down to £3.10, as part of an advertised policy of 'Top brands at sensible prices.'

There are only two visible differences between here and a successful working men's club bar. The first is the toxic propaganda placed on every table. If you agree with Tim Martin's political views – as an older demographic is more likely to do – that's not a problem. Otherwise, wherever you sit, it's like having a pub bore haranguing you about Covid or Brexit whenever you raise your eyes from your pint.

But the second difference is that it also attracts younger people as well as the old men. In London, you don't have to be of pensionable age to appreciate the lure of a cheap pint. People don't know each other, so the sense of community is absent in that respect. But there is still a sense that we're all the same. There are no preeners, posers or sneerers, no one wearing a suit or designer bling.

There are also some little things here that working men's clubs could perhaps learn from: an all-day free refill station for coffee and tea. Cheap food, including breakfast. It's practical, utilitarian, and if I was a local widowed pensioner in search of a quiet pint, I'm struggling to think of a reason why I would choose a club instead of coming here, even if I had such a choice. The nearest surviving club to the White Swan, which is just a few doors down from Highbury and Islington tube station, is the Mildmay, just over a mile away. Later, I find out why.

Destroying working men's clubs was in fact a deliberate strategy for Wetherspoons. 'Oh, I remember it from my days as a sales rep for Bass,' says Ian, a friend of mine who has spent his working life in the beer industry. 'We worked with them to put beers into new openings. They mapped the locations of working men's clubs, which were usually on the estates in the suburbs. If there were two or three clubs spread around a town like this, the strategy was to open in the centre of town, as close to a train station as possible, to suck up the custom from all of them.'

Today, outside the reception of Club Union House, a sign advertises a further 3,000 square feet of office space to let. At the CIU's Annual General Meeting, there are repeated calls to sell off the building as it's clearly no longer needed – the Union's National Executive is just fifteen people now. In 2019, the CIU's accounts showed that the occupancy cost of the building was £280,000, on top of which, that slimmed down Executive Committee was running up £159,000 in expenses. The problem is, whoever leased out this space for 999 years in 2000 (and the Executive today seems not to know who that was) made a huge mistake. The lease was sold on to another property company for £4.5 million. With the ground floor tied up in this lease, the rest of the building is worth only £2.5 million. Without that lease, the CIU would have been able to sell the building for £7.5 million. Now, it's not just the balcony of a club that was never built that's a white elephant: it's the whole CIU building. With their strategy of linking pub names to local history, if Wetherspoons had a sense of humour they'd have chosen a different animal for the pub's name.

* * *

Today in Britain there are over 100,000 clubs of all kinds, 40,000 of which operate from licensed premises. Most are sports clubs, but around 6,000 are social clubs, and of these, 2,000 are working men's clubs. Just 1,500 of all these remain affiliated to the CIU, compared to 4,000 in the 1970s. These CIU clubs between them issue around a million pass and associate cards, down from 7 or 8 million in the 1970s, and that number is declining by around 5 per cent a year. The human need to gather together with like-minded souls, as old as society, is clearly stronger than ever. People still need clubs of some kind, and always will. So why is the traditional working men's club fading away so dramatically?

It would be easy to write a long list of reasons why clubs entered a period of sustained decline from the 1980s onwards. An obvious one is the eradication of industry from the North, with the miners' strike of 1984–5 in particular changing the fundamental nature of working-class communities. The clubs closed when the pits, mills and steelworks did. We can blame the smoking ban and the presence of cheap supermarket booze, and many people do. But if we're blaming deindustrialisation that happened forty years ago, and a smoking ban that happened over a decade ago, for a decline that's still happening now, we're clearly missing something out.

When the traditional industries of the North disappeared, people had less money in their pockets. But eventually these areas recovered – long after they should have, long after they would have if there had been a proper plan in place rather than just shutting everything down and abandoning people – but ultimately people got other jobs, mainly in the service sector.

The long-term issue was that the nature of community and society had changed. The nature of being working class, the idea of class identity, was also different now.

After he describes his working-class communities, the main argument of Richard Hoggart's *The Uses of Literacy* is that, in 1957, he fears a traditional, self-grown working-class culture is about to be swept away by commercialised, mediated leisure. Instead of feeling a sense of community and identity, we would become one class, anonymised by big brands, Americanised pop music, TV, magazines and celebrities, seduced by what Hoggart called 'an invitation to a candy floss world.' There can be little doubt that he was right. It's probably too simplistic to see this universally as being a bad thing – the average working-class person remains far more comfortable and affluent than they were in the 1930s – but the difference between Hoggart's northern terraces and those I grew up in is that TV was the main thing we did with our leisure time, and as a result, when we were kids playing 'Let's pretend' games, we always traded our broad Yorkshire accents for imitations of American ones. Similarly, one reason the club singer's vocal stylings sound ridiculous today is that, from pub karaoke to reality TV shows, they've been replaced by the over-singing of divas like Mariah Carey and Whitney Houston, characterised by a philosophy of why sing one note in a phrase if you can sing five?

Beyond the accent you sing and play in, the broader picture is of a loosening of community ties, particularly between generations. In the twenty years I worked in advertising, the word we used more than any other was 'aspirational.' Since the 1970s, most working-class people above the poverty line have been able to afford enough basic material possessions and comforts, and commercial competition means the things we buy are basically reliable and well-made. So the only way to make you buy more stuff – which brands must do if they are to stay in business – is to make you unhappy with the stuff you already have. You need a better car, a toothpaste that whitens as well as cleans, a pair of shades like David Beckham wears, a can of Coke with your name on it, a smartphone app that themes your gambling around a TV soap. I always find it interesting that on those 'back in time' programmes on TV, where a family lives, dresses and works as families would have done in different decades, at the end of the experiment the kids in particular generally say the 1970s were the best decade, because they had enough stuff – there were appliances that made life convenient, something good on the telly, and lots of presents at Christmas – but the family still behaved as a family, spending time together, before moving into the 1980s and beyond, and slowly growing apart as screens multiplied throughout the household.

Beer advertising in particular changed the way people drank. From the 1970s onwards, the beer you drank said something about you, because there was a greater range of beers to choose from. Because beer brands were not allowed to advertise what we marketers used to call the 'functional benefits' of the product, they advertised a style, attitude or glamorous provenance instead. For every generation since then, the rule for a newly legal beer drinker is that you don't drink what your dad drank. It was a short step from there to not wanting an associate and pass card for your eighteenth birthday.

'World had opened up, hadn't it?' says Ian Clayton. 'The beauty of working men's clubs was that they were so particularly local. End of your street. In the street where I grew up, me grandad always said,

"Never go beyond top o' t' street." I never knew what that meant. I always thought it meant not getting knocked down on t'main road or not meeting any strange people. But what it meant, really, was stay close to where you're from. Admire the world from the top of your street.'

Instead, we moved away from our streets. Large numbers of men working in the same factory, going back to the same streets, the same pubs and clubs, were replaced by men and women commuting to jobs in the service industry where you spent most of the day talking to people you didn't know and people who were not like you. Where once there was a group of miners, there's now a cook, a shop assistant, a delivery driver, a cleaner, a carer, all working different jobs on different shifts with little union support and a diminished sense of collective identity. The barriers between 'us' and 'them' have blurred. More than that, 'I' has become more important than 'us'. You are special. You are unique. You are worth it. You are a brand yourself, and every brand focuses on what makes it different from everything else rather than how it fits in.

The other big shift was that when we got home from work, we increasingly preferred to stay there, and began entertaining people in ways that had been unthinkable in Hoggart's terraces. Without that sense of everyone being on top of each other and knowing each other's business, there was no longer a need for the home to be a private space By the 1990s, you didn't just have to have the latest thing in fashion, hairstyles or cars, but in your tableware and soft furnishings too. If you were stuck for ideas, there was always a makeover programme on TV to inspire you.

The working men's club started to look dull, drab and utilitarian in comparison. As commercial businesses, pubs had to look good and evolve as tastes changed. Theme pubs, sports bars and comfy All-Bar-One-style lounges improved their food and wine offerings. Some got a stack of bar games in the corner, others started running pub quizzes and open mic nights for emerging talent. For those times when you still wanted to go out, the pub felt more aspirational than the club and, in a complete inversion from a few decades ago, also felt safer and more welcoming to women than the club did.

So how did the CIU and its member clubs respond and adapt to this sweeping social and attitudinal change that saw working-class people redefine themselves and the nature of their communities?

Simple: they didn't.

* * *

In the 1970s, racism featured not just in the gags on *The Comedians*, but on primetime, family-friendly sitcoms such as *Love Thy Neighbour*, *Mind Your Language* and *It Ain't Half Hot Mum!* People with different ethnicities were moving into clubland and changing the nature of working-class communities, so attitudes to race were increasingly at the front of people's minds.

Charlie Williams used to live in Royston, the village where I was born and lived until we moved to Mapplewell and/or Staincross when I was six. I remember once my mum coming home from the hairdressers, breathless with excitement, saying that he'd been walking past the window, looked in and saw a room full of women, and walked in and did a twenty-minute set, standing in the doorway.

Williams based his act on the fact that his thick Barnsley accent was so at odds with his appearance, and effortlessly won over club audiences by simultaneously telling overtly racist gags himself and challenging them with lines like 'Enoch Powell said the black man has to go home. Enoch, lad, it's ages till t'bus back to Barnsley,' and 'If yer don't behave I'll come and buy t'house next door to yours.' Similarly, Lenny Henry's act, which he perfected in Midlands clubs before storming *New Faces*, was based on his impressions of famous white men. On his TV debut, he starts a pitch-perfect impression of Frank Spencer from the sitcom *Some Mothers Do 'Ave 'Em* with his back to the audience. Half way through, he turns around and for the first time, the audience realises he's Black. That's the joke. And it gets the biggest laugh of the night.

Comedians could become accepted in clubland if they took the piss with, and out of, their Blackness. Musicians were often not so lucky. In *Not Just Beer and Bingo*, Ruth Cherrington tells the story of Ray

King, Coventry's first Black professional singer. Born Vibert Cornwall in St Vincent, he arrived in Coventry as a teenager in 1963, and was later seen as a key influence on the Two Tone movement. He started playing clubs in Coventry in 1966 and would book gigs without disclosing his ethnicity. There were times when he turned up to sing and was refused admission to his own gigs.

It was common knowledge that some working men's clubs operated a colour bar, but in 1968, the Race Relations Act made racial discrimination unlawful. The CIU maintained its position that the Union itself was apolitical, but also that private members' clubs had the right to accept and reject whomever they liked as members. The issue was put to the test when the East Ham South Conservative Club refused to admit a person of colour. The Preston Docker's Club was also on record as officially operating a colour bar, and both clubs were taken to court. The CIU decided to defend the clubs, even though the Conservative club wasn't even a CIU member. The case went to the House of Lords, and the Union pressed home the principle of the freedom of private membership. They won the case, in what must be chalked up as the most Pyrrhic victory in their existence. It didn't matter that the CIU insisted it wasn't racist: people following the case saw that these clubs were racist, and the CIU was defending their right to be racist. Roy Jenkins, then home secretary, immediately called the Union Executive into his office, and informed them he was bringing a Bill before parliament that would make any form of racial prejudice within clubs illegal.

Finally, the Union issued a policy statement to 'clarify' its position:

The Union Executive, being fully aware of the private nature of a bona fide members' club (which it will at all times seek to protect), considers that conduct by a club committee which is based on colour, race, ethnic or national origins, is unacceptable in that the Union is founded on friendship as is clearly shown on the Union associate card, namely –

HONOUR ALL MEN, LOVE THE BROTHERHOOD, USE HOSPITALITY ONE TO ANOTHER, BE NOT

FORGETFUL TO ENTERTAIN STRANGERS AND HE THAT NEED HAVE FRIENDS MUST SHOW HIMSELF FRIENDLY.

This declaration of purpose, which was first made 100 years ago, is the foundation upon which this great movement has been built and applies today as it did then and must ever be before club committees in their dealings with their fellow men.

In itself, this was a smart solution. But if it had been there on the associate card for a century, and if it was so obvious, why hadn't it been clear when the issue first came up? Why had the Union not taken this position when the two clubs were first taken to court? The CIU's credibility as an organisation was irreparably damaged.

* * *

In 2008, American filmmaker Henry Singer captured the demise of Wibsey Working Men's Club in Bradford, in the film *Last Orders*, which ran as part of the BBC's 'White Season.' The club was in many ways typical of its time: a purpose-built club with a good-sized bar and concert room that would have looked great when it was new in the 1960s but was shabby now. People who had been regular club patrons still went along, but did so less often, arrived later, and spent less. With less money going through the tills, there was no budget for renovation or redecoration, so the club became tattier and less appealing, fuelling the cycle. When the film was made the 2007 smoking ban had just hit, and the club committee was filmed going over the finances, and not coming up with any answers. At one heart-breaking point, the treasurer reveals the club's debt is much higher than he thought and can't be covered by cashing in the club's investments as they had planned.

'Where are we then?' asks one committee member.

'Up shit creek,' says another.

'Right,' says the Chair. Then, after a pause, 'Next item on the agenda …'

Henry Singer, who has become so fond of the club by this point that he drinks there regularly even when he's not filming, can't hide his frustration. 'Maybe they don't like change,' he narrates over images of the committee going through the motions. 'They've got into a routine where ... they become robotic, just doing the same, just going over it, and they're used to it, it's like the norm to them. You couldn't run a company like this. The shareholders would have them drawn and quartered.'

Wibsey club is, obviously, no more. Clubs don't close just because of dwindling custom – like many clubs, Wibsey was still busy when the bingo or the turns were on. Clubs also close because once the decline sets in, there are no good people around to run them. A 1985 Opinion Poll found that 61 per cent of people agreed that club committees attracted 'Little Hitler' types. This was clearly off-putting for other people, because 83 per cent of club members said they had never sat on a committee, reinforcing the cycle where those with a lust for power (over notice boards, pies, cleaning supplies) could usually stand unopposed for committee places. Clubs that allowed women to stand for the committee were in a better position, but despite 85 per cent of people in the same poll saying women should have full membership of clubs, with only 8 per cent disagreeing, it would be another twenty-two years until the creaking machinations of the CIU made it happen. As the world moved on, clubs stood still.

The BBC 'White Season' that kicked off with the Wibsey documentary was an examination of how white working-class people were feeling increasingly marginalised and invisible. At the time, all political parties were focusing on satisfying the floating voters of Middle England. Labour assumed its working-class heartland was theirs no matter what, and the Conservatives thought there wasn't much point trying to challenge that. The only political parties that were bothering to talk to white working-class communities were on the far right. In 2009, Barnsley elected two members of the British National Party among its six MEPs in the European parliamentary elections. If anyone could have been bothered to look, the roots of Brexit and the

2019 collapse of the Labour vote in the North were well-established a decade earlier.

Each of these political earthquakes sent pollsters, journalists and sociologists rushing to the North of England to explore its working-class communities like they hadn't done since the 1950s or 1960s. The books produced as a result of these studies back then would always contain a short chapter dealing with working men's clubs. The books offering an understanding of working-class Britain published more recently don't mention clubs at all. But they do offer deep insight into the reasons for their decline.

After the 2016 Brexit vote, a survey revealed that 60 per cent of the British population thought of themselves as working class, despite only 25 per cent working in routine and manual jobs. That figure hasn't moved since the 1980s. Claire Ainsley, executive director of the Joseph Rowntree Foundation, undertook a study to find out who the twenty-first century working classes were, and what made them tick. Her book *The New Working Class: How to Win Hearts, Minds and Votes* is not aimed at clubmen and doesn't even discuss leisure habits in general, let alone clubs. But it should be mandatory reading for the CIU's National Executive and every surviving club committee.

While the working class is undoubtedly still there, Ainsley says the new working class is 'more disparate, more atomised, and occupies multiple social identities, which makes collective identity less possible.' Essentially then, it's become the opposite of Richard Hoggart's tight, cohesive working class. That his prophecy came true is illustrated perfectly by Ainsley's example of young women in a focus group in Glasgow talking about how 'they bought trainers they could not afford to impress people they did not like for fear of being shamed for their lack of money.' The job for life has gone, replaced by jobs in the service sector with little prospect of advancement. Pretty much the only similarity that remains is that you're still likely to be earning the same at 51 as you were at 21.

Class is about more than just earning and profession, however – as a middle-class writer, I earn less than the average wage of a plumber or electrician. In a 2022 survey, a majority of 18–24 year-olds considered professional footballers to be 'upper class,' while only 6 per cent of over-65s agree. Ainsley works with definitions of class that include social capital (social networks, friendships and associations) and cultural capital (tastes, interests and activities) as well as economic capital (income and wealth). Using this, she outlines three distinct groupings: traditional working class (about 14 per cent of the population); emerging service workers (19 per cent) and a group termed 'the precariat' (15 per cent).

The traditional working class has an average age of 66, doesn't earn much, but has some accumulated wealth, most of it in a house that's worth a lot more than they paid for it, with a mortgage that has now been paid off. They are likely to know a lot of other people, but very few from outside their own class. They're the final generation of Hoggart's working class, and the people I've seen in every working men's club I've visited.

The 'precariat' get their name from the precarious circumstances in which they live. With an average age of 50 and an average annual income of just £8,000, they claim benefits between low-paid service jobs such as cleaners or carers.

Emerging service workers are the youngest and most affluent group, with an average age of 32 and an average income of £21,000. A fifth of them are from ethnic minorities. Socially and culturally, they are quite different from their parents. Hoggart talked again and again about the continuity in working class culture, about how when young couples settle down, 'They have taken over, with remarkably little change, the traditions suitable to their age within their community.' Now, if we were to say that the emerging service industry workers are either literally or metaphorically the children of the traditional working class, it's not just a question of not drinking the same beer as your dad drank, but also enjoying different culture and socialising in different ways.

The biggest difference of all is that they live their social lives online – this is where they build communities and friendships. And this is a major reason why they don't visit working men's clubs, because online, they're even harder to find than some of the clubs I've visited physically. The CIU website looks like it hasn't been redesigned in twenty years. It contains a list of the contact details of the Union's regional branches of which, at the time of writing, there are twenty-two. One of these – South East Metropolitan – has its own website. Of the 1500 CIU-affiliated clubs, a total of sixty-five have active links from the CIU's directory of clubs to a website of their own. Some clubs are on Facebook, but many of these pages are obviously unused. For many younger people, websites and Facebook are irrelevant anyway. On the platforms they use, working men's clubs are simply non-existent.

In pretty much every club I've visited, the committee have talked about the difficulty in attracting younger members. In many clubs, when I've asked how they might go about it, I've been met with blank stares. Guys, I think I might have a suggestion.

Three years after Claire Ainsley completed her study on the new working class, the Conservatives won many seats across the North of England that had been safe Labour seats forever, seats which pollster James Kangasooriam termed 'the Red Wall.' London's political observers and pundits once again got the train north to find out why.

Deborah Mattinson conducted focus groups in various northern towns and summarised the results in her book *Beyond the Red Wall*. She finds communities that feel left behind, cut off, and abandoned by the hated elites in London. The sense of isolation is often literal thanks to a decaying infrastructure – she writes about towns where a twenty-mile train journey can take an hour and twenty minutes.*

In these left-behind towns, people have a proud history, one that's usually linked to industry that has long gone. 'It was long hours, hard work, dangerous work, but you were often doing something important and you were valued – and well-paid for it too,' one man tells Mattinson. Reminders of the glory days are everywhere, but it feels like a tide is going out in these places. There's an astonishing correlation between former Red Wall seats and towns where the local branch

---

* When I go north to do own my research, I beat that: it takes me ninety minutes to travel by public transport from Leeds train station to Ian Clayton's house in Featherstone – a distance of 13 miles.

of M&S has recently closed. The end of being able to occasionally get some new knickers or a posh ready meal symbolises a bigger feeling that we can't have nice things. 'It's all chicken shops, kebab shops, charity shops and pound stores' is a constant refrain in towns that even big retail brands are abandoning.

Where there is desperation, poverty, and nothing else to do, there are also drugs. And where there are drugs, there is a surge in crime. People are scared to go out at night, and there's nowhere to go anyway. A lot of the pubs have closed, and those that remain are little better than drug dens, according to the people Deborah Mattinson talks to. The experience of Sheffield Lane Club, or rather the clubs and pubs that once surrounded it, is not unusual. On the day Chris and I are driving around Yorkshire, we pop into Nailmaker, a craft brewery on the site of the factory where my dad used to work. There, I meet Heath Downing, a lad from my class at school who I haven't seen since we left. I mention that we're visiting working men's clubs, and Heath tells me he once did a spell working behind the bar at the Tin Hat.

'Is it still there?' I ask, thinking of my dad.

'No, it got shut down a while ago.'

'Why?'

'Drugs.'

'What, dealing or selling?'

'Bit of both.'

It's no surprise then that younger working-class people growing up in these communities choose to leave them if they can. The service jobs aren't here; they're in the big cities like Manchester, Leeds or Sheffield, and that's where the social life is too. The younger generation of sociable, mobile working-class people are not just separate from the old working men's clubgoers because they're online – they're increasingly in a different place physically too.

And so, in many northern towns and cities we get a situation where in a domestic context, the Brexit voter labels of 'leaver' and 'remainer' can be reversed. The Red Wall constituencies that voted Conservative in 2019 also voted overwhelmingly to leave the EU. The people in these constituencies are those who remained there as they declined, feeling ever more frustrated and ignored. The younger people in the cities who were more likely to vote to remain in the EU are those who left their hometowns for a more cosmopolitan lifestyle. The 'remainers' resent the metropolitan elites in the cities, except their own children, who did the right thing in leaving so they could make something more of themselves. If there had been prospects for the leavers at home they might not have left, and the Little Hitlers on club committees might have been standing against younger people with fresher ideas and relevant skills – such as knowing how to set up a social media account.

* * *

There's a scene in the Christmas special of *Father Ted* where Ted is presented with the Golden Cleric award for bravery and uses the occasion of his acceptance speech to settle old scores. Hours after he began, most of his audience has drifted away, and he turns yet another page of his script, saying, 'Now we move on to liars …'

Among my friends, we quote this line as shorthand for when anyone is going on a bit or getting above themselves, and it's a line that was constantly in my head when I read *My Life in the CIU* by Derek James Dormer OBE. Dormer spent sixty years working in the CIU and was its president from 1981 to 2003. His memoir details every election and vote he won, and by how many. He settles every old score and presents life on the National Executive of the CIU as an endless round of politicking, jockeying for position and petty squabbles over who gets to chair which sub-committee, all conducted over gallons of free beer from branch breweries.

Like the issue of equal rights for women, Dormer doesn't have much to say about the steep decline in the fortunes of working men's cubs that began on his watch, but he does make a couple of points. He was a fierce opponent of gaming machines being installed in clubs but lost that battle when club committees saw how much money the machines could take. He highlights the temptation to dishonesty that grew up regarding committee men stealing the takings, and states that 'many otherwise decent men with integrity felt they could not associate themselves with people or committees who were suspected or possibly proven to be thieves.' As a consequence, 'it is now rare to have a battle to join the club management team.' While this may be true, it doesn't really come anywhere close to accounting for the wholesale decline in the fortunes of both the CIU and its member clubs that Dormer forgets to include anywhere in his memoirs. But the issue became much more serious after he finished writing them, with accusations of asset stripping made against some of those involved in the clubs' management.

* * *

I finally get to talk to Ken Green, the CIU's current general secretary, in August 2021, eight months after initially contacting the CIU. He's open and honest and happy to answer any questions I have, and he has some firm views on the plight facing clubs.

He thinks that Simon Cowell has had a bigger impact than the smoking ban. 'Turns are not prepared to do their apprenticeship these days. They're just going for instant stardom at extreme cost. A singer will ask for a thousand pounds – you'd have to take five times that across the bar to make it work.'

Changes in the Licensing Act have made it more difficult for clubs, at the same time as attracting unscrupulous people as licensees. Some individuals are alleged to have taken advantage of naïve club members by getting on the committee and selling the club out from under them.

Ken maintains consistently that well-run clubs can survive, and I agree with him entirely. I've seen what can happen when a Glyn Bradshaw turns up at Sheffield Lane or a John Murrie at Greasbrough. The problem is, you need these talented people to join clubs, or there needs to be some way of training then up. As the CIU shrinks, so does the help it can provide its member clubs. What was once a six-month Club Management Diploma is now condensed into three days' teaching.

Every May, the *Club Journal* gives a full account of the Annual General Meeting in Blackpool, which is now attended by 300 to 400 people, down from 2,500 in the 1970s. Even before Covid, exchanges between delegates and the National Executive were testy. The Executive maintain their line that a well-run club can survive, and that the CIU is there to help any club in trouble. The delegates fire back that the CIU is losing money hand over fist, that they won't tell the clubs or the branches what is happening, and that the only answer to increasing operating losses seems to be to increase the subscription paid to the CIU by clubs that are already struggling.

In 2021, following various lockdowns and restrictions, the picture was even worse. A total audience of 100 delegates heard how the 2020 Annual Report showed losses of £800,000, for an organisation that has assets worth £7 to 8 million. Twenty out of twenty-five branches returned net losses. Uto Ekanem, the Union's accountant, read out a litany of losses, and said, 'Without a strategy to address this continued financial decline, the medium-to-long-term health prospects of the Union appear quite bleak.'

Like the long gone Wibsey club, the entire working men's club movement is up shit creek. And it's simply moving on to the next item on the agenda.

11

THE CLUB AND THE FUTURE

Staincross Working Men's Club, Barnsley, South Yorkshire

Garforth Working Men's Club, Leeds

Walthamstow Trades Club, North London

The Mildmay Club, North London

'Who's this – Piss Wet Through?'

'It's Wet Wet Wet, y'daft bugger.'

I thought there might be ghosts here. Chris and I have spent most of a September Friday night and Saturday morning driving around different clubs, or the places they used to be. Coming back to New Road in Staincross, to the club where I worked briefly, the catalyst for my final goodbye to my hometown, was inevitable. But I didn't want to come. We got as far as the bottom of the village, where the shops have changed, before my stomach started churning. The presence of a micropub where Foster's Bakery used to be, and a craft beer bottle shop in place of the little cabin where my mum used to get her knitting wool, should have been reassuring. But they too seemed like unwelcome invaders in a place they didn't belong.

I realise how ridiculous I'm being when Chris and I turn into the car park of Staincross Club, and I imagine my old bar manager standing in the doorway, his eyes fixed on mine, not letting me past and not saying anything until I turn and walk away again. Didn't I get the message last time? Of course, the doorway is deserted.

The building looks the same. New Road tracks up a steep hill, and the car park has been cut out of the slope like a concrete terrace. It's massive, and although it's empty today, the constant scrabble for housing space means it wouldn't still be here if it were no longer needed. A beer garden runs down the top side, perfectly positioned to catch the autumn sun shining across the valley. The club towers twenty feet above the car park in blocky, windowless red brick, barricaded by endless steps and ramps that could have been designed by M. C. Escher.

No one challenges us at the door, and inside I don't recognise it at first – the bar faces a different way from how I remember. Then we go and look at the concert room next door and it comes flooding back – this used to be the main bar. It's empty now in the middle of a Saturday afternoon.

This is when drinkers gather in the games room, slightly smaller and therefore mustering a little more atmosphere. The club is immaculate: freshly decorated and comfortable. The games room glows with a greenish hue thank to the lights reflecting from lime-coloured walls. All the table have lips around their edges to aid the playing of dominoes. We sit across the room from the group of men debating the identities of the bands on NOW 90s. The Stones's is still on the bar and it's tasting good.

For much of my life, I was unaware of the impact I had on other people. I didn't think my presence mattered much, that I was effectively invisible and instantly forgettable. I had to learn the hard way that what I say and do actually affects people, for good or bad. Throughout my visits to working men's clubs, I've been constantly reminding myself that each time I walk into one of these rooms, it causes ripples. Most of the blokes across the room cast sidelong glances in our direction. One man, older than the others, gazes at us steadily.

Their accents aren't as strong as I remember from last time, when I was asked 'Whee't'frum?' People are still proud of their Yorkshire accent, but as Ian Clayton said, 'World opened up, didn't it?' When men lived in the same village, worked in the same pit and drank in the same pubs and clubs, customs and accents reinforced themselves within these sealed groups. When I was a kid, people in pit villages five miles to the north of Barnsley sounded different from those two miles to the south. People from Barnsley still call Sheffielders 'dee dars,' because we hear 'dee' and 'dar' instead of 'thee' and 'tha.' But now, many words and expressions that older people used when I was growing up have disappeared. On a recent thread on a Barnsley Facebook page, some younger commenters were sceptical that that they'd ever existed. Broadcast media, travel to other parts of the country, and jobs in nearby Leeds, Wakefield and Sheffield have all brought the New Road accent a little closer to how mine was last time I was here.

New Road is a deeply residential area. There used to be a pub just across the road and another one at the top of the hill. Both have now succumbed to that thirst for housing. But this place is still here, and despite being quiet mid-afternoon, it looks like it's thriving. I decide to go and ask these men why and explain why I'm asking. I tell them I used to work here in 1988.

'That's year I were born,' replies one.

'If it's for a book, say it's 'cos committee are sitting on a pile o' money,' says the older man, sixtyish, the one who was staring at us.

'We used to do a pub crawl. Cali at top o' t' hill, Masons across road, then in 'ere, darn t' Tin Hat. They've all gone now.'

'So how come this place survived?'

'Cheap beer. It's good beer an' all. Bottom o' town now it's all for tourists. Not that we ever get any tourists. That micropub in t'owd bakery, seven quid a pint in there. Strawberry IPA. We got summat close to lager and sat outside.'

'It's actually quiet in here now. You'd have struggled to get a seat last night.'

'This one's t'best. Turns are good.'

When I check the club's Facebook page later, it's updated almost daily with details of tribute bands and cover bands.

'Pink played here last night. I don't normally come out at night but she were brilliant.'

If I'd been born ten years later, with the end of student grants and the introduction of tuition fees it simply wouldn't have been possible for me to go to university. Would I have found another way to leave Barnsley? Possibly. Or maybe I would have stayed and made my peace with it. Before uni, I always imagined I'd come back here and be a bank manager, for no other reason than that it was a job you could do locally that you had to wear a suit for. If that had happened – well, it never would have, but something like it – I think I would have been happy coming here, taking the piss, drinking Stones's, listening to 'Pink.' The churning in my guts – and the unease that's been there for thirty-four years causing it – has gone.

We finish our pints and say goodbye. Out in the hallway, next to a working coin-operated payphone, posters advertise Top Gun, 'an amazing live 5 piece Classic Pop Rock Band' who play Pink Floyd, Bon Jovi, Thin Lizzy, David Bowie and more, and Manhattan, a 'multi award winning soul and Motown tribute show.'

'When's this book out, then?'

The older guy has followed us out, on the pretext of going to the toilet. I tell him. He nods and says 'I come here because it's *my* club. Every weekend. It's ours. We *own* it.'

* * *

The village of Garforth in West Yorkshire is 22 miles from Staincross. When I was growing up, in our mental geography, it was in another country. Part of me is still amazed that Chris manages to get us there in under half an hour.

Alan Banks has been concert secretary at Garforth WMC for thirty years, but he does a lot more than just booking turns. 'We appreciate our members and they appreciate us. We ask them what they want. We use it as a community space for the kids of members to come in,' he tells us as we fill the time and space before bingo takes over the room.

'Line dancers every Monday and Thursday and we've three snooker teams,' chips in Helen, another of the club's five committee members.

'We've a choir what's coming in, rehearsing,' continues Alan. 'They're going to do a Christmas show for us wi' t' brass band as well. We've got some brilliant cleaners so it always looks good.'

'It feels safe,' says Helen.'

Recently Helen introduced a simple food menu and can now also offer catering for functions booked in the club. Garforth could still improve its social media presence, but it's doing well enough without it, listening to what the community wants, and providing it. By doing so, it's attracting younger members around the same time in their lives it always has: when they have kids and want to go out together as a family to somewhere that's not a pub.

When the bingo starts, Chris and I move to the lounge next door, where the karaoke is about to start. It feels less like a pub, and more like someone's front room where the furniture has all been pushed to the edges to make room. The singing starts with no announcements, no fanfare, just people taking turns to sing their favourites – Neil Diamond's 'Hello,' Patsy Cline's 'Crazy' of course – each one with an echo on the mic that makes it sound like it's being sung in a cave, adding a bit of polish. Every song is sentimental, a sucker punch to the heart, but sung plaintively, with none of the histrionics of either Richard Hoggart's 'big dipper' or its modern, American-originated equivalent. It is a bit cramped in here. We don't risk waiting around for 'Human.'

* * *

Both Garforth and Staincross working men's clubs seem to be thriving. They prove that Ken Green is right to an extent – with good people on the committee, clubs can thrive. The problem is, if the club is already struggling, how do you get those good people in to rescue it?

Too often, if an institution like a pub or club is struggling, they attempt to appeal to people's better nature to 'save' the place, with slogans like 'use or lose it.' But this makes supporting a club seem like an act of duty, a chore that only magnifies the fact that it's struggling. It's human nature that we tend to avoid being associated with failure. Instead, clubs need to make people *want* to come to them. Maybe if I had stayed in Yorkshire and become involved with the committee of a struggling club, based on what I've seen on my travels for this book, I could think of various initiatives to turn it around.

1. Embrace social media

This is the biggest failing across clubland, and the easiest problem to fix. You simply can't reach or engage with younger audiences if you're not present in the space where they spend most of their time. I'm no fan of Facebook, but 66 per cent of the entire UK population use it. A fifth of those are aged 55 and over, so if a club isn't on Facebook, it's not even reaching a chunk of its core audience, let alone potential new members.

2. Promotion to community groups

Every town and village has associations such as yoga groups, mother and baby groups, play groups, weightwatchers, sports clubs, wargaming clubs, scouts and guides. There are also people wanting to hold jumble sales, craft markets, beer festivals and coffee mornings, people who want to practice singing, form a band, hold an art class, and countless other hobbies and pastimes that Orwell would celebrate as aspects of the British at play. Years of austerity have left communities without communal spaces such as youth clubs and community centres. Public libraries, to our shame as a nation, are disappearing faster than any other community asset (time to bring back the reading rooms too?) Many working men's clubs are now closed during the day, and even on weekday evenings, most have concert rooms and lounges that are empty with the lights off. I think I can see a solution to many problems here. And if a club's response is 'Yes but we'd have to pay a member of staff to open up' or 'what about the cost of the electricity?' then they've already given up.

3. Create some atmosphere

It's fun to take the piss out of municipal decoration and strip lighting so bright it exposes your soul. But working men's clubs used to be places where men went when their houses weren't pleasant spaces to spend much time. If the working men's club is now not as nice to be in or to look at as your own home, why would you go there? Lounge bars were named after comfortable rooms in houses, not airport departure lounges.

4. Hold open days

I've met so many people who have walked into working men's clubs and been amazed by what they've discovered there. And I've visited so many clubs myself that were physically difficult to find. The very nature of a private members' club is that you assume if you're not a member, you won't be allowed in. I've never once been asked to show my associate and pass card at a single one of the clubs I've visited over the past year and a half, but I didn't know that would be the case until I got there. Some clubs have big signs outside saying 'New Members Welcome' or 'Public Welcome,' and somehow, these tend to be busier than those that don't. Incredibly, some clubs who have told me they are desperate for new members but don't know how to attract them don't have such signs outside their doors. I found so many stories in local and regional press about clubs closing down. That's because clubs were once a significant aspect of a local journalists' beat. I'm sure the same titles would be just as responsive to a story about a club opening its doors and inviting people in.

5. Food

Clubs have always competed against pubs, and pubs on average now make more money from food than they do from drink. Not every club has the facilities to cook food on the premises, but if they do, they should. If they can't, then I'm struggling to think why any club wouldn't figure out an alternative solution given that every single club performer from the 1960s and 1970s was interrupted by the announcement that the pies have come. Where are the pies now? I know pubs that have cutlery and a set of takeaway menus behind the bar, because it's better to let someone order a pizza in and stay for two more drinks than watch them leave and go to a restaurant. Craft beer bars and brewery tap rooms make arrangements with food vans to come and park up outside – and charge them money to do so. Why not clubs?

None of this is wishful thinking. Any successful club today is doing at least one of these things. Just imagine what a club could be like if it did them all.

Any individual club can only do what its members are capable of. The story of the working men's club movement has constantly swung between the stories of ordinary people and the clubs they create, and the extraordinary story of the Club and Institute Union. It's heart-breaking to see the state of the CIU now. Clubs can and do survive without the CIU – many are realising this and leaving the Union – but it would be a shame if they all had to do so. The CIU has been a unique organisation that has taken the power of individual clubs and multiplied it, providing working-class people with help and opportunities for advancement they wouldn't have had otherwise. Its reputation may be tarnished, and it may be seemingly doing nothing to stem what seems like an inevitable decline, but it too could be saved with an injection of fresh thinking and younger members.

The impossible situation it finds itself in with its London HQ has no ideal solution, but maybe a positive one would be to move out and rent out the whole thing. The majority of clubs are in the North, and it's clear from reading the transcripts from successive AGMs that they hate London and all it stands for (some branch executives cheerfully admit to never having visited the capital). Moving to cheaper premises in the North, financed by renting out the London building, would not just help the financial situation – it would also bring the CIU closer to its clubs both physically and symbolically.

It would also be useful if the CIU could indicate its awareness of the twenty-first century. Like its member clubs, it urgently needs to up its online game. The website looks ancient and is difficult to navigate. It has no social media presence whatsoever, and neither do any of its key officeholders.

Also, if clubs are to prosper, the CIU needs to extend the education it provides in matters of club law and accountancy to also cover the commercial aspects that any organisation needs in order to survive. It could easily appoint people to provide training in social media and marketing, designing template posters and ads that clubs could download and adapt. Even before that, it could offer computer literacy to the clubs that still do everything on paper. These are basic skills that clubs need to survive, that many don't have. In some ways, the CIU is needed more than it ever was.

* * *

As the nature of being working-class shifts, and t'world continues to open up, some working men's clubs in London are once again reinventing themselves, challenging the North to regain control of the narrative. Walthamstow Trades Club, founded in 1919 by a group of trade union members, today has a modern, up-to-date website, which advertises dance lessons, choir rehearsals and mums' fitness classes, as well as comedy nights, dance clubs, DJ sets and regular turns. I arrange to meet the club's president and secretary on a regular 'General Echo' sound system night, when guest DJs are invited to come and dig into 'dub, dancehall, roots, rockers, ska, rocksteady and other bass transmissions on two turntables and a space echo.' As Debbie Smith, former bassist of nineties Britpop band Echobelly, sorts out her records on stage at one end of the large room, we head away from the dance floor and past the pool table to sit at the back and talk about how the club has changed over the last few years.

'Financially it was on its knees,' says Abby, the club secretary, 'It had been so successful. In the seventies and eighties, you couldn't become a member, the waiting list was too long. But it had this history of different factions taking over, which has continued.'

Club president Julia had lived in the area for thirty-five years and had heard of the Trades but never been in until 2015. 'I heard someone needed a DJ for a fiftieth birthday, as theirs had dropped out, so I said I'd do it. I'd been looking for a venue to start a disco night for people of a certain age. And I walked in here and it was like, this is the place. And that's how I got involved.'

The disco night brought in lots of new people who had also never been in the club before. Its fortunes began to turn around.

Abby was one of the people who came to Julia's night in 2016, and on walking in, fell in love with the place. 'I thought, there's something mad about this place. I asked Julia to DJ for my birthday and we've been friends since then.'

The two women stood for the committee because the president asked for younger people (meaning people in their forties and fifties) to get involved. Abby and Julia choose their words very carefully, talking about weirdness and 'things not being right.' Some older members wanted the club to fail, because they believed that if it did, it would be sold off and, as they owned the club, they would share the money. There was a protracted power struggle which ended when the two became president and secretary. They could understand accounts, and they knew how to run popular events. Abby and Julia clearly enjoyed the latter more than they enjoyed finance, politics and the battle for control, but they loved the club, and so they persisted. Unlike in some clubs, neither Abby nor Julia are paid for their roles, yet the hours they put in are like having a second job.

In the club's diary, tea dances rub shoulders with heavy dub disco. The club is one of the area's best venues for live music, and also organises fund-raising events for charity. Unlike some other clubs that have managed to reinvent themselves, there are strong links between old and new.

'When I did my disco night, I had to accept that I had to stop for the bingo, so now I incorporate it into my night,' says Julia. 'Eileen, the bingo caller, she's ninety. So when it's time, I play "Come on Eileen" by Dexy's and she gets up and dances her way onto the floor.'

Clubs like Walthamstow, the Langham and the Mildmay all bene-fit from the new energy that comes from people who often didn't grow up in the area. The 'leavers' from declining communities still want some kind of connection, some notion of community that their parents and grandparents enjoyed back home but doesn't seem open to them now. Having severed their – or rather, our – roots, we seek to put them down again somewhere new. We stumble across fading clubs, almost by accident, and find these incredible spaces bursting with potential. And we see people like us, maybe from different parts of the country but often with a similar experience, and we can relax.*

Some clubs, like Hedben Bridge Trades Club, completely reinvent themselves and break with the past. The Trades is no longer a working men's club, but an 'Independent socialist collective club' and one of the best gig venues in West Yorkshire. The Brudenell Social Club in Leeds is also independent from the CIU, and is also a popular gig venue, but it still performs the functions of a social club, so old men can be spotted playing dominoes while up-and-coming indie bands play on stage. There's a games room and lounge bar with darts, pool and snooker. The craft beers and local cask ales mix with traditional working men's club smoothflow beers, and there are even pies, now supplied by Pieminister. In 2021 Tom Jones went back to his clubland roots with a secret fan club gig here to launch his new album. Apparently, he said to the crowd, 'Last time I was here, I got paid up.'

Other clubs take this reinvention further. Bethnal Green Working Men's Club has an arch, ironic take on traditional clubland entertain-ment. The turns are generally alternative cabaret and burlesque, sometimes featuring comedians playing grotesque caricatures of the traditional northern club comic.†

---

* Obviously, divisions and conflict still sometimes remain. Shortly after our chat, Abby and Julia were ousted from their posts, though the club seems to be continuing in the direction they set.

† I'd love to be able to say that 'Bethnal Green Working Men's Club' isn't just taking the piss out of working-class culture to make some hipsters laugh, but as the people who run the club ignored all attempts to contact them, even when introduced by mutual friends, I wasn't able to confirm this.

Older members often resist the change, which they see as gentrification or 'yuppiefication,' but for most clubs there's not really an alternative. Clubs with an ageing demographic need to attract younger people to survive, and these days, each younger generation wants something different from what their parents or grandparents wanted. The club either accommodates changing tastes or it doesn't get new members. A queer indie disco may not be the biggest draw in every club, but if that's what packs them in in Bethnal Green, then that's what Bethnal Green Club should put on. Any outcry that greets it is no different from 120 years ago, when the same clubs were putting on music hall singers and comedians instead of improving lectures. The beauty of a club is that it can be more than one thing: at the Mildmay, you can sit in the main bar with a pint or play a few games of snooker in the games room with no idea that Miss Bonnie Fleur is presenting her Tickle My Fancy Cabaret in the main hall.

* * *

'One thing I've been asking myself,' I say 'is have working men's clubs done their job? Do we need them anymore? The early founders wanted to elevate working men out of their condition and get them out of the pubs. Did the club actually succeed?'

'Well we're not a classless society are we?' replies Ruth Cherrington when I put this to her as we sit in the bar at the Mildmay. 'We do need clubs, we need different spaces where people feel they can share their lives with people like them. Henry Solly says somewhere that we will no longer need clubs when working men have decent homes to live in where they can socialise at home and they don't need to go out. So maybe that's happened. But a lot of the welfare state has been disbanded. Services for older people have gone. Everything is so business-oriented. Clubs are needed more now, but they've got to adapt.'

The Mildmay has adapted. It's safe now, looking at soon achieving a total membership of over a thousand, compared to a couple of hundred when we had Liz's party here. One of the people who made that happen is Laurence Fryer, a friend of Ruth's who joins us now.

Laurence has been coming to clubs since he was a teenager and came to the Mildmay with his mates Harry and Bob the Polisher to play snooker on Monday nights.

Ten years later, he was asked to stand for the committee. He wasn't part of the ruling clique, but elections were often unopposed, so he put his application in at the last minute, just before they closed.

'It quickly became clear the club wasn't going anywhere,' says Laurence. 'Things that broke weren't being replaced, and we were being told the club didn't have a future. It was too big for its members, things like that.'

When the old president fell ill, Tom Jones (not that one) stood for president and Laurence for vice-president. This was the injection of new energy the club needed. They stepped up a long-needed programme of repairs, in particular a new roof to replace the one that allows the club to be soaked through in heavy rain, opened up the membership, and started looking for other sources of revenue.

When Stewart Lee used the Mildmay for his *Comedy Vehicle*, not only was that a significant source of revenue for the club in its own right, it put the club on the map, attracting the attention of film, TV and fashion shoot location scouts. When they realised how potentially lucrative this was, the Mildmay hired someone on a commission basis to promote the venue as a filming location. It's featured in films such as *Made in Dagenham* and TV shows like *Killing Eve* and played host to Renée Zellweger when she was filming a biopic of Judy Garland. All the revenue from being a location has gone into steadily improving the facilities. But not everything can happen at once. At the time of the Judy Garland shoot, there was no green room for the talent.

'We left her in the women's toilets,' say Laurence. 'It was a bit grim and we had to put sheets up to cover the worst bits. As long as it wasn't raining, nothing would have landed on her head.'

The money from these shoots means the club now has a more salubrious green room.

So does Laurence believe clubs like the Mildmay have a future?

'People can relax and chat and feel that they're not pressured to drink a lot. They can play games, read a newspaper, you don't have to drink at all if you don't want to. You can be as involved or as uninvolved as you want to be. A well-run club can be a mirror to the local community.'

It's a Tuesday night. Upstairs, the main hall where we had Liz's birthday party has been hired by a group who put on a Swing Dance Jazz Club. There are lessons for beginners at 8pm, then the doors open at 8.30 and a live band plays three sets. Laurence sneaks us up to the balcony before he heads off to the next task on his endless list, and I watch as hipsters dressed in immaculate 1950s threads swing across the floor. As I head to the toilet, an elderly Jewish man emerges dressed just like them, and the younger men totally lose their shit around him, because he's been wearing these clothes and dancing to this music in clubs like this since before they were born, and it's as if the hipsters have been visited by a jazz god, someone who can actually remember the times they're attempting to recreate.

Equidistant in age between the hipsters and the old jazzman, I look from them to him, and suspect we've all found home.

FURTHER READING

Books

Ainsley, Claire, *The New Working Class: How to Win Hearts, Minds and Votes*, Policy Press, Bristol, 2018

Anderson, Neil, *Dirty Stop Out's Guide to Working Men's Clubs*, Dirty Stop Outs Guides, Sheffield, 2017

Bailey, Peter, *Leisure and Class in Victorian England*, Routledge & Kegan Paul, London, 1978

Barfe, Louis, *Turned Out Nice Again: The Story of British Light Entertainment*, Atlantic, London, 2008

Barfe, Louis, *The Trials and Triumphs of Les Dawson*, Atlantic Books, London, 2012

Beaven, Brad, *Leisure, Citizenship and Working Class Men in Britain, 1850–1945*, Manchester University Press, Manchester, 2005

Burke, Barry, and Worpole, Ken, *Working Class Club Life and Politics in Hackney 1870–1900*, Centerprise Trust Ltd, London, 1980

Capstick, Sheila, *A Woman's Right to Cues*, Yorkshire Arts Circus, Yorkshire, 1988

Cherrington, Ruth, *Not Just Beer and Bingo! A Social History of Working Men's Clubs*, Authorhouse, Bloomington, Indiana, 2012

Clayton, Ian, *Bringing It All Back Home*, Route Publishing, Pontefract, 2008

Clayton, Ian (ed.), *The Red Shed: Fifty Years a Socialist Club*, Route Publishing, Pontefract, 2015

Clayton, Ian, *It's the Beer Talking*, Route Publishing, Pontefract, 2018

Coekin, Chris, *Knock Three Times: Working Men, Social Clubs and Other Stories*, Dewi Lewis, Stockport, 2006

Collins, Michael, *The Likes of Us: A Biography of the White Working Class*, Granta, London, 2004

Dawson, Les, *A Card for the Clubs*, Sphere, London, 1974

Dennis, Norman, Henriques, Fernando, and Slaughter, Clifford, *Coal is our Life: An Analysis of a Yorkshire Mining Community*, Eyre & Spottiswoode, London, 1956

Dormer, Derek, *My Life in the CIU*, Fastprint Publishing, Peterbrough, 2018

Elkins, Ted, *So They Brewed Their Own Beer: The History of the Northern Clubs & Federation Brewery Ltd*, Northern Clubs & Federation Brewery Ltd, Newcastle, 1970

Hall, B. T., *Our Sixty Years*, WMCIU, London, 1922

Hamp, Johnnie, *It Beats Working for a Living: A Lifetime in Showbusiness*, Trafford Publishing, Victoria, Canada, 2008

Hoggart, Richard, *The Uses of Literacy*, Penguin, London, 2009 edition

Jackson, Brian, *Working Class Community: Some General Notions Raised by a Series of Studies in Northern England*, Routledge & Kegan Paul, London, 1968

Jackson, Lee, *Palaces of Pleasure: How the Victorians Invented Mass Entertainment*, Yale University Press, London, 2019

Lynne, Dame Vera, *Some Sunny Day: My Autobiography*, HarperCollins, London, 2009

McDonald, Jane, *Riding the Waves: My Story*, Virgin, London, 2019

Mass Observation, *The Pub and the People*, Victor Gollancz, London, 1943

Margolis, Jonathan, *Bernard Manning: A Biography*, Orion, London, 1996

Mattinson, Deborah, *Beyond the Red Wall: Why Labour Lost, How the Conservatives Won and What Will Happen Next?* Biteback, London, 2020

Peppin, T. S., *Club-Land of the Toiler, Exemplified by the Workmen's Club and Institute Union*, J. M. Dent & Co, London 1895

Prest, Maureen, *King of Clubs*, Route Publishing, Pontefract, 2017

Solly, Henry, *These Eighty Years: The Story of an Unfinished Life*, publisher unknown, 1893, reprinted by Pranava Books, India

Solly, Henry, *Working Men's Social Clubs and Educational Institutes*, WMCIU, London, 1867

Solly, Henry, *Working Men: A Glance at Some of their Wants, with Reasons and Suggestions for Helping Them to Help Themselves*, London, 1863

Taylor, John, *From Self-Help to Glamour: The Working Man's Club, 1860–1972*, History Workshop Pamphlets, Ruskin College, Oxford, 1973

Tremlett, George, *Clubmen: The History of the Working Men's Club and Institute Union*, Secker & Warburg, London, 1987

Starling, Boris, *The Official History of Britain: Our story in numbers as told by the Office of National Statistics*, HarperCollins, London, 2020

Whitbread & Co., *Your Club*, Whitbread & Co, London, 1950

Yeo, Eileen and Stephen, *Popular Culture and Class Conflict 1590–1914*, Harvester Press, Brighton, 1981

Articles and Papers

Cherrington, Ruth, 'We Are Not Drinking Dens!': Working Men's Clubs and the Struggle for Respectability, 1862–1920s', *Brewery History*, The Brewery History Society, 2013

Hall, Richard, 'Being a Man, Being a Member: Masculinity and Community in Britain's Working Men's Clubs, 1945–1960', *Cultural and Social History*, Routledge, London, 2016

Wilson, Paul, 'The Law of Optics: The Fall, the Northern Working Men's Club and the Refining Powers of Rational Recreation', in Norton, Tessa and Stanley, Bob, (eds), *Excavate! The Wonderful and Frightening World of The Fall*, Faber & Faber, London, 2016

Video

'1982 Vintage Film, Batley Variety Club, The History': https://www.youtube.com/watch?v=wjGzSruor2Y

'Memories of Greasbrough Social Club' – excerpt from BBC *Panorama*, 1965: https://www.youtube.com/watch?v=9Hrsu WeTPKc&t=291s

'Wheeltappers & Shunters Social Club – Granada TV – Series 1 Episode 1': https://www.youtube.com/watch?v=6jChufJu7 fo&t=1795s

'Last Orders' – excerpt from Henry Singer's 2008 documentary on Wibsey Club: https://www.youtube.com/watch?v=MUxbonn4waU

ACKNOWLEDGEMENTS

It's taken almost twenty years – my entire career as a writer – to finally tell this story. As always, I had to lean on quite a lot of people for help and support in making it happen.

For stories, help, inspiration, advice, and support both moral and practical, thanks to Jane Alexander, Louis Barfe, Richard Boon, Tom Campbell, Ken Capstick, Ruth Cherrington, Ian Clayton, Bernie Clifton, Steve Davis, Les Dennis, Travis Elborough, Laurence Fryer, Chris Garnsworthy, Chris Gittner, Kenneth Green CMD ACM, Brenda Haywood, Stewart Lee, Kate Manning, Ben Metcalf, Dusty Miller, Jude Rogers, Dave Stone, Adrian Tierney-Jones, Richard Thomas, Ben Wilkinson, Andrew Whitehead, and all the club committee men and women who gave up their time and allowed me in. Thanks to Sean Ferris for all the advice and help he was able to give after keeping *Club Mirror* and the *Club Journal* thriving, modern and relevant.

Thank you to Jonathan de Peyer and all at HarperNorth for finally giving this book a home, and to my agent Jim Gill for always having my back.

Biggest thanks as always to my greatest fan, sternest critic, sometime editor, and collaborator – my wife Liz Vater. I think I owe you another party at the Mildmay.

London, May 2023

Harper
North

BOOK CREDITS

HarperNorth would like to thank the following staff
and contributors for their involvement in making
this book a reality:

Laura Amos
Hannah Avery
Fionnuala Barrett
Claire Boal
Caroline Bovey
Charlotte Brown
Sarah Burke
Alan Cracknell
Jonathan de Peyer
Anna Derkacz
Tom Dunstan
Kate Elton
Mick Fawcett
Simon Gerratt
Monica Green
Tara Hiatt
Graham Holmes

Ben Hurd
Patricia Hymans
Megan Jones
Jean-Marie Kelly
Oliver Malcolm
Alice Murphy-Pyle
Adam Murray
Genevieve Pegg
Agnes Rigou
Emma Rogers
Florence Shepherd
Zoe Shine
Eleanor Slater
Emma Sullivan
Katrina Troy
Phillipa Walker
Kelly Webster

For more unmissable reads,
sign up to the HarperNorth newsletter at
www.harpernorth.co.uk

or find us on Twitter at
@HarperNorthUK

Harper
North